W9-API-915

The Complete Guide to
CHRISTIAN
DENOMINATIONS

RON RHODES

HARVEST HOUSE PUBLISHERS

EUGENE, OREGON

Unless otherwise indicated, all Scripture quotations are taken from the HOLY BIBLE, NEW INTERNATIONAL VERSION®. NIV®. Copyright©1973, 1978, 1984 by the International Bible Society. Used by permission of Zondervan. All rights reserved.

Verses marked KJV are taken from the King James Version of the Bible.

Verses marked NASB are taken from the New American Standard Bible ®, © 1960, 1962, 1963, 1968, 1971, 1972, 1973, 1975, 1977, 1995 by The Lockman Foundation. Used by permission. (www.Lockman.org)

Cover by Terry Dugan Design, Minneapolis, Minnesota

THE COMPLETE GUIDE TO CHRISTIAN DENOMINATIONS
Copyright © 2005 by Ron Rhodes
Published by Harvest House Publishers
Eugene, Oregon 97402
www.harvesthousepublishers.com

Library of Congress Cataloging-in-Publication Data

Rhodes, Ron.
    The complete guide to Christian denominations / Ron Rhodes.
        p. cm.
    Includes bibliographical references and index.
    ISBN 0-7369-1289-4 (pbk.)
    1. Protestant churches—United States. 2. Protestant churches—Doctrines. I. Title.
    BR516.5.R47 2005
    280'.4—dc22   2004017507

All rights reserved. No part of this publication may be reproduced, stored in a retrieval system, or transmitted in any form or by any means—electronic, mechanical, digital, photocopy, recording, or any other—except for brief quotations in printed reviews, without the prior permission of the publisher.

Printed in the United States of America

05 06 07 08 09 10 11 12 13 / VP-KB / 10 9 8 7 6 5 4 3

*In honor of the head of the church (Ephesians 5:23),
who purchased the church with His own blood (Acts 20:28)—
Jesus Christ*

ACKNOWLEDGMENTS

Researching every denomination in this book required considerable effort. Representatives of many of these denominations made the task easier by pointing me to helpful information regarding their groups. To these individuals—too many to list— I offer a heartfelt thanks.

Kerri, David, and Kylie (my wife and children)—as always, I could not have written this book without your continued support. God has used you mightily in my life!

Contents

BEGINNINGS: THE EMERGENCE OF CHRISTIANITY AND DENOMINATIONS

THE WORD *CHRISTIAN* IS USED only three times in the New Testament, most importantly in Acts 11:26 (see also Acts 26:28 and 1 Peter 4:16). In Acts 11:26, we are told simply and straightforwardly, "The disciples were called Christians first at Antioch." This would have happened around A.D. 42, about a decade after Christ died on the cross and rose from the dead.

Until this time, the followers of Jesus had been known among themselves by such terms as "brothers" (Acts 15:1,23), "disciples" (Acts 9:26), "believers" (Acts 5:12), and "saints" (Romans 8:27). Now, in Antioch, they were called Christians.

The term is loaded with significance. Among the ancients, the *ian* ending meant "belonging to the party of." Herodians belonged to the party of Herod. Caesarians belonged to the party of Caesar. Christians belonged to Christ. And Christians were loyal to Christ, just as the Herodians were loyal to Herod and Caesarians were loyal to Caesar (see Mark 3:6; 12:13).

The name *Christian* is noteworthy because these followers of Jesus were recognized as a separate group. They were distinct from Judaism and from all other religions of the ancient world. We might loosely translate the term *Christian*, "those belonging to Christ," "Christ-ones," or perhaps "Christ-people." They are ones who follow the Christ.

Those who have studied the culture of Antioch have noted that the Antiochans were well-known for making fun of people. They may have used the word *Christian* as a term of derision, an appellation of ridicule. Nevertheless, history reveals that by the second century, Christians adopted the title as a badge of honor. They took pride (in a healthy way) in following Jesus. They had a genuine relationship with the living, resurrected Christ, and they were utterly faithful to Him, even in the face of death.

The city of Antioch was a mixture of Jews and Gentiles. People of both backgrounds in this city became followers of Jesus. What brought these believers unity was not their race, culture, or language. Rather, their unity was rooted in the personal relationship each of them had with Jesus. Christianity crosses all cultural and ethnic boundaries.

If a Christian is one who has a personal relationship with Jesus Christ, then Christianity is a collective group of people who have personal relationships with Jesus Christ. This may sound simplistic, but from a biblical perspective, this is the proper starting point.

In the New Testament, the early Christians never referred to their collective movement as Christianity, even though they used the term *Christian* with greater frequency as the movement grew in numbers. By the time of Augustine (A.D. 354–430), the term *Christianity* appears to have become a widespread appellation for the Christian movement.

The Birth of the Church

Scripture refers to both the universal church and the local church. The universal church is a company of people who have one Lord and who share together in one gift of salvation in the Lord Jesus Christ (Titus 1:4; Jude 3). It may be defined as the ever enlarging body of born-again believers who comprise the universal body of Christ, over which He reigns as Lord.

Although the members of the church—and members of different denominations—may differ in age, sex, race, wealth, social status, and ability, true believers are all joined together as one people (Galatians 3:28). All of them share in one Spirit and worship one Lord (Ephesians 4:3-6). This body is comprised of only believers in Christ. The way one becomes a member of this universal body is to simply place faith in Christ. If you are a believer, you are in!

The word *church* is translated from the Greek word *ekklesia*. This Greek word comes from two smaller words. The first is *ek*, which means "out from among." The second is *klesia*, which means "to call." Combining the two words, *ekklesia* means "to call out from among." The church represents those whom God has called out from among the world. And those God has called come from all walks of life. All are welcome in Christ's church.

Many theologians believe the church did not exist in Old Testament times (I think they are right). Matthew 16:18 cites Jesus as saying that "I will build" my church (future tense). This indicates that at the moment He spoke these words, the church was not yet existent. This is consistent with the Old Testament, which includes no reference to the church. In the New Testament, the church is portrayed as distinct from Israel in such passages as Romans 9:6, 1 Corinthians 10:32; and Hebrews 12:22-24. Therefore, we should not equate the church with believing Israelites in Old Testament times.

Scripture indicates that the universal church was born on the Day of Pentecost (see Acts 2; compare with 1:5; 11:15; 1 Corinthians 12:13). We are told in Ephesians 1:19-20 that the church is built on the foundation of Christ's resurrection, meaning that the church could not have existed in Old Testament times. The church is thus called a "new man" in Ephesians 2:15.

The one *universal* church is represented by many *local* churches scattered throughout the world. For example, we read of a local church in Corinth (1 Corinthians 1:2), and another in Thessalonica (1 Thessalonians 1:1). Only a few local churches existed at first, but due to the missionary efforts of the early Christians, churches soon cropped up around the globe.

FAST FACTS ON
the Church

	Universal Church	Local Church
Membership	Embraces all believers from Pentecost to the rapture	Embraces believers in a specific locale who meet for fellowship and worship
Living or Dead	Includes living and dead believers	Includes living believers only
Denominational Relationship	Includes all true believers, regardless of denominational affiliation	Normally identified with a specific denomination or movement
Joining	One becomes a member by faith in Christ.	One becomes a member by profession of faith in Christ, plus any requirements unique to the denomination, such as baptism.

The New Testament strongly urges believers to attend local churches. Hebrews 10:25 specifically instructs us not to forsake meeting together. The Christian life as described in Scripture is to be lived within the context of the family of God and not in isolation (Acts 2; Ephesians 3:14-15). Moreover, by attending church, we become equipped for the work of ministry (Ephesians 4:12-16). The Bible knows nothing of a "lone ranger" Christian. As the old proverb says, many logs together burn very brightly, but when a log falls off to the side, the embers quickly die out (see Ephesians 2:19; 1 Thessalonians 5:10-11; and 1 Peter 3:8).

The Spread of Christianity

Christianity experienced phenomenal growth following the death and resurrection of Jesus Christ. We learn in Acts 1:15 that about 120 Jewish believers in Christ gathered in Jerusalem. A bit later, after Peter's powerful sermon, 3000 people became believers on the Day of Pentecost (Acts 2:41). The number soon grew to 5000 (Acts 4:4). Soon enough, the Samaritans—viewed as "unclean" by the Jews—were added to the church (see Acts 8:5-25), as were the Gentiles (see Acts 10; 13–28).

In Acts 1:8 the Lord instructed His disciples: "You will receive power when the Holy Spirit comes on you; and you will be my witnesses in Jerusalem, and in all Judea and Samaria, and to the ends of the earth." The rest of the book of Acts is a historical account of how Paul, Peter, and others empowered by the Holy Spirit spread Christianity among both Jews and Gentiles around the northern Mediterranean, including Samaria (Acts 8:5-25), Phoenicia, Cyprus, Antioch (9:32–12:25), Phrygia and Galatia (13:1–15:35), Macedonia (15:36–21:16), and Rome (21:17–22:29). Despite persecution by Roman authorities, Jewish authorities, and others (2:13; 4:1-22; 5:17-42; 6:9–8:4), Christianity spread like wildfire.

The apostle Paul went on three missionary tours (Acts 13:1–14:28; 15:36–18:22; 18:23–21:17), spreading God's Word in strategic cities like Antioch, Perga, Iconium, Lystra, Derbe, Troas, Philippi, Thessalonica, Berea, Athens, Corinth, Ephesus, Galatia, and Miletus. One of Paul's strategies was to visit major Roman capitals that were easily reached by existing trade routes, a strategy that resulted in the gospel spreading out to other areas through these routes. One local church popped up after another.

Fast-forward to the twenty-first century. Christianity has continued to grow and expand from the first century to the present, and it is now variously represented in some 300 denominations in the United States alone. And this number is in flux because new denominations are constantly forming, and other denominations disappear from the religious landscape.

With so many denominations sprinkled across the land, keeping track of their similarities and differences has become increasingly difficult. That is one reason I wrote this book. You will find this book a handy guide that provides a brief history and doctrinal summary of the mainstream denominations in the United States.

What Is a Denomination?

The English word *denomination* comes from the Latin word *denominare* which means "to name."[1] In this book, you will find that the names of denominations are diverse, reflecting a wide range of distinctive beliefs and practices.

A denomination can be defined as "an association or fellowship of congregations within a religion that have the same beliefs or creed, engage in similar practices, and cooperate with each other to develop and maintain shared enterprises."[2] Seen in this light, Presbyterians are Presbyterians precisely because they share the same beliefs, engage in similar practices, and cooperate with each other to develop and maintain shared enterprises. Likewise, Roman Catholics are Roman Catholics for the same reasons.

Though the church experienced some sectarianism even in early New Testament times (see 1 Corinthians 3:3-7), formal denominations are actually a relatively recent development. One reason for this is that in many countries of the world, governmental authorities believed that civic harmony hinged on religious conformity. The recipe for a healthy society, they believed, included "one king, one faith, and one law."[3] This is why so many countries have had state churches. They resisted the idea of allowing people to have freedom of religious belief, for they thought such a policy would be disruptive to society. Only with the emergence of the United States did all this change in a significant way.

The United States promises every American the free exercise of religion. This is one of the things that makes America so great. The First Amendment, ratified in 1791, affirmed that "Congress shall make no law respecting an establishment of religion or prohibiting the free exercise thereof."[4] In keeping with this, James Madison, who became the fourth president of the United States (1809–1817), wrote, "The religion…of every man must be left to the conviction and conscience of every man…. We maintain, therefore, that in matters of religion no man's right is [to be] abridged by the institution of civil society."[5]

This policy is one reason so many people immigrated to the colonies in the early years of our country. As these people arrived, they brought with them their churches and denominations. Frank S. Mead and Samuel S. Hill note that "among the English colonists there were Congregationalists in New England, Quakers in Pennsylvania, Anglicans in New York, Presbyterians in Virginia, and Roman Catholics in Maryland. In addition, there were

Dutch, Swiss, and German Reformed [and] Swiss and German Lutherans."[6]

Maintaining their former churches on American soil served to help these immigrants adjust to their new surroundings. They were able to stay grounded in a familiar spiritual environment even while getting used to their new physical environment. Eventually these various churches took on an American flavor and adapted to fit in with American society.

With the passing of time, new denominations continued to emerge on American soil as a result of splits and mergers. Why do denominations split? The answer is simple. Wherever human beings congregate, they will have differences of opinion about what to believe and how faith should be practiced. This book will illustrate how, in many cases, churches split off from a parent denomination because of differences in belief and/or practices, thereby giving rise to entirely new denominations.

What Are Protestants?

The three major divisions of Christianity are Roman Catholicism, Protestantism, and the Orthodox Church. In the chapters on Roman Catholicism and the Orthodox Church, I provide a full history of how these respective groups emerged (see chapters 4 and 14). However, the great majority of denominations in this book—including those affiliated with the Methodists, the Baptists, the Presbyterians, and the Lutherans—are Protestant. Therefore, an introductory history of Protestantism may be helpful.

Protestantism refers to a broad system of the Christian faith and practices that emerged in the sixteenth century. It began as a movement seeking to bring reform to the Western Church.

The term *Protestant* was first coined in 1529 at the Diet of Speyer, an imperial assembly. Just three years earlier, another diet (or formal assembly) had granted tolerance to the Lutherans, allowing them to determine their own religious position. At the Diet of Speyer, the Roman Catholic majority of delegates rescinded this tolerance.

Consequently, six Lutheran princes and the leaders of fourteen German cities signed a protest against this action, and it was then that Lutherans became known as *Protestants*. Gradually, however, the term *Protestant* came to embrace all churches not affiliated with (and who have separated from) Roman Catholicism or Eastern Orthodoxy. This small beginning eventually mushroomed to embrace over 400 million people (as of A.D. 2000). About one-fifth of all Christians are Protestant.

One religious researcher suggests that "if the Christian church you're sitting in isn't Orthodox or Roman Catholic, then you are in a Protestant church of one variety or another. The thing to remember about Protestants is that they *protest*."[7] One cannot deny the "protest" element in the history of Protestantism. Many scholars are quick to note, however, that the term *protest* etymologically carries the idea "to testify" or "to affirm." Robert McAfee, in his book *The Spirit of Protestantism*, gives us this interesting insight:

> The verb "to protest" comes from the Latin *pro-testari*, and means not only "to testify," but, more importantly, "to testify on behalf of something." *Webster's Dictionary* gives as a synonym, "to affirm." *The Oxford English Dictionary* defines it, "to declare formally in public, testify, to make a solemn declaration." The notion of a "protest against error" is only a subsidiary meaning. Thus, the actual word itself is charged with positive rather than negative connotations. "To protest," then, in the true meaning of the word, is to make certain affirmations, to give testimony on behalf of certain things.[8]

The point, then, is that Protestantism is not simply a reactionary, negative movement. To be sure, the early Reformers did take a stand against the teachings of the Roman Catholic Church. But Protestants predominantly testify to what they consider to be the truth!

Distinctive Emphases of Protestantism

Protestants have strong convictions on quite a number of doctrines, but three are particularly important. These three serve to distinguish Protestantism from Roman Catholicism.

1. *The Exclusivity of the Bible.* Protestants view the Bible as the only infallible rule of the Christian life and faith. It is considered the sole source for spiritual teachings. This is in obvious contrast to Roman Catholicism, which places heavy emphasis on the authority of tradition and the *ex cathedra* pronouncements of the pope.

2. *Salvation by Grace Through Faith.* Protestants have always emphasized that the benefits of salvation are by grace alone through faith alone (Romans 4; Galatians 3:6-14; Ephesians 2:8-9). By contrast, Roman Catholics have historically placed a heavy emphasis on meritorious works in contributing to the process of salvation. This is not to say that Protestants view good works as unimportant. They simply believe good works are by-products of salvation (Matthew 7:15-23; 1 Timothy 5:10,25).

3. *The Priesthood of All Believers.* In Roman Catholicism, the priest is the intermediary between the believer and God. For example, a person must confess sins to a priest, who then absolves that person of sin. By contrast, Protestants believe each Christian is a priest before God and thus has direct access to Him without need for an intermediary (see 1 Peter 2:4-10).

Divisions Within Protestantism

The independent spirit intrinsic to Protestantism has been both a strength and a weakness. It has been a strength in that it has had a revitalizing effect on church members who are free to directly interact with God and serve Him freely in the church. It has been a weakness in that such independence has led to numerous denominational splits throughout history.

Today, Protestantism includes many denominations—each having some distinctive beliefs and histories. Lutheran churches, for example, emerged out of the reforming work of Martin Luther in the early sixteenth century in Germany. Churches in both the Presbyterian and Reformed traditions emerged largely from the Calvinistic side of the Reformation. The Methodist church grew out of the holiness teachings of John Wesley. The work of several influential Christian leaders gave rise to new denominations.

Fast Facts on
Influential Religious Leaders

Historical Person	Date	Denomination
Pope Leo I	400–461	Early pope of the Roman Catholic Church, during whose reign claims of papal authority over all other churches were first made.
Michael Caerularius	d. 1058	Patriarch of Constantinople in power when the Eastern Orthodox Church split off from Roman Catholicism.
Martin Luther	1483–1546	German Reformer. Followers became the Lutherans.

Menno Simons	1496–1561	Dutch leader. Followers became the Mennonites.
King Henry VIII	1509–1547	King responsible for the Church of England's break with the Roman Catholic Church. (Anglican and Episcopal churches emerged out of the Church of England.)
John Calvin	1509–1564	French Reformer. Led to rise of Presbyterian churches and Reformed churches.
George Fox	1625–1691	Mystical preacher. Led to rise of Friends churches.
Jakob Amman	1656–1730	Swiss Mennonite bishop. Led to rise of Amish churches.
John Wesley	1703–1791	Evangelist and missionary. Led to rise of Methodist churches.
Thomas Campbell Alexander Campbell Barton Stone	1763–1854 1788–1866 1772–1844	Three individuals instrumental in founding Christian or Disciples of Christ churches.
William Miller	1782–1849	Itinerant preacher. Led to rise of Adventist churches.
Phoebe Palmer	1807–1874	Itinerant speaker. Led to rise of Holiness churches.
Dwight L. Moody John Nelson Darby Cyrus Scofield	1837–1899 1800–1882 1843–1921	Three individuals instrumental in the rise of fundamentalist Bible churches.
William J. Seymour	1870–1922	Evangelist whose Azusa Street Revival in Los Angeles led to Pentecostal churches.

How to Use This Book

This book is divided into 17 alphabetized groupings of denominations—Adventist churches, Baptist churches, Brethren churches, Catholic churches, Christian churches, Congregational churches, Episcopal and Anglican churches, Friends (Quaker) churches, Fundamentalist and Bible churches, Holiness churches, Lutheran churches, Mennonite churches, Methodist churches, Orthodox churches, Pentecostal churches, Presbyterian churches, and Reformed churches. In each case, I provide a brief history of the emergence of the group as a whole before dealing with specific denominations that fall within that group. For example, I provide a brief Baptist history before providing information on relevant Baptist denominations.

This book is *not* intended as an apologetic critique of each denomination. Rather, it is intended to provide a brief history and doctrinal summary of the major denominations in North America. This means that just because a denomination is listed in this book does not mean that I personally endorse the teachings of that denomination.

Unlike some other denomination handbooks, this book does not provide information about denominations from Judaism, world religions like Islam, or cultic groups. So, for example, you will not find listed in this volume information on the Mormons or the Jehovah's Witnesses. These groups may claim to be Christian but in fact are not Christian because they deny one or more of the essential doctrines of Christianity as taught in the 66 books of the Bible.[9]

For each denomination I provide statistics on church membership and the number of congregations within the denomination. Please note, however, that these statistics should not be taken as "gospel truth." Some churches, in their membership roles, count *all* baptized persons, including infants. Others exclude infants and include only adults who have made a formal profession of faith in Christ. Some churches include only members in good standing. Others include people who officially joined the church but rarely ever attend services. Some churches are not careful about excluding the deceased or those who have left their congregations. In some cases, one person may be on the membership roles of more than one church.[10] Such factors make exact figures extremely difficult, if not entirely impossible, to obtain. Nevertheless, the figures presented in this book are good "guestimates."

Though I seek to provide helpful doctrinal summaries of the various denominations I cover in this book, some of them publish less information than others regarding their beliefs. For this reason, some denominations in this book have briefer doctrinal summaries than others.

You will notice several "Fast Facts" charts scattered throughout the book. These are intended to provide general information in a concise format. An index of these charts is provided at the back of this book.

For most denominations, a Web address is provided so you can easily obtain more information. The bibliography includes additional websites and other resources. The website addresses are accurate as of the time of publication. A regularly updated list of denominations' website addresses is available at www.ronrhodes.org.

1

ADVENTIST CHURCHES

WILLIAM MILLER WAS BORN in Pittsfield, Massachusetts, in 1782. He grew up to be a good citizen, a responsible farmer, and a respected soldier in the War of 1812.

Miller was a nominal churchgoing Baptist. Some of his skeptic friends, however, managed to talk him out of his faith, and he became a deist. Deism involves belief in a God who created the world out of nothing but is now uninvolved with the world or its events, a God who governs the world only through unchangeable, eternal laws.

During the Second Great Awakening (1816), Miller experienced a powerful conversion to Christianity. He became a fervent student of the Bible with special interest in prophetic portions of the Bible such as Daniel and Revelation. His personal Bible had study notes that espoused the chronology of Bishop Ussher, who dated the creation of the world at 4004 B.C. Miller came to believe that since the precise dates of Noah's Flood, Israel's sojourn from Egypt, and other notable events were laid out prophetically in Scripture, the precise date of Christ's second coming must also be prophesied in the Bible.

Miller believed he found what he was looking for in Daniel 8:14: "Unto two thousand and three hundred days; then shall the sanctuary be cleansed" (KJV). Miller fixed the beginning date of this period at 457 B.C., which was the year of Cyrus' command to rebuild Jerusalem (Ezra 1:1; Isaiah 44:28; 45:13; Daniel 9:25). He was convinced that a day in prophecy was equal to a year (Ezekiel 4:6) and proclaimed that the cleansing of the sanctuary would take place within a year after March 21, 1843 (457 B.C. + 2300 years = A.D. 1843). He believed the cleansing of the sanctuary was a metaphorical way of referring to the personal return of Jesus Christ, who would cleanse the world (or perhaps just the church) of its evil and then establish His kingdom in place of the kingdoms of this world.

Miller's chronology caught on like wildfire. By 1843, nearly 100,000 people were following his lead, and the sense of expectancy was growing by the day. Miller became an itinerant preacher, going on speaking tours to Baptist, Methodist, and Congregationalist churches, all the while using elaborate charts to illustrate his prophetic scheme. He was quite sure the second coming would occur by the spring of 1844.

In anticipation of this, he wrote a book entitled *Evidences from Scripture and History of the Second Coming of Christ about the Year 1843: Exhibited in a Course of Lectures*. The book gave increased impetus to the movement, and other preachers joined in on the prophetic crusade.

March 21, 1844 came and passed, and nothing happened. There was great disappointment. Miller lamented to his followers, "I confess my error, and acknowledge my disappointment; yet I still believe that the day of the Lord is near, even at the door; and I exhort you, my brethren, to be watchful, and not let that day come upon you unawares."[1]

Some people left the movement. Some went back to their former churches. Hope for many was renewed, however, at a meeting in Exeter, New Hampshire, when some prominent individuals in the sect stood up and claimed that the coming of the

Lord, according to their calculations, was to occur on the Festival of the Atonement on October 22, 1844, and not on the Jewish New Year, as Miller had argued. The excitement was reignited. People made extensive preparations and sought to let the world know of the impending event. Some gave up their jobs to engage in evangelism.

Sadly, October 22 came and passed, and nothing happened. So devastating was the prophetic failure that it became known as "the great disappointment." The movement was left in chaos and Miller again acknowledged the prophetic error. He refused to engage in further prophetic speculation. Some gave up on Adventism; others gave up on Christianity altogether.

Despite the prophetic failure, a solid core of believers retained Miller's basic theology (minus the precise timetables regarding the Lord's return). These met in April of 1845 in Albany, New York, in order to take inventory of their convictions and define their basic beliefs concerning the coming advent of Christ, the resurrection, and the coming renewal of the earth. They agreed on these points:

- The present world will be destroyed by fire and a new earth will be created.

- There are only two advents of Jesus Christ, and both are visible and personal.

- The second coming of Christ is imminent.

- The condition of participating in the millennial reign of Christ is repentance, faith, and a godly, watchful life.

- There will be two resurrections—that of believers at the second coming of Christ, and that of unbelievers after the millennium.

- Departed believers do not enter paradise in soul and spirit until the final blessedness of the everlasting kingdom is revealed at the second coming of Christ.

Despite these agreements, many at the meeting continued to disagree over other issues:

- Do the wicked suffer eternally in hell, or are they annihilated?

- Are the dead conscious or unconscious?

- Is the Sabbath on the first day or the seventh day?

Controversies over issues such as these gave rise to a variety of Adventist denominations (some of which I summarize below). Miller died in 1849. He was promptly succeeded by the controversial "prophetess" and "visionary" Ellen G. White. Whereas Miller had sought only to interpret the Scriptures, White went far beyond this and set forth her own new revelations. As will become clear below, some Adventist denominations accept White, but others reject her.

ADVENT CHRISTIAN CHURCH
Founded: 1860
Members: 26,264
Congregations: 303

Beginnings

The Advent Christian Church is one of the denominations that emerged when Adventists regrouped in 1845 following "the great disappointment" of 1844 (see above). William Miller, though not the founder of this denomination, nevertheless provided the doctrines that serve as the theological backbone of the group. The first Advent Christian Church General Conference was held in 1860.

Beliefs

Bible. The writings and prophecies of Ellen G. White are rejected. The Bible alone is inspired and is considered revelation from God. Prophecies in the Bible will be literally fulfilled.

God. God is the Creator and is eternally existent in three persons: the Father, the Son, and the Holy Spirit.

Jesus Christ. Jesus is the Son of God. In the Incarnation, He was conceived by the Holy Spirit and born of the Virgin Mary. He died for sinners, was bodily raised in resurrection, and ascended into heaven.

Holy Spirit. The Holy Spirit is the divine Comforter whose ministries include convicting the world of sin, sanctifying believers, and sealing them unto the day of redemption.

Sin and Salvation. Though man was created to experience immortality, he forfeited this blessing through sin. Because of Adam's sin, death spread to all humanity. Only through repentance and faith in Jesus can people be restored to God and become partakers of the divine nature, thereby enabling them to live forever with God. Believers will receive immortality when they receive their resurrection bodies at Christ's coming.

Church. The church is an institution of divine origin and includes all true Christians, of whatever name. Local churches must be independent of outside control (not in submission to a bishop or pope). Church government is congregational. The proper day of worship and rest is Sunday, the day of the Lord's resurrection.

Sacraments. Baptism is for believers only and is by immersion. The Lord's Supper constitutes a memorial celebration in recognition of the significance of Christ's death.

End Times. When people die (whether righteous or unrighteous), they remain in an unconscious state until a future day of resurrection that will take place when Christ returns. Christ will literally, visibly, and gloriously come again. Then the righteous will receive everlasting life and dwell forever on a new, restored, sinless earth, which Christ Himself will renovate. The wicked will suffer for a time and then be punished with "everlasting destruction"—that is, they will experience a complete extinction of their being. We should not set dates, but Scripture does seem to indicate that we are living in the general time of Christ's coming.

Website

www.adventchristian.org

FAST FACTS ON
Styles of Church Government

National Church	The state or nation rules over the church.
Episcopal	A church hierarchy rules the church. Bishops play a key role.
Presbyterian	The congregation vests power in a ruling board of elders.
Congregational	All decisions are by congregational vote.

SEVENTH-DAY ADVENTIST CHURCH

Founded: 1845
Members: More than 12 million
Congregations: 51,086

Beginnings

This denomination (some today call it a Christian cult[2]) emerged out of the Millerite movement. As noted previously, Miller believed the second coming of Christ would occur in 1844. Though Christ obviously did not come ("the great disappointment"), many nevertheless remained Adventists because they believed the second coming is still imminent. Unlike Miller, who interpreted Daniel 8:14 to mean that the second coming would occur in 1844, Seventh-day Adventists interpreted the verse to mean that Christ cleansed the heavenly sanctuary and began a heavenly judgment (the "investigative judgment"—see below) in 1844 that will end prior to the second coming.

This denomination began in 1845 with a small group of believers in New England led by founder Ellen G. White and some of her associates. They chose the name "Seventh-day" because they believe the Old Testament Sabbath, Saturday, is the proper day of worship and rest. They believe that observing the Sabbath is the proper way to await the soon advent of the coming Lord.

Beliefs

Bible. The Old and New Testaments are inspired by God and constitute the written Word of God. The Bible is an infallible expression of God's will, an authoritative revealer of biblical doctrines, and an accurate record of God's acts in history.

God. The one God is the Creator, Sustainer, and sovereign Governor of the universe. He exists as a unity of three coeternal persons: Father, Son, and Holy Spirit.

Jesus Christ. Jesus is the eternal Son who became incarnate (fully God and fully man), lived a perfect life, suffered on the cross of human sin, rose from the dead, and ascended into heaven.

Holy Spirit. The Holy Spirit inspired Scripture, empowered Christ during His ministry, convicts the world of sin, and transforms believers into God's image. Through the Holy Spirit, God gives spiritual gifts to believers to equip them for ministry. One of these gifts is prophecy, which was manifest in Seventh-day Adventist leader Ellen G. White, who claims to have witnessed visions and received messages from heaven. Her writings are considered by church members to be authoritative, especially concerning the workings of heaven.

Sin and Salvation. Our first parents fell into sin, and the image of God in them became marred. They then became subject to death and passed a fallen nature on to all their descendants.

Salvation is found in Jesus Christ. Christ lived a perfect life, suffered on the cross, and was resurrected from the dead. Christ thereby provided the only means of atonement for human sin. Christ's death was substitutionary (in our place) and expiatory (satisfying God's righteous demands).

As the Holy Spirit leads, people come to recognize their need, acknowledge their sinfulness, repent of transgressions, and place faith in Jesus as Lord and Christ. Through faith in Christ, people are justified (declared righteous in God's sight). Through the Holy Spirit, believers are born again and are sanctified. The saved receive immortality when they are resurrected on the last day.

God's law expresses His will and purposes regarding human conduct and relationships. His commands are binding upon people of all ages. Salvation is by grace, but obedience to the commands is the fruit of salvation.

Church. The church is the community of believers who confess Jesus as Lord and Savior. It is the family of God, the body of Christ (of which Christ is the head), and the bride of Christ.

God rested on the seventh day, following six days of creation. He thereby instituted the Sabbath for people as a memorial of creation. God's fourth of the Ten Commandments is an unchangeable law, and so even today the seventh day (Saturday) is the proper day of worship.

Church government is presbyterial. Each local church is part of a local conference, local conferences combine to form regional conferences, and all these are subsumed under a general conference. Women are not ordained.

Sacraments. Baptism is by immersion and is contingent on personal faith in Christ. It constitutes a confession of faith and testifies to the death of sin in one's life. The Lord's Supper is celebrated as an expression of faith in Jesus, and Jesus Himself is present in the ceremony to strengthen His people. The ritual of foot washing takes place in preparation for the Lord's Supper.

End Times. Christ ministers on our behalf in a sanctuary in heaven. In 1844, Christ moved from the Holy to the Most Holy Place in the heavenly sanctuary and began the work of investigative judgment. This judgment reveals who among the dead are asleep in Christ and who among the living are abiding in Christ. These belong to God's kingdom.

Christ will soon come again literally, personally, and visibly. The righteous will be resurrected and receive immortality, but the unrighteous will be destroyed in the lake of fire rather than suffer eternally in a burning hell. Until then, all people who have died—both the righteous and unrighteous—are in an unconscious state.

A new earth will one day become the eternal home of the redeemed. God will dwell there with His people.

Website

www.northamerica.adventist.org

FAST FACTS ON
the Sabbath Debate

Worship Should Be on the Sabbath	Worship Should Be on the Lord's Day
God made the Sabbath at creation for all people (Genesis 2:2-3; Exodus 20:11).	New Testament believers are not under the Old Testament Law (Romans 6:14; Galatians 3:24-25; Colossians 2:16).
Christ observed the Sabbath (Mark 1:21) and is the Lord of the Sabbath (Mark 2:28).	Jesus was resurrected and appeared to some of His followers on a Sunday (Matthew 28:1).
The apostle Paul preached on the Sabbath (Acts 17:2).	Jesus made continuing resurrection appearances on succeeding Sundays (John 20:26). John had his apocalyptic vision on a Sunday (Revelation 1:10).
Gentiles worshipped on the Sabbath (Acts 13:42-44).	The descent of the Holy Spirit took place on a Sunday (Acts 2:1).
Matthew, Mark, and Luke, writing after the resurrection, spoke of the Sabbath as an existing institution (Matthew 24:20; Mark 16:1; Luke 23:56).	The early church was given the pattern of Sunday worship, and this they continued to do regularly (Acts 20:7; 1 Corinthians 16:2).

SEVENTH-DAY ADVENTIST REFORM MOVEMENT

Founded: 1925
Members: More than 24,000
Congregations: Unknown

Beginnings

This denomination emerged as a result of a conflict that developed with the leadership of Seventh-day Adventism regarding whether members should participate in war. Seventh-day Adventists have traditionally taught that in view of the sixth of the Ten Commandments (which prohibits the taking of life), members should never participate in war or bloodshed. However, during World War I (1914–1918), church leadership changed its position, and 98 percent of church members followed their lead and supported military service. The 2 percent who remained faithful to the original church position were disfellowshipped. After the war, these few members made an attempt at reconciliation with the larger body but without positive results. They had no choice but to separate from the main body of Seventh-day Adventists and form the Seventh-day Adventist Reform Movement in 1925.

Beliefs

Bible. The Bible is inspired by God and is an all-sufficient revelation from God. It is the only unerring rule of faith and practice.

God. The eternal Godhead is comprised of the Father, the Son, and the Holy Spirit. The Father is the Creator and is infinite in perfections.

Jesus Christ. The Son, Jesus, is eternal deity and is one in nature with the Father. He took on a human nature in the Incarnation, died for human sin at the cross, rose from the dead, and ascended to heaven.

Holy Spirit. The Holy Spirit is Christ's representative on earth and is the Regenerator in the work of redemption.

Sin and Salvation. Because of the sin of our first parents, human beings became separated from the source of life (God) and are therefore mortal by nature. At death, human beings—both the righteous and the unrighteous—enter into "sleep," remaining unconscious until the future day of resurrection. To be saved, humans must experience the new birth. This occurs when one repents of sin, yields to the work of the Holy Spirit, trusts in Christ, and experiences a desire to live in obedience to God's will.

The Ten Commandments are an expression of God's will and describe humankind's duty to God and fellow human beings. This law is binding upon humans of all ages. Obedience to the law does not save, but through Christ's strength Christians are enabled to render obedience.

Church. The church is a visible and organized body of believers led by and edified by elected officers. People become members of the church by a profession of faith and baptism. The offices of elder and bishop are for men only.

The fourth of the Ten Commandments requires worship on the seventh day (Saturday). It is both a day of rest and a memorial of God's work of creation.

Sacraments. Those who experience the new birth are to be baptized by immersion. This represents the death, burial, and resurrection of Jesus, as well as the death of the "old man" and resurrection of the "new man" in the life of a Christian. The Lord's Supper commemorates Christ's suffering and death on the cross. It is only for members in good standing. It is preceded by the ceremony of foot washing, an ordinance of humility.

End Times. In 1844, Jesus began the investigative judgment, an examination of the lives of professed children of God through the ages. Those found to be true and worthy become participants in God's kingdom. All others will experience eternal death.

Christ will one day come again visibly, physically, and gloriously, at which time the saints of all ages will be resurrected and taken to heaven. Christ will establish His glorious kingdom. Following a 1000-year period during which the unrighteous remain in the dust of the desolated earth, they will be resurrected, only to be exterminated by fire. God will then restore the earth to its Edenic beauty, and it will become the eternal home of the redeemed.

Website

www.sdarm.org

2

BAPTIST CHURCHES

BAPTIST SCHOLARS ARE not in agreement regarding Baptist origins. There are three basic theories:

1. The Jerusalem-Jordan-John Theory. This view—common among Landmark Baptists—says that Baptists have existed ever since the days of John the Baptist's ministry along the Jordan River in the first century.[1] If this theory is correct, then the Baptist church long predates the emergence of Protestantism. The problem with this theory is that it lacks convincing historical support. Certainly there are some similarities between the beliefs of Baptists and the first-century church, but this does not prove a direct line of descent.

2. The Anabaptist Spiritual Kingship Theory. This theory seeks to trace a spiritual relationship from the long line of Anabaptist sects—including the German, Dutch, and Swiss Anabaptists, the Waldensians and Petrobrusians, the Henricians, the Novations, and the Donatists—to modern-day Baptists.[2] Anabaptists are so-named because they required that those who were baptized as infants be rebaptized as adults following a profession of faith.

The problem with this theory is that Baptists have long disagreed with key theological positions held by the Anabaptists.

Baptist scholar Robert Torbet observes that "Baptists have not shared with Anabaptists the latter's aversion to oath-taking and holding public office. Neither have they adopted the Anabaptists' doctrine of pacifism, or their theological views concerning the Incarnation, soul sleeping, and the necessity of observing an apostolic succession in the administration of baptism."[3] Such factors make a direct lineage from the Anabaptists to the Baptists unlikely.

3. *The English Separatist Descent Theory.* According to this view, the Baptists emerged out of certain seventeenth-century English Separatists who had a congregational polity, believed the church should be made up of only a regenerate membership, and considered believers' (adult) baptism alone as valid according to the Scriptures.[4] The theology of the early Baptists supports this third theory.

John Smyth (1570–1612) founded the first Baptist church on English soil in 1611, the same year the King James Version was produced. These first Baptists were Arminian in their theology, emphasizing that Christ died for all people and that salvation was possible for all. These early Baptists were appropriately called General Baptists (salvation was *generally* available to all people).

FAST FACTS ON
Arminianism

Doctrine	Explanation
Election Based on Foreknowledge	God elected those whom He foreknew would, of their own free wills, believe in Christ and persevere in the faith.
Unlimited Atonement	In His atonement, Christ provided redemption for all humankind, making all humans saveable. Christ's atonement becomes effective only in those who believe.
Natural Inability	Humans cannot save themselves; the Holy Spirit must effect the new birth.
Prevenient Grace	Prevenient grace from the Holy Spirit enables a person to respond to the gospel and cooperate with God in salvation.
Conditional Perseverance	Believers have been empowered to live victoriously, but they are capable of turning from grace and losing salvation.

Later, in the 1630s, Particular Baptist churches emerged in England, teaching that Christ died only for the elect, and salvation was not possible for all people. (Salvation was limited to *particular* individuals.) This viewpoint—called "limited atonement"—is associated with the teachings of John Calvin (1509–1564). Theological controversy between Calvinism and Arminianism has continued to the present day.

FAST FACTS ON
the Five Points of Calvinism

Doctrine	Explanation
Total Depravity	Humans are not completely devoid of good impulses, but every human is engulfed in sin to such a degree that he or she can do nothing to earn merit before God.
Unconditional Election	God's choice of certain persons to salvation is not dependent upon any foreseen virtue on their part but rather is based on His sovereignty.
Limited Atonement	Christ's atoning death was only for the elect.
Irresistible Grace	Those whom God has chosen for eternal life will, as a result of God's irresistible grace, come to faith and thus to salvation.
Perseverance of the Saints	Those who are genuine believers will endure in the faith to the end.

The earliest Baptist churches on American soil were founded by Roger Williams (Providence, Rhode Island, 1639) and John Clarke (Newport, Rhode Island, 1648). By the 1680s, the Baptists had infiltrated the middle colonies, and in 1714 the first Baptist church was founded in the south. As was true in England, these first Baptist churches in America were Arminian in theology. They believed people were given a free will by God so they could freely choose for or against the gospel, as opposed to the strict predestination view of Calvinists.

With the passing of time, through the 1700s and after, the Baptists experienced tremendous growth. By the time of the American Revolution, they were the third-largest grouping of denominations in the colonies. Their growth was largely the result of their appeal to the poor and lower classes of people. Presently Baptists are the second largest Christian family in the United States, second only to Roman Catholicism.

AMERICAN BAPTIST ASSOCIATION
Founded: 1924
Members: 275,000
Congregations: 1760

Beginnings

The American Baptist Association is a fellowship of Missionary Baptist churches who hold to distinctive "Landmark" theology (see "Beliefs" below). These Landmark believers stood against the convention system in general and the policies of the Southern Baptist Convention in particular. In the early 1920s, Southern Baptist Convention loyalists were committed to the empowerment of the convention, whereas those affiliated with Landmarkism argued for a stronger emphasis on the local church. They believed that missionary work—indeed, the fulfillment of the Great Commission—was to be done through local churches as opposed to being overseen by a convention board. Conventions, they believed, should be servants of the local churches, controlled by the local churches. Each local church should be absolutely sovereign regarding its own doings. The idea of an ecclesiastical authority higher than local congregations was viewed as patently unbiblical.

In view of all this, an attempt was made to convert the Southern Baptist Convention to Landmark views concerning how missions work should be done. Their failed attempt led to their decision to associate together in the American Baptist Association in 1924.

Beliefs

Bible. The entire Bible is inspired by God and is inerrant and infallible. It is the all-sufficient rule for faith and practice.

God. God is a personal triune being, with each of the three persons in the Godhead equal in every divine perfection. The Father is the divine Creator.

Jesus Christ. Jesus is absolute deity. In the Incarnation, He was virgin-born, had a sinless life, suffered a substitutionary death on the cross, rose from the dead, and ascended into heaven.

Holy Spirit. The Holy Spirit convicts sinners, regenerates believers, indwells them, and seals them for salvation.

Sin and Salvation. Our original parents fell into sin by voluntary transgression, resulting in all humans being born in sin. Salvation is available by faith in Christ based on God's grace. All who trust in Jesus are secure in their salvation.

Church. Jesus Himself established the church. In keeping with Landmarkism, the church is *always* a local, visible assembly of scripturally baptized believers who are in a covenant relationship with God to carry out the Great Commission. Local churches and the kingdom of God are essentially the same. Only Baptist churches are true churches. A direct succession of Missionary Baptist churches stretches from the time of Christ and the apostles to the present day.

Pastors can be ordained only in legitimate Baptist churches. Only valid ministers can administer the Lord's Supper and baptism. Each church is autonomous and is responsible to Christ alone, not to a convention. The two officers of the church are pastor and deacon, both of which must be men. Church government is congregational. The association meets annually.

Sacraments. Baptism is by immersion and is for penitent believers. It must be administered in a scriptural Baptist church to be legitimate. The Lord's Supper is a memorial of Christ's death and is restricted to church members. Non-Baptists cannot participate.

End Times. Christ will one day come again personally and visibly. At His return, the righteous will be resurrected. Following the millennium, the unrighteous will be resurrected and then experience eternal punishment in the lake of fire.

Website

www.abaptist.org

AMERICAN BAPTIST CHURCHES IN THE USA

Founded: 1907
Members: 1,484,291
Congregations: 5836

Beginnings

This denomination began in 1907 as the Northern Baptist Convention and was formed to coordinate the efforts of various Baptist societies. The name was changed in 1950 to the American Baptist Convention and in 1972 to the American Baptist Churches in the USA. Presently most of the churches in the denomination are in the northern United States. It is about one-tenth the size of the Southern Baptist Convention and ranks sixth among the largest Baptist bodies.

Beliefs

Doctrinal Diversity. There is great doctrinal diversity within this body of churches. The doctrinal spectrum ranges from conservative to liberal among pastors. Overall, this is a much less conservative denomination than the Southern Baptist Convention. It rejects creeds and statements of faith that might hinder the ability and freedom of members to interpret the Bible as they see it.

Bible. Many believe the Bible is God's divinely inspired Word. It is an authoritative guide to knowing God and living the Christian life.

God. God is triune: Father, Son, and Holy Spirit (Creator, Redeemer, and Sustainer). The Father is the Sovereign of the universe.

Jesus Christ. Jesus, the Lord and Savior, atoned for human sin at the cross and then rose from the dead.

Holy Spirit. The Holy Spirit gives guidance to help people understand Scripture.

Church. The church is the fundamental unit of missionary work in the world. Each church is autonomous, formulating its own doctrine, mission, and worship style. The denomination does not dictate policy to local congregations but rather exists as a resource for missionary efforts. Women can be ordained.

Sin and Salvation. Because of humanity's sin, Jesus came to make atonement at the cross. Those who believe in Him are assured of salvation.

Sacraments. Baptism is by immersion and is reserved for those mature enough to understand its significance (resurrection unto new life in Jesus). The Lord's Supper is a memorial of Christ's broken body and shed blood at the cross. The ordinances are not necessary for salvation.

End Times. Jesus will one day come again in glory. Opinions vary on end-time events. Many pastors in the denomination, though not all, believe that heaven is reserved for believers. Many, though not all, believe hell is reserved for nonbelievers.

Website

www.abc-usa.org

FAST FACTS ON
Liberal vs. Conservative Christianity

	Liberal Christianity	Conservative Christianity
Bible	The Bible is a fallible, human document.	The Bible is verbally inspired by God, inerrant, and infallible.
Miracles	Miracles are not possible.	Miracles are possible.
Human Beings	Human beings are fundamentally good.	Human beings are fallen in sin and are in need of salvation.
Jesus	Jesus is not God but is a good moral teacher.	Jesus is eternal God and is the divine Savior and Messiah.
Jesus' Death	Jesus' death has a positive moral influence on human beings.	Jesus' death was an atoning substitutionary sacrifice for the sins of humankind.
God	God's primary attribute is love.	God's primary attribute is holiness. Because of His holiness, unredeemed (fallen) man cannot fellowship with Him.
Hell	There is no eternal hell.	All who have rejected Jesus Christ will suffer for all eternity in hell.

BAPTIST GENERAL CONFERENCE

Founded: 1852
Members: 194,610
Congregations: 880

Beginnings

The Baptist General Conference emerged out of the nineteenth-century Pietistic movement in Sweden. This movement was characterized by simple faith in the Bible, a rejection of dead formalism, and vibrant evangelism.

A middle-aged schoolteacher named Gustaf Palmquist immigrated from Sweden to the United States, became baptized, and was ordained to ministry in early 1852. Along with three other immigrants from Sweden—two males and a female—they organized a Swedish Baptist congregation in Rock Island, Illinois, on August 18, 1852. Before long, other such congregations cropped up due to the continued influx of Swedish immigrants into America. In 1864, 11 churches were affiliated with the movement, primarily in the upper Midwest and Northeast.

In 1879, the first annual (national) meeting of these churches took place—the Swedish Baptist General Conference. It was held in Village Creek, Iowa, and involved some 65 churches.

Following World War I, the denomination went through a bilingual stage, with both Swedish and English being used among the churches. Since the 1940s, however, English has become the exclusive language. Members became more comfortable with their American identity, and the word "Swedish" was dropped from the denomination name in 1945. With English as the exclusive language, the denomination took on greatly accelerated growth.

Beliefs

Bible. The Bible is the inerrant Word of God and is inspired in the words of the original manuscripts. It is the supreme authority in matters of faith and conduct.

God. The one true God exists eternally in three persons who are equal in the divine nature and divine attributes. The Father is an infinite and personal spirit who is perfect in holiness, wisdom, power, and love.

Jesus Christ. Jesus is the Father's only begotten Son who, though eternal deity, was born on earth through a virgin, conceived by the Holy Spirit, and lived a sinless life. He died as a substitutionary sacrifice on the cross and thereby atoned for human sin. He then rose from the dead and ascended into heaven.

Holy Spirit. The Holy Spirit proceeds from the Father and the Son. He convicts the world of sin, regenerates believers, sanctifies them, indwells them, empowers them to live for Jesus, and comforts them throughout life.

Sin and Salvation. Human beings are by nature sinful due to the sin of Adam and Eve. All are under just condemnation. Those who repent of their sins and trust in Christ are regenerated by the Holy Spirit. Their salvation in Jesus is secure.

Church. The universal church is the living spiritual body of Christ of which Christ is the head. It is made up of all regenerate Christians. The local church is made up of baptized believers. Its primary task is communicating the gospel to a lost world. Each local church is autonomous and should be free from interference from any ecclesiastical authority. Church government is congregational. Churches can cooperate with other churches—in and outside the denomination—to further the cause of Christ. Women can be ordained.

Sacraments. Baptism is by immersion and is only for those giving a credible profession of faith. The Lord's Supper commemorates the sacrificial death of Christ and is to be celebrated until Christ returns. Each church is free to determine how often the Lord's Supper is celebrated.

End Times. Jesus will one day return personally and visibly and establish His kingdom. Humans will be resurrected from the dead and face a final judgment. The righteous will experience eternal bliss in heaven. The wicked will experience endless suffering in hell.

Website

www.bgcworld.org

GENERAL ASSOCIATION OF GENERAL BAPTIST CHURCHES

Founded: 1870
Members: 66,296
Congregations: 1133

Beginnings

This denomination grew out of the theology of Benoni Stinson (1798–1869). Stinson had originally been a member of the United Baptist Church in Kentucky. His affiliation with this Calvinistic church eventually ended because of his Arminian theology—a theology that emphasizes human free will instead of predestination, and Christ's atonement for the sins of all humankind and not just those of the elect. In his heart, Stinson was a "general Baptist" because of his belief in a general atonement for all humankind.

Stinson accordingly left his church in 1823 and founded a new one—Liberty Church in Evansville, Indiana. This church was made up of like-minded Arminian enthusiasts. Other congregations soon cropped up, and the movement quickly spread into Illinois and Kentucky.

In 1824, these various churches joined to form the Liberty Association of General Baptists. Decades later, in 1870, they were renamed the General Association of General Baptists, adopting 11 articles of faith formulated by the Liberty Association, adding a few small changes.

Beliefs

Bible. The Bible is the inspired and infallible Word of God, fully authoritative in the life of the believer. It is the only reliable guide to Christian faith and conduct.

God. The one true living God is eternally revealed as Father, Son, and Holy Spirit.

Jesus Christ. Jesus, the second person of the Trinity, is humankind's Savior, having tasted death for everyone.

Sin and Salvation. Because of the disobedience of our first parents, human beings have become fallen, sinful, and depraved, unable to save themselves. Salvation is received through repentance toward God and faith toward Jesus. There is no final assurance of salvation. Only those who continue to abide in Christ, maintaining faith, persevering to the end, are assured of salvation. Those who lose faith and fall into apostasy lose their salvation.

Church. The church universal is the body of Christ, which includes all believers. The local church is a fellowship of Christians, all of whom are a part of the body of Christ and who voluntarily band together for worship, mutual nurture, and service to members of the body. Each church is autonomous. Government is congregational. Local churches are organized into local associations, and these in turn are organized into a general association. These associations are only advisory in nature.

Sacraments. Baptism is by immersion and is only for those who have demonstrated a personal relationship with Christ. The Lord's Supper is a memorial of Christ's atoning work at the cross, the bread representing Christ's broken body, the wine representing His shed blood. It constitutes an open confession that one has put away sin and put on Jesus Christ. Some members of the denomination practice a third ordinance: foot washing.

End Times. Jesus will one day return. The dead will be resurrected, and all humankind will face judgment. The righteous will be rewarded with eternal life. The wicked will suffer eternal torment in hell.

Website

www.generalbaptist.com

GENERAL ASSOCIATION OF REGULAR BAPTIST CHURCHES

Founded: 1932
Members: 155,757
Congregations: 1417

Beginnings

This association was founded in 1932 as a result of a number of churches withdrawing from the American Baptist Convention over doctrinal differences. These churches believed the convention had defected from the truth in that it refused to affirm adherence to the nineteenth-century New Hampshire Confession of

Faith (1833), widely accepted by Baptists in the northern and western states who were concerned that the convention had become theologically liberal and had succumbed to modernism. As well, the convention had drifted away from the Baptist emphasis on the independence and autonomy of local Baptist congregations.

Once the General Association of Regular Baptist Churches was formed, it adopted the New Hampshire Confession for its articles of faith but added a premillennial ending to the last article. The new association required all churches wanting to join to subscribe to these articles of faith and required them to separate themselves from any modernist groups. The association also rejected dual membership, thus barring all member churches from participating with any organization tainted by modernism. The term "regular" in the association's title separates it from those who hold to the "irregular" position of theological liberalism. This association is committed to the "regular" Baptist (conservative) position regarding the truth of Scripture.

Beliefs

Bible. The Bible is verbally and fully inspired and is infallible and inerrant in all matters which it addresses. It is the supreme standard for human conduct and doctrine.

God. The one true God is an infinite Spirit. He is the Maker and Ruler of all things and is intrinsically holy. In the unity of the Godhead are three coequal persons: the Father, the Son, and the Holy Spirit. They share equally in the divine perfections but are involved in different but harmonious offices.

Jesus Christ. Jesus is fully God. In the Incarnation, He was begotten of the Holy Spirit and virgin-born. He is both the Son of God and God the Son. He was crucified, rose from the dead, ascended into heaven, and is now our High Priest at the right hand of the Father.

Holy Spirit. The Holy Spirit is a divine person who restrains evil, convicts humans of sin, bears witness to the truth, is the agent of the new birth, seals believers, guides and teaches them, and sanctifies them.

Sin and Salvation. Adam fell and catapulted the entire human race into sin. Humans are thus totally depraved and are under just condemnation. Salvation is wholly of God's grace through Jesus Christ, who voluntarily took on Himself our sins such that by shedding His blood, He satisfied the just demands of a holy God. Faith in the Lord Jesus is the only condition of salvation, but repentance is an integral part of saving faith. The evidence of salvation includes fruits of repentance. All who are truly born again are kept by the Father for Jesus Christ.

Church. The local church is an organized congregation of baptized believers. Each church is autonomous, free of interference from any hierarchy. The only Ruler over the church is Jesus Christ. Church government is congregational. Its two offices are pastor and deacon. There is an annual convention. Churches can and should cooperate with each other for the furtherance of the gospel.

Sacraments. Baptism is by immersion for believers only. The ritual shows our identification with the crucified, buried, and risen Savior—representing our death to sin and rising to a new life in Jesus. It is a prerequisite to the privileges of church membership. The Lord's Supper commemorates Jesus' sacrificial death on the cross. It is preceded by solemn self-examination. Only immersed (baptized) believers can celebrate the Lord's Supper.

End Times. Church members believe in the premillennial return of Christ. The dead in Christ will be raised, and the living in Christ will be glorified without tasting death. This takes place at the rapture. After this is the tribulation period followed by the second coming, at which time Christ will set up His millennial kingdom. Following this kingdom the eternal state begins. Believers will enjoy heaven forever, while the wicked will suffer eternally in the lake of fire.

Website

www.garbc.org

NATIONAL ASSOCIATION OF FREE WILL BAPTISTS

Founded: 1935
Members: 197,919
Congregations: 2470

Beginnings

This denomination can be traced to Baptists from England who settled in the colonies in the 1700s and were Arminian in their theology—holding to the doctrines of free grace, free salvation, and free will. They believed *any* person is free to believe in Jesus, as opposed to the Calvinistic view that God predestines only the elect to salvation. They interpreted *election* to mean that God determines from the beginning of time to save all those who comply with the conditions of salvation, and that human beings *become* His elect by opting for the salvation He offers. These Baptists also rejected "irresistible grace"—the idea that God's grace irresistibly moves only a select group of people to believe. Rather, they believed *any* human being could accept or reject the grace of God. From the early 1700s through the early 1900s, a series of splits and mergers took place, with a major stream of Free Will

Baptists finally coming together in 1935 to form the National Association of Free Will Baptists in Nashville, Tennessee.

Beliefs

Bible. The Bible is inspired by God and is without error in all that it touches on—including history, geography, and even matters relating to science. It is the infallible rule of faith and practice.

God. The one true living God is eternally revealed in three persons: the Father, the Son, and the Holy Spirit.

Jesus Christ. Jesus is God manifest in the flesh, fully divine and fully human. He is the Mediator between humankind and God. He was crucified for human sin, rose from the dead, ascended into heaven, and was glorified.

Holy Spirit. The Holy Spirit, the third person of the Trinity, has all the attributes of deity. He is involved in a variety of ministries among the people of God.

Sin and Salvation. Adam and Eve were created in a state of innocence, but they fell into a state of sin and condemnation. All humans since that time have inherited a fallen nature and are thereby guilty before God. Through Christ's life, sufferings, death, and resurrection, redemption has been provided for humankind.

Whoever wills can be saved. The condition for salvation is repentance or sincere sorrow for sin (and a renunciation of it) and faith in Christ as Lord and Savior with the purpose of loving and obeying Him in all things, continuing in faith and obedience unto death. Humans are not secure in this salvation. Only believers who through grace persevere in holiness to the end of life are assured salvation. If a saved person wrongly uses his freedom of will and stops trusting in Jesus for salvation, he or she can fall from grace and once again be lost.

Church. Local churches are autonomous and self-governing. They voluntarily choose to cooperate as Free Will Baptists.

Sacraments. The three ordinances are baptism, the Lord's Supper, and foot washing. Baptism is by immersion. It represents the burial and resurrection of Jesus as well as the death of Christians to the world, the washing of their souls from sin, and their rising to a new life in Jesus. The Lord's Supper commemorates Christ's death, the bread representing His broken body and the wine representing His shed blood. Foot washing is a universal obligation to be administered to all true believers. The ritual teaches humility and reminds believers of the necessity of a daily cleansing from sin.

End Times. Jesus will come again personally and visibly at the end of the gospel dispensation. All humans will be resurrected. The righteous will experience a resurrection unto life, and the wicked will experience a resurrection unto eternal punishment.

Website

www.nafwb.org

NATIONAL BAPTIST CONVENTION OF AMERICA

Founded: 1895
Members: 3,500,000
Congregations: 2500

Beginnings

Three conventions led to the eventual formation of the National Baptist Convention of America. In 1880, the Foreign Mission Baptist Convention was created in Montgomery,

Alabama. In 1886, the American National Baptist Convention was formed in St. Louis, Missouri. In 1893, the Baptist National Educational Convention was formed in the District of Columbia. In a merger in 1895, these three conventions joined in Atlanta, Georgia, to form the National Baptist Convention of America. It constitutes the second-largest association of African-American Baptists in the United States.

With 3,500,000 members in 2500 congregations, the association is comprised of more than 30 affiliate state conventions. Its objectives include (1) bringing unity to its membership and the larger Christian community by proclaiming Christ's gospel, (2) promoting Baptist faith and practice, and (3) encouraging the scholarly and creative skills of church members in writing for publication.

Beliefs

Bible. The Bible is inspired by God and is without error in all that it touches on.

God. The one true living God is eternally revealed in three persons: the Father, the Son, and the Holy Spirit.

Jesus Christ. Jesus is God manifest in the flesh, fully divine and fully human. He is the Mediator between humankind and God. He was crucified for human sin, rose from the dead, ascended into heaven, and was glorified.

Holy Spirit. The Holy Spirit, the third person of the Trinity, has all the attributes of deity. He is involved in a variety of ministries among the people of God.

Sin and Salvation. Adam and Eve were created in a state of innocence but fell into a state of sin and condemnation. All humans have inherited from them a fallen nature and are thereby guilty before God. Through Christ's life, suffering, death, and resurrection, redemption has been provided for humankind. Salvation comes through faith in Christ.

Church. Local churches are independent, autonomous congregations of baptized believers. (Only saved people can be members.) The work of the church is to get people saved, baptize them, and teach them Scripture.

Sacraments. Baptism is by immersion and must be given by a proper administrator. The Lord's Supper is a memorial of Christ's broken body and His blood, shed on the cross.

End Times. Jesus will come again personally and visibly. All humans will be resurrected. The righteous will experience a resurrection unto life, and the wicked will experience a resurrection unto eternal punishment.

Website

www.nbcamerica.org

NATIONAL PRIMITIVE BAPTIST CONVENTION

Founded: 1907
Members: 1,000,000
Congregations: 1530

Beginnings

During the Civil War years, black slaves in the South worshipped with white slave owners. Following the emancipation of slaves, their white Baptist brethren assisted them in setting up their own churches and ordained ministers and deacons from among their own people. By the early 1900s, many of these churches were ready to unite into a convention.

In 1906, a number of black elders—including Clarence Sams, George Crawford, and James Carey—issued a call for others to attend a strategic meeting in Huntsville, Alabama, that was to take place in July of 1907. Some 88 elders from seven southern states attended and organized the National Primitive Baptist Convention.

The convention is a loosely structured organization with no central authority and no common confession. Accordingly, some variation exists among members regarding doctrine and practice. A primary difference of opinion exists among members regarding the issue of social involvement.

Beliefs

Bible. The Bible is inspired by God and is the only rule of faith and practice. It is fully sufficient to make one "wise unto salvation."

God. The one true God is externally manifest in three persons: the Father, the Son, and the Holy Spirit.

Jesus Christ. Jesus died on the cross to provide salvation for the elect. He rose from the dead and ascended into heaven.

Sin and Salvation. Adam fell into sin, and his sinful nature was communicated to his posterity by ordinary generation. All human beings are now fallen in sin.

Before the foundation of the world, God specifically elected certain individuals in the human race for salvation. These chosen in Christ will be effectually called, regenerated, and born again by the Holy Spirit. At the moment of belief in Christ, they are justified—Christ's own righteousness is imputed to them by faith. Good works are the fruit that give evidence of faith. All the elect will persevere to the end and will finally be saved.

Church. Local churches are independent congregations of baptized believers. Only saved people can be members. The work of the church is to get people saved, baptize them, and teach them Christ's principles. The officers of the church are pastors and deacons (or deaconesses). Church government is congregational. There are local associations and a national convention.

Sacraments. Baptism is by immersion and must be given by a proper administrator. The Lord's Supper is a memorial of Christ's broken body and His blood, shed on the cross. Foot washing takes place after the Lord's Supper (as it did at the Last Supper in the upper room).

End Times. The end will include a general judgment of both the just and the unjust. Eternal joy awaits believers in heaven. Eternal punishment awaits the unsaved.

Website

www.natlprimbaptconv.org

NEW TESTAMENT ASSOCIATION OF INDEPENDENT BAPTIST CHURCHES

Founded: 1965
Members: Not available
Congregations: 126

Beginnings

In the 1950s and 1960s, many members of the Conservative Baptist Association of America expressed dissatisfaction with the convention. They felt the association, instead of separating from churches and theological beliefs that are aberrant, was becoming increasingly inclusive with other churches and was growing too ecumenical in spirit. Further, many of these members wanted the association to take a stand for premillennialism and pretribulationism (that is, a pretribulational rapture).

In 1964, representatives of these dissenters met at Marquette Manor Baptist Church in Chicago, Illinois, to explore possible courses of action. A committee was then appointed to make plans for the establishment of a new association. The New Testament Association of Independent Baptist Churches was provisionally constituted in 1965 at Beth Eden Baptist Church in Denver, Colorado, and some 27 churches affiliated with the association at this first meeting.

Beliefs

This denomination has a policy of separation and disavowal in regard to interdenominationalism, liberalism, Covenant and Reformed theology, amillennialism and postmillennialism, and the posttribulational and midtribulational theories of the rapture.

Bible. The Bible is God's Word. It is the only rule Christians have for faith and practice.

God. The one true God is eternally revealed in three persons: the Father, the Son, and the Holy Spirit. The three, though distinct persons, are one in essence (or nature).

Jesus Christ. Jesus is fully God. In the Incarnation, He became a man while fully retaining His deity. He was crucified for human sin, was buried, and rose from the dead.

Holy Spirit. The Holy Spirit, the third person of the Trinity, convicts people of sin, indwells believers, and empowers them for service.

Sin and Salvation. By virtue of Adam's sin, all human beings are born in sin. Jesus was crucified for the sins of humanity, and those who believe in Him become recipients of salvation. One who is truly born again is eternally secure in Christ.

Church. The universal church is the body of Christ. The local church is made up of a regenerate membership (all are believers). The local church is autonomous, and government is congregational. Only men can be ordained and serve as pastors.

Sacraments. Baptism is by immersion in the name of the Father, Son, and Holy Spirit. It points to a believer's faith in the crucified, buried, and risen Savior, and it represents the participant's death to sin and resurrection unto a new life. It is a prerequisite to the privileges of church membership. The Lord's Supper commemorates the death of Jesus and is to be preceded by a solemn self-examination. It is for church members only.

End Times. Eschatology is interpreted from a dispensational, premillennial, and pretribulational viewpoint. At death, the spirits of believers go to heaven with Christ and enjoy conscious joy until the future rapture. At the rapture, believers receive their resurrection bodies. Following the rapture, God's judgments will be poured out on humankind during the tribulation. Christ's second coming will then occur, after which He will set up the Davidic kingdom (the millennial kingdom). Israel will be saved and restored as a nation. Following the millennial kingdom is the eternal state. Believers will live forever in heaven. Unbelievers will suffer eternally in the literal flames of hell.

Website

Unknown

NORTH AMERICAN BAPTIST CONFERENCE
Founded: 1865
Members: 66,359
Congregations: 398

Beginnings

The North American Baptist Conference was established in the nineteenth century by Germans who immigrated to the United States. Konrad Anton Fleischmann founded the first

German-speaking Baptist congregation in Philadelphia in 1843. After founding this church, Fleischmann traveled around founding other churches throughout Pennsylvania, New Jersey, and New York. In 1865, delegates of these like-minded churches met in Wilmot, Ontario, and organized the North American Baptist Conference. At that time, the German language was exclusively used among the churches. The shift from German to English occurred rather rapidly following World War I, and today nearly all congregations within the denomination speak English (though a few are bilingual).

Beliefs

Bible. The Bible is the Word of God, inspired by Him. It constitutes God's revelation to humankind and is trustworthy, sufficient, and without error. It is the supreme authority and guide for doctrine and conduct.

God. The one true God is perfect in wisdom. He is sovereign, holy, just, merciful, and loving. He exists eternally in three persons: the Father, the Son, and the Holy Spirit. The Father reigns with providential care over all things in the universe.

Jesus Christ. Jesus is the Son of God who, in the Incarnation, became a man, having been conceived of the Holy Spirit and born of the Virgin Mary. He revealed the Father through a sinless life, many miracles, and teachings. He provided salvation for humankind through His atoning death on the cross. He rose from the dead and ascended into heaven, where He now intercedes on behalf of believers.

Holy Spirit. The Holy Spirit inspired the Scriptures, convicts humans of sin, indwells believers, seals them for salvation, empowers them for service, guides and teaches them, and produces spiritual fruit in them.

Sin and Salvation. Adam disobeyed God and brought sin and death to all humans. All people are born with a sin nature and are in need of reconciliation with God. Salvation is provided by the redemption wrought by Christ and is a free gift of God to all people. It is received personally through repentance and faith in Jesus Christ. True believers are secure in their salvation.

Church. The universal church is the body of Christ, of which Christ is the head. All who believe in Christ are members of the universal church. Christians who are baptized upon profession of faith become members of a local church for mutual encouragement and growth in discipleship. Each local church is autonomous under the lordship of Christ. Church government is congregational. A triennial conference of all churches is the chief administrative body.

Sacraments. Baptism is by immersion in the name of the Father, Son, and Holy Spirit. It symbolizes the believer's identification with the death, burial, and resurrection of Jesus Christ. The Lord's Supper involves partaking of bread and the cup as a memorial of the broken body and shed blood of Christ.

End Times. Jesus is coming soon, personally and visibly. The dead will be raised and Christ will judge all humankind. The righteous will receive rewards from Christ and dwell forever in heaven. The unrighteous will be consigned to everlasting punishment in hell.

Website

www.nabconference.org

PRIMITIVE BAPTISTS

Founded: 1827
Members: 72,000
Congregations: 1000

Beginnings

The Primitive Baptists emerged in the nineteenth century as a reaction against money-based missionary societies. These Baptists argued that the New Testament does not mention missionary societies, and no Scripture verse tells Christians to form such societies. They are mere human inventions, and because they have no biblical support, Christians should not have them today. The Primitive Baptists at the Kehukee Association in North Carolina (1827) took the lead in condemning such societies as going against Christ's teachings.

Primitive Baptists are "primitive" not in the sense of being backward, as the word is sometimes interpreted. Rather, "primitive" is intended to communicate the idea of originality—that is, the goal is to recapture the original faith and practice of the original New Testament apostles.

Beliefs

Bible. The Bible is the divinely inspired Word of God and is infallible in all matters, including history and science. It is the sole rule of faith and practice. The 1611 King James Version is considered the superior English translation of the Scriptures.

God. The one true God is eternal, infinite, incomprehensible, and almighty. God is eternally manifest in three persons: the Father, Son, and Holy Spirit.

Jesus Christ. Jesus is the true Messiah and Savior. He was manifested in the flesh, born of a woman, and died on the cross for the elect only. He rose from the dead, ascended into heaven, and now makes intercession for believers from heaven.

Holy Spirit. The Holy Spirit, the third person of the Trinity, is involved in various ministries, including teaching believers the Word of God.

Sin and Salvation. Since Adam's time, all humans have been born with a corrupted nature, utterly dead to spiritual things. Sinners can do nothing to gain merit before God. Yet God has unconditionally elected specific individuals to receive salvation. This choice was not based on foreseen merit of human beings but rather was based entirely on God's sovereignty. In God's plan, the blood of Christ is sufficient to both procure and secure salvation for all for whom it was shed. All of the elect will finally be saved.

Church. The local church is made up of believers. Each church is autonomous, and no association has authority over them. Church government is congregational. Ministers of each church are called elders. These are chosen by individual congregations from among male members who have proven themselves faithful to the church. They are self-educated in the Word of God under the guidance of the Holy Spirit.

No musical instruments are used during services. There are no Sunday school classes (for none are mentioned in the New Testament). There is no organized program for the entertainment of youth. There are no crucifixes or pictures of Jesus in the church, for such would be idolatry. No one can join the church that is a member of a secret society. Sermons are often delivered in a dramatic singsong voice.

Sacraments. Baptism is by immersion and follows a profession of faith. It represents the death, burial, and resurrection of Jesus. People who come to the church from another denomination must be rebaptized (Acts 19:1-7). Communion (using wine and unleavened bread) commemorates the sufferings and death of Jesus and follows a time of personal self-examination. Foot washing takes place after communion, just as Jesus washed the feet of the disciples after the Last Supper (John 13:14-15).

End Times. Jesus will one day come again personally and visibly. The dead will be resurrected and judged based on their works, whether good or bad. Heaven is reserved for the saved, while eternal suffering in hell is the fate of the unsaved.

Website

www.pb.org

PROGRESSIVE NATIONAL BAPTIST CONVENTION

Founded: 1961
Members: 2,500,000
Congregations: 2000

Beginnings

This convention was formed in 1961 as a result of five years of continued dispute regarding the tenure of the presidency of the National Baptist Convention of the USA, as well as other administrative and procedural issues. There was also growing tension related to the civil rights movement. The National Baptist Convention of the USA had been following a policy of noninvolvement regarding civil rights.

Before 1961, concerned ministers had met several times, seeking solutions to their concerns regarding the convention. Their goal was to continue working within the framework of the convention, with no intention of withdrawing membership. At subsequent convention meetings, however, the breach widened. In one session, delegates actually threw chairs around.

The Reverend L.V. Booth of Zion Baptist Church in Cincinnati, Ohio, promptly sent a letter out to urge fellow pastors to come to Cincinnati for a meeting. He called for all who were interested in peace, fellowship, and progress to attend. Though the meeting was opposed by leading ministers in the convention, 33 delegates from 14 states attended. At this meaning, attendees formed the Progressive National Baptist Convention and elected Reverend Booth as its first president. Within a short five years, some 660 affiliate churches and 31 affiliate associations, conventions, and fellowships joined the convention.

Not unexpectedly, the convention became a strong supporter of Martin Luther King Jr. It became very active in seeking social justice, not only in the United States but also around the world. The convention took a strong stand against the apartheid of South Africa.

Beliefs

Bible. The Bible is inspired by God and is without any mixture of error. It is the supreme standard against which all human actions should be judged.

God. The one true God is the Creator and Ruler of the universe. He is eternally manifest in three persons: the Father, the Son, and Holy Spirit.

Jesus Christ. Jesus is the Son of God, who atoned for human sin by His death on the cross. He then rose from the dead and ascended into heaven.

Sin and Salvation. Adam sinned and catapulted the entire human race into sin. Every human being now has an inherently sinful nature. Jesus, however, provided redemption at the cross. The salvation He provided is to be received by personal faith.

End Times. Christ will one day come again personally and visibly. Humans will be resurrected from the dead and face the judgment. Believers will spend eternity in heaven, while unbelievers will suffer endless punishment in hell.

Website

www.pnbc.org

REFORMED BAPTIST CHURCH

Founded: 1954
Members: Not available
Congregations: 350

Beginnings

The Reformed Baptist Church is more of a theological movement than a denomination, but between 300 and 400 churches have aligned themselves with it. All such churches hold to five-point Calvinism as represented in the London Confession of 1689 and the Philadelphia Confession of Faith (1772). As noted previously, the five points of Calvinism are total depravity, unconditional election, limited atonement, irresistible grace, and perseverance of the saints.

The movement formally began in 1954 in Ashland, Kentucky, where a series of meetings conducted by Rolfe Barnard (1904–1969) led to the first conference meeting.

Beliefs

Bible. The Bible is the Word of God and is fully inspired. It is inerrant regarding not only faith and practice but also history and science.

God. The one true God exists eternally in three persons: the Father, the Son, and the Holy Spirit.

Jesus Christ. Jesus is full deity. He is the eternal Son of God. In the Incarnation, He took on an additional human nature and atoned for the sins of the elect at the cross.

Sin and Salvation. Man is a sinner who is totally depraved. He can do nothing to merit favor before God. Those whom God sovereignly elected to salvation will, as a result of God's grace, come to faith and thus to salvation. From the individual's perspective, this salvation is received through repentance and faith. All true saints will persevere to the end in faith, repentance, and holiness.

Church. The local church is autonomous and is headed by pastors (teaching elders) and ruling elders (lay elders). The election of church officers is by congregational vote.

Sacraments. Baptism is by immersion. The Lord's Supper is open to all who are genuine Christians and members in good standing of evangelical churches.

End Times. Jesus will bodily come again in glory. Dispensational eschatology is specifically rejected. Church members do not take a particular millennial view. In the future there will be a literal new heavens and new earth that will be the final inheritance of God's people. Hell is reserved for the wicked, who will suffer eternal punishment there.

Website

www.vor.org

SOUTHERN BAPTIST CONVENTION
Founded: 1845
Members: 15,900,000
Congregations: 41,500

Beginnings

The Southern Baptist Convention was established in 1845 in Augusta, Georgia. It was formed by Baptist congregations in the southern United States during the years leading up to the Civil War. Some of the southern congregations separated from the American Baptist Home Mission Board because the board refused to send slave owners into the missionary field. Members of southern congregations felt slave owners should be able to become missionaries on the foreign field. They believed they were no less eligible than others to serve as missionaries, and missionary boards had no right to judge their moral character. The Southern Baptist Convention was thus formed, and it established its own boards for foreign and home missions. Some 300 churches in eight southern states entered the new convention.

The Southern Baptist Convention today seeks to be a supportive organization that provides help to affiliate churches in evangelism and missionary work. It is the largest Baptist body in the United States and the largest Protestant denomination in the United States. About half of all the Baptists in the United States belong to churches affiliated with the Southern Baptist Convention.

At one time, all the churches affiliated with the convention were from the South. Today, however, affiliate churches are in all 50 states, working through some 1200 local associations and 41 state conventions who share common beliefs and a commitment to the Great Commission. The term "Southern" is no longer truly descriptive of the organization.

In 1995, the Southern Baptist Convention adopted a resolution renouncing and condemning its racist origins and apologized to African-Americans for the racist policies of its founders. Today, some 1900 congregations in the convention are predominantly African-American.

Beliefs

Churches in the Southern Baptist Convention are bound by no creed, but they share a confession of faith based on the New Hampshire Confession. Most member churches are conservative in their theology—more so than Northern Baptists.

Bible. The Bible was written by men who were divinely inspired, and therefore God is ultimately the author of Scripture. It is authoritative and constitutes God's full revelation to humankind. It contains truth without any mixture of error.

God. The one true living God is eternally revealed as Father, Son, and Holy Spirit. Though distinct persons, these three are without division of nature, essence, or being. The Father reigns supreme with providential care over the entire universe.

Jesus Christ. Jesus is the eternal Son of God who, in the Incarnation, was conceived of the Holy Spirit and born of the Virgin Mary. He died on the cross for human sin and secured salvation for humankind. He then rose from the dead and ascended into heaven.

Holy Spirit. The Holy Spirit exalts Christ, convicts men of sin, enlightens the minds of believers, and empowers them for service.

Sin and Salvation. By free choice, Adam sinned and brought sin and death upon the entire human race. Salvation is offered freely to all who accept Jesus as Lord and Savior. Salvation includes regeneration, sanctification, and glorification. All true believers endure to the end and will not fall away from their salvation.

Church. The universal church is the body of Christ and includes the redeemed of all ages. The local church is made up of baptized believers who are associated by covenant in the faith and fellowship of the gospel. Each local church is autonomous but cooperates with other churches. Government is congregational. Only men participate in pastoral roles.

Sacraments. Baptism is by immersion and is for those who have given a public profession of faith. It symbolizes the believer's faith in the crucified, buried, and risen Savior, and it represents the believer's death to sin, burial, and resurrection to a new life in Jesus. The Lord's Supper memorializes the death of Jesus and anticipates His second coming.

End Times. Jesus will personally and visibly return. The dead will be raised, and Christ will judge all human beings. The righteous will receive rewards and dwell forever with the Lord in heaven. The unrighteous will be consigned to eternal suffering in hell.

Website

www.sbc.net

3

BRETHREN CHURCHES

THE BRETHREN CHURCH SEEKS to be a company of brothers and sisters joined in a fellowship and community of love and mutual edification. The Spirit of God within believers binds them together. Many Brethren enjoy a simple and unadorned life, dressing in plain clothing, covering women's heads at church services, and making moral purity a high priority among members. They generally abstain from worldly amusements, do not engage in lawsuits or go to war, and often greet each other with a holy kiss.

Alexander Mack (1679–1735) and seven other German believers founded the Brethren movement in Schwarzenau, Germany, in 1708. All of them had been heavily influenced by the Pietists, who abhorred dead orthodoxy and said Christianity was a faith to be lived and experienced, and by the Anabaptists, who wanted not to reform the existing church but to build a New Testament church from the ground up. Mack and his friends felt the churches in their area had become spiritually stagnant, and they sought a spiritual awakening. They wanted to return to the vitality and commitment of the first-century church. With the New Testament as their only creed, they stressed personal discipleship and desired that their lives be shaped by a vibrant faith in Jesus Christ.

Their movement started with small meetings in peoples' homes for the purpose of prayer and Bible study. They referred to themselves as *Brüder-Gemeinde* ("Community of Brothers"). Mack was their first leader and minister. The new movement experienced rapid expansion in Germany.

Because they were not supporting the state church, their actions were interpreted by German authorities as disloyalty to the state, and they began to suffer persecution. This persecution took the form of confiscation of members' property and the imprisonment of some in the movement. They were eventually driven out of Germany, and in 1723 they migrated to Germantown, Pennsylvania.

In their new locale, their zeal, honesty, and hard work yielded many conversions, and the movement expanded at a fast pace. Soon enough, congregations emerged in Kentucky and Ohio (1790s), in Missouri and Illinois (1810s), and in California and Oregon (1850s).

CHURCH OF THE BRETHREN
Founded: 1708
Members: 134,828
Congregations: 1070

Beginnings

In 1908 the Brethren movement started by Alexander Mack and his associates in 1708 (see above) adopted the name "Church of the Brethren." "Brethren," to church members, was reflective of the brotherhood that existed in New Testament times. The term portrays Christians as kindred spirits.

In the early years of the movement, a number of factors distinguished the Brethren from other Christians. Church leaders were not salaried or expected to receive a formal theological education. They had a strong commitment to church discipline when members fell into sin. Members opposed any involvement in the military, avoided taking any oaths, and separated themselves from all secular influences. They dressed quite plainly, and their living arrangements avoided extravagance.

In the 1900s, the Brethren made some changes. At their 1911 conference, the dress code was modernized, and people were now allowed to wear whatever they wanted. Church leaders started earning a salary and were formally trained. In 1957, women became eligible for church ordination.

Despite such changes, the denomination remained committed to following Christ in simple obedience in all things. They took Romans 12:2 very seriously: "Do not be conformed to this world" (NASB). To this day, they continue to remember the instruction of Alexander Mack that people in the world would recognize the Brethren "by the manner of their living."

Beliefs

Bible. The Bible is divinely inspired. What is meant by *inspiration* is debated. Some in the denomination believe in verbal, plenary inspiration. Others believe the biblical writers merely had a heightened sense of spiritual awareness when they wrote. In any event, the Bible is viewed as a sufficient formulation of truth.

God. The one true God is the Creator and Sustainer of all things. He is triune in nature. Reference is made to the fatherhood of God, the lordship of Christ, and the empowerment of the Holy Spirit.

Jesus Christ. Jesus, the Son of God, is both Lord and Savior. He is the head of the church.

Holy Spirit. The Holy Spirit is God's active presence in the world. He guides believers in every aspect of life, thought, and mission.

Sin and Salvation. All humanity is fallen in sin. To be saved, human beings must repent and believe in Jesus Christ as Lord and Savior.

Church. The church is a fellowship of redeemed and baptized believers. It is a community of faith and commitment. By undergoing baptism, a person becomes a full member of the Brethren congregation and of the larger body of Christ. Government is both presbyterial and congregational. Final authority rests in the annual conference of elected delegates.

Sacraments. Baptism is by a threefold forward immersion. The person kneels in the water of the baptistery, publicly acknowledges his decision, and is immersed three times in the name of the Father, the Son, and the Holy Spirit. (The Brethren are often referred to as "dunkers.") Baptism is for confessing believers only and is a symbol of the believer dying with Christ and being raised to engage in Christ's work.

Communion is celebrated once or twice a year and follows the threefold actions of Christ in the upper room. First is a foot washing, which symbolizes humility and servanthood. Then comes a common fellowship meal, which symbolizes family. Following this is the sharing of the bread and cup, symbolizing the Savior. The service closes with a hymn.

End Times. Heaven is a place of blessing reserved for believers. Hell is the place of final punishment for the wicked. Some in the denomination believe God may eventually empty hell so that all souls will be restored to heaven.

Website

www.brethren.org

FAST FACTS ON
Biblical Hymnology

- Moses and the Israelites sang praise to God in response to His deliverance of the Israelites from Egyptian bondage (Exodus 15:1-21).

- Deborah and Barak sang praise to God in response to being delivered from the Canaanites (Judges 5:1-12).

- Many of the psalms were originally accompanied by music.

- Isaiah's songs of praise most often focus on God's deliverance of Israel from exile and His future blessings on the nation (Isaiah 12:5,6; 27:2; 30:29; 42:10-11; 44:23).

- Believers are exhorted to sing new songs of praise (see Psalm 33:3; 40:3; Revelation 5:9; 14:3).

BRETHREN CHURCH (ASHLAND, OHIO)
Founded: 1883
Members: 10,381
Congregations: 120

Beginnings

In 1882, some progressive-minded members of the Church of the Brethren (see above) withdrew from the main body because they desired a church which, unlike their present church, had an educated and paid clergy, Sunday school classes, a missions program, a congregational church government, and more liberty and freedom in the worship service (including more freedom in how one dresses).*

Within a year, these dissenting Brethren organized a convention called the Brethren Church. They allowed more modern dress, developed a missions program, and allowed an educated and salaried ministry leadership. Their present headquarters is in Ashland, Ohio.

The denomination emphasizes that how one lives the Christian life is more important than doctrine. Jesus' Sermon on the Mount (Matthew 5–7) plays a major role in showing believers what the Christian life should look like.

Beliefs

Bible. Both the Old and New Testaments are inspired by God. The Bible is authoritative, trustworthy, and true in every respect. The New Testament is the final rule of faith and life for the church.

God. The one true God is eternal, infinite, personal, and perfect. He is the Creator of the universe. He is eternally manifest in three persons: the Father, the Son, and the Holy Spirit.

Jesus Christ. Jesus is God from all eternity. He eventually became flesh, was born of a virgin, and lived a perfect life. He was the ultimate revelation of the Father. At the cross, He gave His life as a ransom for human sin. He was then resurrected, ascended into heaven, and now intercedes on behalf of believers.

Holy Spirit. The Holy Spirit inspired Scripture, assisted Jesus during His three-year ministry, and opens the minds of believers so they can understand Scripture. He empowers believers for service, fills, seals, and baptizes them, gives them spiritual gifts for service, and enables them to grow in Christlikeness.

---

* As noted previously, the Church of the Brethren eventually updated its dress code, began paying its clergy, and allowed for clergy eduction.

Sin and Salvation. Because of Adam's sin, the effects of guilt and corruption have passed on to every human being. Sin dwells in all people, making them unable to please God in their own efforts. The penalty for sin is spiritual death (spiritual separation from God).

People receive salvation by repentance from sin and personal faith in Jesus Christ, both witnessed by water baptism. God adopts these individuals into His family, forgiving their sins. Believers demonstrate the genuineness of their faith by obeying Christ's commands.

Church. The church is a visible body of God's followers, composed of those who have received Jesus as Lord. This body finds expression in local communities of believers (local churches). Through mutual submission they covenant together for worship, spiritual nurture, evangelism, and service. Government is congregational. Churches are semiautonomous. Conferences do not have authority over local churches accept in those areas that the local churches authorize. Women can be ordained, though this issue is debated among many congregations.

Sacraments. Baptism is by immersion three times (in the name of the Father, the Son, and the Holy Spirit). Communion takes place in the evening service and has three components based on Jesus' example in the upper room: foot washing, which symbolizes cleansing and the need for humility, a common fellowship meal, and the sharing of the bread and cup.

End Times. Jesus will one day return personally and visibly as King of kings. All people will be resurrected and face judgment. Believers will enjoy eternal life, living with the Lord in the new heavens and new earth. The wicked will be confined to eternal punishment.

Website

www.brethrenchurch.org

FELLOWSHIP OF GRACE BRETHREN CHURCHES

Founded: 1939
Members: 30,371
Congregations: 260

Beginnings

The Brethren Church (Ashland, Ohio) suffered a division in 1939. The conservatives of the denomination spoke out against what they perceived to be liberal tendencies of the Brethren Church. These "liberals" (the mainstream of the Ashland group) were Arminian in their theology, while the conservative dissenters (the "grace" group) were Calvinist in theology. The "grace" group split off and in 1939 founded the Fellowship of Grace Brethren Churches.

Beliefs

Bible. The Bible is verbally inspired in all parts. It is the infallible Word of God, wholly without error in the original manuscripts. It is the only authority for doctrine and practice.

God. The one true God is infinite in perfections. He exists eternally in three persons: the Father, the Son, and the Holy Spirit.

Jesus Christ. Jesus is eternal God and Lord. In the Incarnation, He became a man, begotten of the Holy Spirit and born of a virgin. He lived a sinless life and died a substitutionary death on the cross. He was resurrected bodily and ascended into heaven, where He now intercedes for believers at the right hand of the Father.

Holy Spirit. The Holy Spirit baptizes and indwells believers at the moment of regeneration. He fills and empowers them for Christian life and service.

Sin and Salvation. Adam fell into sin, thereby becoming spiritually dead. As a result, all humankind is dead in sin. A new birth is necessary for salvation. Salvation is received as a gift of God through personal faith in Christ and His finished work. Salvation is secure in Jesus.

Church. The church is the body and bride of Christ, composed of all true believers of the present age. Members are organized in local churches for worship, edification, and a worldwide gospel witness. Each church is autonomous but cooperates with other churches in fellowship and in working toward fulfilling the Great Commission. Church government is congregational. Churches send delegates to the denomination's annual convention.

Sacraments. Each believer is baptized by a threefold forward immersion in the name of the Father, the Son, and the Holy Spirit. Baptism is a testimony of one's conversion and obedience to Jesus. Communion includes a threefold service: foot washing, a common fellowship meal, and the sharing of the bread and cup.

End Times. There will be a pretribulational and premillennial coming of Christ. In the end, all people will be resurrected and judged. Believers will be rewarded and experience eternal life in heaven. Unbelievers will suffer eternal punishment.

Website

www.fgbc.org

FAST FACTS ON
the Blessings of Heaven

- Sharing in Christ's glory (Romans 8:17)
- No more death (1 Corinthians 15:54)
- A reunion with Christian loved ones (1 Thessalonians 4:13-17)
- Praising and worshipping God and Christ (Revelation 7:9-10)
- Satisfaction of all needs (Revelation 7:16-17)
- Serene rest (Revelation 14:13)
- Intimate fellowship with God and Christ (Revelation 21:3)

BRETHREN IN CHRIST CHURCH

Founded: 1778
Members: 24,000
Congregations: 269

Beginnings

This denomination was founded in 1778 in Lancaster County, Pennsylvania. It emerged out of the spiritual awakening in Pennsylvania during the late 1700s. This revival was rooted in the preaching of German Reformed minister Philip Otterbein (1726–1813) and Mennonite evangelist Martin Boehm (1725–1812). These and other individuals—heavily impacted by the Pietists and Anabaptists—had grown discontent with the formalism and spiritual dryness that predominated in the churches of their area. By 1767, a loosely structured movement of people impacted by the revival had emerged. About a decade later (1778), this loose movement solidified into the Brethren in Christ Church. (However, Otterbein and Boehm themselves became affiliated with another Brethren denomination—the Church of the United Brethren in Christ.)

Beliefs

Bible. The Bible is inspired by the Holy Spirit. It is the authoritative and reliable Word of God, and is the final authority for faith and practice for believers.

God. The one true sovereign and living God is the Creator and preserver of all things. He is all-knowing and all-powerful, and He transcends time and space. He is perfect, just, good, and holy. He is self-existent as a perfect unity of three persons: the Father, the Son, and the Holy Spirit.

Jesus Christ. Jesus is eternal God. He has perfect equality and unity with the Father and the Holy Spirit. In the Incarnation, He became fully human, having been conceived by the Holy Spirit and born of a virgin. He lived without sin, died as an atonement for sin at the cross, was resurrected from the dead, ascended to heaven, and now intercedes for us.

Holy Spirit. The Holy Spirit eternally coexists with the Father and Son. He convicts sinners, awakens sinners to their need for salvation, regenerates the penitent, empowers and fills believers, illumines the Word of God so believers can understand it, equips believers for service, produces virtuous character (fruit) in believers, and intercedes for them.

Sin and Salvation. Because of Adam's sin, a sinful nature has been transmitted to all his descendants. Moral depravity and death thus became an inherent part of human experience. All humans are corrupted by a sinful nature and are unholy, self-centered, self-willed, and rebellious toward God.

Redemption is found only in Jesus. All who repent and turn to Christ in faith are born again, receive the Holy Spirit, and become children of God. They are acquitted of guilt (justified) and become part of the church. Those who walk in obedience to Christ's lordship are secure in their salvation. Those who persistently rebel against God can lose salvation.

Church. The church consists of all who have trusted in Jesus as Lord and Savior. It is a covenant community, a redeemed community—God's new community. As a covenant community, believers practice mutual accountability among members. The functions of the church are worship, fellowship, discipleship, and missionary work. The local church is largely autonomous, but it receives guidance from bishops. Churches submit to the general conference, which is the highest authoritative body in the denomination. Women can be ordained.

Sacraments. Baptism involves three forward immersions in the name of the Father, Son, and Holy Spirit. It symbolizes the believer's submission to Jesus and identification with His death and resurrection. Communion is open to all the saved and commemorates the Lord's death and resurrection. Christians are to examine their lives before partaking of the elements. Foot washing is also practiced, an ordinance that shows humility and service to one another.

End Times. Christ will return in power and glory, though no one knows the day or hour. The dead will be resurrected and judged. Believers will experience eternal joy and rewards in heaven. The unsaved will suffer everlasting destruction and punishment, being shut out eternally from God's presence.

Website

www.bic-church.org/index.htm

CHURCH OF THE UNITED BRETHREN IN CHRIST

Founded: 1800
Members: 47,000
Congregations: 600

Beginnings

As noted previously, during the late 1700s and early 1800s a spiritual revival occurred among the Germans who migrated into the Pennsylvania area. These revivals were largely led by German Reformed minister Philip Otterbein (1726–1813) and Mennonite evangelist Martin Boehm (1725–1812). These and other individuals had been discontent with the formalism and spiritual dryness that predominated in the churches of the area.

In 1800, Otterbein and Boehm—along with other clergymen who withdrew from their respective denominations, including Presbyterian, German Reformed, Mennonite, and Lutheran—associated to form the Church of the United Brethren in Christ. Otterbein and Boehm were elected as the first bishops.

The denomination experienced significant internal disruption from the 1840s through the 1880s as they debated whether members could join Masonic Lodges and secret societies. The General Conference of the denomination was asked to ratify its constitution to allow membership in such societies, and a majority of members went along with this. Eventually, however, this majority group merged in 1946 with the Evangelical Association to form the Evangelical United Brethren Church, which in turn merged with the Methodist Church in 1968 to form the United Methodist Church.

Though the majority of members in the denomination merged with other denominations, a minority of the United Brethren in

Christ remained. They adhered to the original constitution of the denomination, prohibiting membership in secret societies. Presently, the heaviest concentration of churches in the denomination is in Pennsylvania, Ohio, Indiana, and Michigan.

Beliefs

Bible. The Bible is the Word of God. It is the only rule and guide of the Christian faith and contains the only true way of salvation.

God. The one true God is the Creator, Sustainer, and Governor of the universe. He is eternally revealed in three persons: Father, Son, and Holy Spirit, who are equal in the divine nature.

Jesus Christ. Jesus is fully God. In the Incarnation, He became a man, having been begotten of the Holy Spirit and born of a virgin. He provided full atonement at the cross, was buried, rose again, and ascended to heaven. He now sits at the right hand of the Father, where He makes intercession for believers.

Holy Spirit. The Holy Spirit is equal in being with the Father and the Son. He comforts the faithful and guides them into all truth.

Sin and Salvation. In Adam all human beings are fallen in sin. Through Christ alone we can receive eternal life. To become a Christian, one must repent and believe in Christ. Eternal security is not an official teaching of the denomination, though many within the denomination hold to the doctrine.

Church. The Christian church is a communion of saints. The Lord's Day is to be kept holy by church members, spending it in exercises of devotion. Government is of a modified episcopal style (denominational bishops assign ministers to congregations instead of congregations choosing them). The highest authority is the General Conference, held triennially. Women can be granted ministerial credentials.

Sacraments. Baptism is celebrated, but the mode of baptism is up to the individual. Communion, which memorializes the sufferings of Christ, is celebrated, but the manner of remembrance is up to the individual. Foot washing is an optional practice.

End Times. Jesus will return one day to judge the living and the dead. There is a literal heaven and hell.

Website

www.ub.org

FAST FACTS ON
Ministries of the Holy Spirit

- Convicts people of sin, righteousness, and judgment (John 16:8-11)

- Guides believers (Romans 8:14)

- Intercedes for believers (Romans 8:26)

- Indwells believers (1 Corinthians 6:19)

- Gives spiritual gifts to believers (1 Corinthians 12:11)

- Baptizes believers (1 Corinthians 12:13)

- Produces spiritual fruit in believers (Galatians 5:22-23)

- Seals believers for the day of redemption (Ephesians 4:30)

- Fills believers (Ephesians 5:18)

- Regenerates believers (Titus 3:5)

CHURCH OF GOD (ANDERSON, INDIANA)

Founded: 1880
Members: 234,311
Congregations: 2353

Beginnings

Beginning in 1880, Daniel S. Warner (1842–1925) and some like-minded associates sought to foster a movement that would restore unity and holiness to the church of their day. Influenced by the holiness emphasis of Pietism and Wesleyan theology, these individuals did not originally intend to begin a new denomination (though a new one did eventually emerge) but rather to turn people's complete attention to Jesus Christ. They felt that loyalty should be to the Lord alone, not to denominations.

Their basic authority was not a creed or denominational statement of faith but rather the Word of God alone, as illuminated by the Holy Spirit. As the movement continued to grow, it eventually formalized as a denomination, taking the name Church of God (Anderson, Indiana).* However, it continued to reject the formulation of a creed or doctrinal statement that would be binding on all affiliate churches. For this reason, some minor variation exists today in the beliefs of affiliate churches. The denomination has no official registration of members, and, in fact, membership is not required.

Beliefs

Bible. The Bible is the Word of God and is divinely inspired. It provides the content and guidelines of the Christian faith.

God. The one true God is triune in nature.

Jesus Christ. Jesus is fully God and became man to bring about our redemption.

---

* Note that this denomination is not related to the Pentecostal churches that go by the name "Church of God."

Holy Spirit. The Holy Spirit indwells all true believers.

Sin and Salvation. Humans are sinners as a result of the fall. Forgiveness is available as a result of Christ's atonement on the cross. To be saved, one must confess sins to God in prayer, ask for forgiveness, and invite Jesus to come into one's life as Savior and Lord.

Church. The church is a fellowship and community of believers who gather for regular times of worship, instruction, prayer, and fellowship. When a person accepts Jesus as Savior, he or she is born into God's church. The church has no formal initiation rite and no formal membership.

Worship services are informal, involving expository preaching and singing. Government is congregational. Churches voluntarily associate with other churches. The General Assembly is the highest authority in the denomination. Women are accepted in the ministry.

Sacraments. The ordinances are not mandatory for being a Christian or for being a member of God's family. They are symbolic of things God has done for us in Jesus Christ. Baptism is by immersion. By this ritual, the believer testifies to his regeneration in Christ and his entrance into God's family. Communion is for all believers and is a celebration of the liberating death of Jesus by which our salvation is made possible. Foot washing is symbolic of the servant attitude God desires us to have toward other Christians.

End Times. Christ will personally return, but not to set up a millennial kingdom. This denomination is amillennial, meaning that members believe God's kingdom is here and now; it is an ongoing reality. There will be a general resurrection of the dead and a general judgment. The righteous will be rewarded and the unrighteous will be punished.

Website

www.chog.org

FAST FACTS ON
God's Judgment of Christians

- We will all stand before God's judgment (Romans 14:10).

- Actions will be judged (Psalm 62:12).

- Words will be judged (Matthew 12:36).

- Thoughts will be judged (Revelation 2:23).

- Knowledge of God's will is taken into consideration (Luke 12:48).

- Salvation will not be lost (1 Corinthians 3:15).

- Christians should seek to run the race well (1 Corinthians 9:24-25).

- Rewards will be received or lost, depending on faithfulness (1 Peter 5:4).

EVANGELICAL COVENANT CHURCH
Founded: 1885
Members: 101,003
Congregations: 800

Beginnings

Several theological and religious streams led to the formation of the Evangelical Covenant Church, including the Protestant Reformation, the religious revivals in Scandinavia in the early nineteenth century, and the home Bible study movement affiliated with the Lutheran State Church of Sweden. Those who became a part of this movement had been discontent with the lack of spiritual vitality and the formalism of the Lutheran church in Sweden. They decided to meet in small groups to study Scripture, pray, and sing together. There they found the spiritual vitality they had been lacking.

In the mid-nineteenth century, many of those affiliated with this movement immigrated to the United States. At first, they attempted to stay within Lutheran synods, but their ties to the Lutheran church eventually weakened and dissolved. They began to form their own churches.

In 1885 these churches joined to form a new denomination—the Evangelical Covenant Church. The denomination values the historic confessions of Christianity, especially the Apostles' Creed. They utilize such creeds instead of their own statement of faith.

The denomination describes itself as evangelical but not exclusive, biblical but not doctrinaire, traditional but not rigid, congregational but not independent. Affiliate churches unite to obey the Great Commandments and to fulfill the Great Commission.

Beliefs

Bible. The Bible—including the Old and New Testaments—is the Word of God. It is the only rule of faith, doctrine, and practice.

God. The one true God is triune in nature.

Jesus Christ. Jesus is fully divine and is the only begotten Son of God. He is the Lord and Savior of humankind. He died for humankind's sins.

Holy Spirit. The Holy Spirit empowers believers to be Christlike, guides them, and gives them gifts to serve fellow believers.

Sin and Salvation. Human beings are fallen in sin. By placing faith in Jesus, people are acquitted of the guilt of sin, and the righteousness of Christ is imputed to them. Following salvation, believers continue to grow in sanctification through the ministry of the Holy Spirit.

Church. The church is a fellowship of believers. It is characterized by a mutual participation in and sharing of the new life believers have in Christ. Membership in the church is by confession of personal faith in Jesus as Savior and Lord. Each church is autonomous. Government is congregational. The highest authority in the church is the annual meeting. Women can be ordained.

Sacraments. Baptism can be by either immersion or pouring. Both infant baptism and adult (new believer) baptism are permitted. All pastors in the denomination respect and administer baptism according to the individual wishes of members. Communion is also celebrated and commemorates the Lord's suffering at the cross.

End Times. Christ will return in glory, after which He will judge the living and the dead. Heaven is reserved for the saved, while hell is the eternal destiny of the unsaved.

Website

www.covchurch.org

EVANGELICAL FREE CHURCH OF AMERICA

Founded: 1950
Members: 150,000
Congregations: 1300

Beginnings

In the late 1800s there was a wave of immigration from Scandinavia into the United States. Many of these immigrants left the

Lutheran State Church to come to America. Eventually two denominations emerged among these immigrants. The first was the Swedish Evangelical Free Church, established in 1884 in Boone, Iowa. The second was the Norwegian-Danish Evangelical Free Church Association, established in 1912 in Boston, Massachusetts.

In 1950 these two denominations merged near Minneapolis, Minnesota, to form the Evangelical Free Church of America. Some 275 local congregations from these two denominations united, based on their common principles, policies, and practices.

The title of the denomination is significant. The term "Evangelical" points to the denomination's continual proclamation of the gospel and its commitment to the authority of the Bible. The term "Free" points to the congregational form of government of each affiliate church (they are "free" to govern their own affairs).

Beliefs

Bible. The Bible is the Word of God. The Scriptures are infallible and inerrant in the original manuscripts. They have absolute authority and are the final rule for faith and practice.

God. The one true God is infinitely perfect. He is the Creator of all things. He is triune in nature, with each person in the Trinity being of one divine essence.

Jesus Christ. Jesus is true God. In the Incarnation, He became true man, having been conceived by the Holy Spirit and born of the Virgin Mary. He died for human sin and accomplished a vicarious atonement. He was then resurrected from the dead and ascended into heaven. He now intercedes from heaven as our High Priest and Advocate.

Holy Spirit. The Holy Spirit glorifies Jesus. He also regenerates believing sinners. He indwells, guides, instructs, and empowers them for godly living.

Sin and Salvation. Humankind fell into sin and is therefore lost. Salvation and justification are based on the shed blood of Jesus for all who believe. By receiving Jesus by faith, people can be born of the Holy Spirit and become children of God. Some in the denomination believe in the eternal security of the believer, while others do not.

Church. The true church is composed of persons who have been regenerated by the Holy Spirit and are united together in the body of Christ. Only those who are members of the body of Christ are eligible for membership in the local church. Membership requires commitment to sound doctrine as expressed in the statement of faith of the denomination. However, the church allows for legitimate differences in the fine points of theology. Each church is autonomous. Government is congregational. Churches elect delegates to an annual conference.

Sacraments. Both baptism and the Lord's Supper are celebrated, though neither one is viewed as being necessary for salvation. Baptism is generally by immersion. Communion is for believers only, is celebrated once a month, and symbolizes Christ's sufferings at the cross.

End Times. Christ's coming is imminent, and it will be premillennial. After He comes, He will reign during the millennium for 1000 years. There will be a bodily resurrection of believers to everlasting blessedness and a resurrection of unbelievers to judgment. Believers are destined for heaven, but unbelievers will suffer eternally in hell.

Website

www.efca.org

MORAVIAN CHURCHES

Founded: 1457
Members: 28,000
Congregations: 102

Beginnings

The Moravian church was established in Moravia and Bohemia—what is today the Czech Republic—in 1457. Centuries earlier, these countries had converted to Greek Orthodox Christianity as a result of the work of two missionaries—Cyril and Methodius. By the early 1700s, the Moravian church became established in what is today Germany.

In the mid-1700s, German Moravian missionaries came to Georgia in the United States under the leadership of Augustus G. Spangenberg (1735). They relocated to Pennsylvania (1740) and later established a settlement in North Carolina (1753). The movement experienced healthy growth in these areas with significant evangelism among the Native Americans.

During this general time, Spangenberg came up with a plan called "The Economy" to make the American Moravians self-supporting communities in the United States. He developed a communal system in which church members gave their time, their talents, and their labor to the church. In return, they were given a home, food, clothing, and church fellowship. The community was supervised by Spangenberg and a board of directors. This lasted for some two decades before the arrangement dissolved.

The movement experienced increased growth over the next century as waves of new immigrants arrived from Germany. New congregations quickly formed in Wisconsin, New Jersey, Minnesota, and North Dakota. The motto of the church became "In essentials, unity; in nonessentials, liberty; in all things, love."

Beliefs

Bible. The Bible is the inspired Word of God. It is the sole guide for doctrine and faith.

God. The one true and infinite God is triune in nature.

Jesus Christ. Jesus is the Lord and is the ultimate revelation of God. He redeemed humanity at the cross, rose from the dead, and ascended to heaven.

Sin and Salvation. Humankind is fallen in sin. To be saved, human beings must come into a personal relationship with Jesus Christ by faith.

Church. Moravian churches offer a diversity of styles of worship. Churches are organized into provinces, with the highest authority being a worldwide synod. Women can be ordained in the church.

Sacraments. Both infant baptism and adult (new convert) baptism are acceptable. In baptism, the believer is united to Christ in His death and resurrection, representing death to sin and newness of life. The usual mode of baptism is sprinkling. Communion celebrates the benefits Christians experience as a result of Christ's sufferings and death.

End Times. Christ will one day return. When this will occur is unclear.

Website

www.moravian.org

4

CATHOLIC CHURCHES

ROMAN CATHOLICS BELIEVE IN an unbroken continuity from the early New Testament church to modern Catholicism. Because all the Catholic denominations in this chapter derive from the broader Roman Catholic Church, the historical introduction for this chapter is found in my discussion of Roman Catholicism below.

ROMAN CATHOLIC CHURCH

Founded: first century
Members: More than 62,000,000
Congregations: More than 19,000

Beginnings

New Testament churches were governed by a plurality of elders (1 Timothy 5:17; 1 Peter 5:1). One of these elders typically rose to a position of authority over the others. He became a "first among equals," akin to a chairman of the elders. This individual eventually came to be known as a bishop, an office distinct from that of the elder. This hierarchy facilitated the practical running of the church.

As churches in the larger cities continued to grow numerically, they divided into a number of smaller congregations spread throughout the city, with an elder overseeing each of them. The bishop of the city exercised authority over all the congregational elders of the city.

Eventually, some bishops attained greater authority than others. In some cases this was due to the simple fact that the bishop was a strong personality who exerted powerful leadership skills. In other cases, the bishop became prominent because the city in which the church was located was prominent. This was the case in Alexandria, Antioch, Rome, and Carthage.

The office of bishop became solidified by the middle of the second century, and consequent historical developments served to greatly enhance the office. For example, when Constantine (288–337) divided his empire into four praetorian prefectures (governmental provinces), the bishops of the capital cities in these provinces gained significant influence. As well, the Council of Nicea (sixth canon) gave the Alexandrian, Antiochan, and Roman bishops authority over the bishops in the broader territories of which these cities were centers. This set the stage for the eventual elevation of the Roman bishop.

The Rise of the Bishop of Rome. The bishop of Rome eventually became the head of the entire church. A number of factors led to this development. First, as the capital of the empire, Rome was strategically located ("all roads lead to Rome"). Further, this was the only Western church to have received an epistle from the apostle Paul. Still further, Catholics believe Peter took up residence in Rome in A.D. 42, became its first bishop, and remained there until his martyrdom in A.D. 67. When Jerusalem fell in A.D. 70, Rome's authority was further enhanced. Add to this the fact that the Roman church had attained significant wealth and great power, and one can easily perceive how Rome's bishop was destined for greatness.

In the fourth century, the claims of authority for the bishop of Rome increased. In the fifth century, Pope Leo I claimed authority over all other churches.

Ups and Downs in the Medieval Church. In the late sixth and early seventh centuries, Pope Gregory I expanded the authority of the Roman Catholic Church to include military and civil power. However, from the mid-seventh to the eleventh centuries, the Roman Empire suffered a decline in power, and this was accompanied by a general decline in the authority of the bishops of the Roman Catholic Church. By the late eleventh century, however, a reformed papacy was able to restore episcopal power.

The East-West Split. In A.D. 1054 the Eastern and Western churches split. Prior to 1054, the bishop of Rome served as the head of the Western church while the bishop of Constantinople served as the head of the Eastern church. Neither one asserted authority over the other. However, a consensus eventually developed in the Western church that the *entire* church should be ruled by a single ecclesiastical institution with a single head (the Roman bishop). The bishop of Constantinople—Michael Caerularius—was not impressed with this idea. Because the two bishops could not come to an agreement, they promptly excommunicated each other, and their churches went their separate ways.

The Reformation. Martin Luther (1483–1546), during his doctoral studies, uncovered what he believed to be significant differences between the teachings of the Bible and those of Roman Catholicism. He therefore set out to motivate the Roman Catholic Church to reform its theology and practices so it would be more in line with the Word of God. His concerns included the power of the pope, the abuse involved in the sale of indulgences, and the teaching that souls are in purgatory. In 1517, Luther posted his famous 95 Theses on the door of Wittenberg Castle Church.

The theses caused a firestorm. The Roman Catholic pope and religious authorities pressured Luther to recant his views, but he refused. Luther had hoped to bring *reformation* to the church, but he ended up bringing *division* to the church. Both the pope and Luther were unbending. The pope excommunicated Luther, and Luther refused to recognize the authority of the pope. Western Christianity became splintered.

The Council of Trent. The Council of Trent was an ecumenical council of the Roman Catholic Church held in 25 sessions between A.D. 1545 and 1563. During these sessions, many distinctive Roman Catholic doctrines were defined for the first time, and the Church's present ecclesiastical structure was codified. At this council, anathemas were pronounced against those who differed with the church concerning the doctrine of justification and salvation. A notable outcome of Trent is that from this time forward, the pope became the foundation of stability, unity, and authority in the church.

Emergence in the United States. Roman Catholicism initially emerged in the United States as a result of Spanish explorers infiltrating Central and South America in the sixteenth century. Catholic missionaries always accompanied these explorers, and Catholicism quickly grew in what would become Florida, Texas, New Mexico, and California. These settlements became centers of Catholic evangelism among Native Americans. The first Catholic parish was established in St. Augustine, Florida, in 1565. Meanwhile, French missionaries evangelized among Native Americans in what is now Maine and New York.

Geometric growth of Catholicism took place in the United States in the nineteenth century. During this time, there was a massive Catholic immigration from such countries as Ireland, Italy, and Germany. During the hundred-year period between 1820 and 1920, some ten million Catholics immigrated.

Vatican Council I. Pope Pius IX convened the First Vatican Council in 1869 in St. Peter's Basilica in Rome. More than 800 Roman Catholic priests from around the world attended. Perhaps the most significant outcome of this council is that the doctrine of the supremacy and infallibility of the pope was formulated.

Vatican Council II. The Second Vatican Council was an ecumenical council of the Roman Catholic Church held in Rome in four sessions: the first during the pontificate of Pope John XXIII in 1962 and the other three during the pontificate of Pope Paul VI in 1963, 1964, and 1965. Some 2500 Roman Catholic priests attended. Guests from other Christian churches were invited to observe.

Vatican II allowed priests to celebrate the Mass in the language of the people (instead of Latin). It allowed modern methods of biblical study and interpretation, it encouraged the laity to be involved in parish life, and it allowed Roman Catholics to enter into ecumenical and interfaith dialogue. It also addressed the Catholic view that Mary was the Blessed Mediatrix and Mother of the church.

Significantly, this council decided that all who are named "Christian" (including non-Catholics) are a part of God's family. Non-Catholics are now considered "separated brethren." The council concluded that "the church knows that she is joined in many ways to the baptized who are honored by the name of Christian, but who do not however profess the Catholic faith in its entirety or have not preserved unity which unites them to Christ."[1]

Beliefs

Diversity. Not all Roman Catholics believe the same things. Ultratraditional Catholics defend "old time" Catholicism and are critical of the changes brought about by Vatican II. Traditionalist

Catholics, while critical of liberalism and modernism within the church, are generally accepting of the reforms of Vatican II. Liberal Catholics have replaced the Bible and church authority with the authority of human reason and have questioned the infallibility of the pope, church councils, and the Bible itself. Charismatic and evangelical Catholics affirm conservatively orthodox doctrines and emphasize the gifts of the Holy Spirit, the importance of being baptized in the Holy Spirit, and the Spirit-filled life. Cultural Catholics are "womb-to-tomb" Catholics—that is, they are born, baptized, married, and buried in the Catholic church, but they are relatively unconcerned about spirituality. Popular folk Catholics predominate in Central and South America and are very eclectic in their beliefs—combining elements of an animistic or nature religion with a traditional medieval Catholicism. The discussion of doctrines below reflects the official teachings of the Roman Catholic Church.

Bible. A body of truth was passed down to the pope and bishops in two ways—tradition and the written Word. Tradition refers to information in *unwritten* form, such as the oral teachings, oral worship, and oral prayers of the apostles. God's *written* Word, by contrast, is what we find recorded in the pages of Scripture. Catholics believe that *both* written Scripture *and* oral tradition *together* form the Word of God. They together constitute the "sacred deposit of faith."

The *written* Word of God is found not only in the Old and New Testaments but also in the apocryphal books—seven complete books and four partial books, many of which originated in the period between the Old and New Testaments. These books were canonized at the Council of Trent (A.D. 1545–1563).

God. The one God, the Almighty, is triune in nature.

Jesus Christ. Jesus is Lord, the only Son of God, and is one in being with the Father. Through Him all things were made. In the

Incarnation He took on a human nature. In His humanity, He was begotten of the Holy Spirit and born of the Virgin Mary. He was crucified, was resurrected three days later, and ascended into heaven, where He now sits at the right hand of the Father. He will one day come again to judge the living and the dead.

Holy Spirit. The Holy Spirit is the third person of the Trinity, who proceeds from the Father and Son and is the Giver of life. With the Father and Son, He is worshipped and glorified. He has spoken through all the biblical prophets.

Sin and Salvation. When Adam and Eve fell into sin, they lost the divine life God had bestowed upon them through sanctifying grace. Since then, every human being born into the world has been born without this divine life or sanctifying grace. For a person to be saved, there must be a restoration of sanctifying grace.

Toward this end, the salvation process starts out with "first actual grace." This grace is "first" in the sense that it is God who initially reaches out to a person and gives him the grace that will enable him to seek God, have faith, and prepare his soul for baptism and justification. It is "actual" in the sense that good acts are the goal.

This grace does not have an automatic influence. A person must respond to it—yield to its influence—for it to become effectual. Should a person cooperate with this grace, he or she will end up performing "salutary acts" that prepare the soul for baptism and justification. If he rejects this grace and ends up dying, he is lost.

When a person is finally baptized, original sin is removed from the soul, and in its place sanctifying grace is "infused." At this point the person experiences "initial justification." No one can merit or earn this grace, so this initial aspect of justification is said to be by grace. When the soul is infused with this sanctifying grace of God, inherent righteousness becomes one of the soul's characteristics.

Following initial justification, a second aspect of justification occurs throughout life as the person continues to cooperate with God's grace and progresses in good works, thereby meriting the further grace that is necessary for him or her to enter eternal life. This means the person must sustain his new relationship with God and continue cooperating with God's grace to gain full and final justification. He must be cautious along the way not to commit a mortal sin (a conscious, deliberate, serious sin), which has the effect of erasing grace from the soul. (Only in the sacrament of penance—involving confession and acts of penance—can a Catholic be absolved from such a sin.) The believer will only know for certain that he or she is finally justified at the end of the process (that is, when he or she dies).

Church. Roman Catholics have traditionally believed that their church is the only true church where salvation may be found. After all, Rome's bishops are said to be the successors of Christ's 12 apostles, and the Catholic pope is said to have inherited his throne from Peter (Matthew 16:18). In the twelfth century the Fourth Lateran Council thus affirmed: "There is only one universal Church of the faithful, outside which none will be saved."[2] In 1854, Pope Pius IX declared, "It is to be held as a matter of faith that no one can be saved outside the Apostolic Roman Church. It is the only ark of salvation and anyone who does not enter it must sink in the flood."[3] As noted earlier, however, since Vatican II Roman Catholics acknowledge that all who are named "Christian" (including non-Catholics) are viewed as a part of God's family. Non-Catholics are now considered to be "separated brethren."

Power in the Roman Catholic Church centers in the pope, the "Supreme Pontiff." He is said to be the "Vicar of Christ" on earth. (*Vicar* literally means "one serving as a substitute or agent.") The pope as Vicar of Christ acts *for* and *in the place of*

Christ. As successor to the apostle Peter, the pope exercises authority over the 3250 bishops in the church. When he speaks *ex cathedra* (Latin, meaning "from the chair") on issues pertaining to faith and morals, he is believed to be infallible.

The pope is assisted by top advisors and administrators called cardinals who oversee the Roman Curia—the administrative and judicial offices of the Vatican. If the pope should die, this group of cardinals would elect a new pope.

Below the pope and cardinals are the archbishops, who preside over one or more dioceses in a given territory. They are typically addressed, "Your Excellency." Among other things, they have the authority to call bishops to provincial councils and to act as first judge of appeal over a decision of one of the bishops.

The bishops are viewed as the successors of Christ's apostles. According to the Second Vatican Council, the bishops "have by divine institution taken the place of the apostles as pastors of the Church, in such wise that whoever listens to them is listening to Christ and whoever despises them despises Christ and him who sent Christ."[4] When they speak "with one voice" (in agreement with each other), they *as a group* are viewed as infallible in matters of doctrine.

Below the pope, cardinals, archbishops, and bishops are the priests who serve in individual parish churches. Their primary task is to administer the sacraments (especially the Mass and penance) and pastor the flock of God.

Sacraments. There are seven sacraments: baptism, penance, the Eucharist, confirmation, matrimony, holy orders, and the anointing of the sick. These sacraments are believed to be containers of grace, and this grace is infused into the believer when participating in the sacraments. The *Catechism of the Catholic Church* states: "The Church affirms that for believers the sacraments of the New Covenant are necessary for salvation."[5]

The Eucharist (or Mass) is perhaps the most important of the Roman Catholic sacraments. It involves a "re-presenting" or "renewing" of the sacrifice of Jesus over and over again. Catholics believe the sacrament constitutes a "true and proper sacrifice,"[6] and in every single Mass God is appeased. It is believed that during the Mass, the bread and wine miraculously turn into the actual body and blood of Christ (transubstantiation). This happens at the prayer of consecration of the priest.

Baptism, another important sacrament, is thought to confer initial justification and the new birth (regeneration). It purifies one from sin, makes him a new creature, renders him an adopted son of God, and infuses sanctifying grace into his soul.

In the sacrament of penance, the priest and confessing parishioner go through a programmed ritual in which each verbalizes responses and prayers. In the course of the ritual, the parishioner verbally confesses his sins, admits how often they occurred, and acknowledges sorrow for such moral failure. Following this, the parishioner is assigned some acts of penance and is instructed to say an "Act of Contrition"—a penitential prayer that indicates personal sorrow for the sins committed. The priest then extends his right hand toward the parishioner and absolves him of his sins.

Distinctives. A distinctive of Roman Catholicism is that Mary is viewed as having been "immaculately conceived" (and is thus beyond sin altogether), remained perpetually a virgin, is the "Mother of God," is a co-redeemer and mediatrix of grace, and was "bodily assumed" into heaven at the end of her life. In view of the above, Mary is venerated by Catholics worldwide. Catholics say the veneration given Mary *(hyperdulia)* is less than the adoration given God *(latria)* but is nevertheless higher than that rendered to angels and other saints *(dulia).*

End Times. Jesus will one day come again in glory and judge the living and the dead. Heaven is for the finally righteous. Hell is for the unrighteous. Purgatory exists for those who die in God's friendship but are still imperfectly purified, so that, following a time of purging, they can finally enter the joys of heaven.

Website

www.vatican.va

EASTERN RITE CATHOLIC CHURCH
Founded: 1500–1700
Members: 500,000
Congregations: Unknown

Beginnings

The Eastern Rite Catholic Church embraces Eastern Orthodox believers who have returned to, and established a union with, the Roman Catholic Church—but retain their distinctive rites, practices, sacred art, spirituality, and married clergy. The Roman Catholic Second Vatican Council Decree on the Catholic Eastern Churches reaffirmed the pledge of earlier popes regarding the legitimacy of these Eastern churches with their distinctive rites and practices. Like Roman Catholics, Eastern Rite Catholics accept the pope as the head of the church, celebrate the seven sacraments, and accept the Roman Catholic faith.

In the sixteenth, seventeenth, and eighteenth centuries, a number of Orthodox groups united with the Roman Catholic Church. This includes the Ruthenians in east-central Europe (1595), the Romanians of Transylvania (1698), and the Melchites (Syrian Christians) (1724). The largest and most significant union took place in 1596 when the majority of Ukrainian Orthodox bishops accepted the primacy of the pope, as ordered by the Polish Catholic king.

Beliefs

Aside from holding to the primary theological doctrines of Roman Catholicism (see above), the Eastern Rite Catholic Church emphasizes five theological distinctives:

1. A belief in the call of the Christian to be "divinized," being united to Christ and indwelt by the Holy Spirit. Believers are invited to live the very life of God.

2. Union with God through the Holy Mysteries (the sacraments). These sacraments are viewed as actual encounters with God.

3. A public life of worship, fellowship, and service.

4. A secret life of prayer, fasting, and mutual sharing of goods. In one's secret life of prayer, one can speak honestly with God.

5. The need for spiritual warfare (for example, learning to submit one's weaknesses to the divinizing power of the Holy Spirit at work within them).

Website
Unknown

OLD CATHOLIC CHURCH
Founded: 1871
Members: More than 600,000
Congregations: Unknown

Beginnings

Many Swiss, German, and Austrian priests were excommunicated from the Roman Catholic Church in 1871 because they refused to accept the "new" doctrine of papal infallibility instituted at the First Vatican Council (1870). One of the outstanding Roman Catholic scholars of the time, church historian J.J.I. von Dollinger at the University of Munich, was a formidable opponent of this doctrine. Though he himself did not form any separatist churches, his extensive influence laid the groundwork for the emergence of Old Catholic churches in Germany, Switzerland, Austria, and elsewhere. These churches sought a restoration of the "old ways."

Less than two decades later, in 1889, the Declaration of Utrecht was published as the doctrinal statement of Old Catholics. Catholic distinctives up to the year A.D. 1000 were affirmed in this declaration. They accepted the Apostles' and Nicene creeds, as well as the dogmatic decisions of the first seven ecumenical councils. Newer doctrines—including papal infallibility, celibacy of the priesthood, the necessity of confession to God in the presence of a priest, and the immaculate conception of Mary—were rejected.

The movement eventually made its way to the United States via Joseph René Vilatte (1854–1929), who was responsible for founding a few Old Catholic parishes in Wisconsin. The movement grew from there. Since then, however, the Old Catholics have split into a number of bodies, including the Old Roman Catholic Church of North America, the North American Old Catholic Church, and the North American Old Roman Catholic Church.

Beliefs

God. The one true God is almighty and infinite in perfections. He is the Maker of heaven and earth and is triune in nature.

Jesus Christ. Jesus is the Son of God, the second person of the Trinity, and of one substance with the Father. In the Incarnation, He was born of a virgin, was crucified for our sins, was buried, rose again on the third day, and ascended into heaven. He is now at the right hand of the Father.

Holy Spirit. The Holy Spirit proceeds from the Father and is the Giver of life. Along with the Father and the Son, He is worshipped and glorified. He spoke through all the prophets of biblical times.

Sin and Salvation. As a result of Adam's fall, sin and death came upon all humanity. We all share in the effects of Adam's sin and are alienated from God. Jesus died on the cross to redeem human beings from sin and death.

Church. The church is a divinely instituted community of believers united by the Catholic faith, the law of God, and the sacraments. Jesus is the head of the church.

Sacraments. There are seven sacraments: baptism, confirmation, the Eucharist, penance, holy orders, matrimony, and anointing of the sick. Each sacrament is a holy act through which grace works supernaturally upon man.

End Times. Jesus will one day return again in glory. Those who have done good will experience a resurrection of life, while those who have done evil will experience a resurrection of damnation. All humans will face Jesus at the judgment.

Website

www.oldcatholic.org

POLISH NATIONAL CATHOLIC CHURCH OF AMERICA

Founded: 1897
Members: 270,000
Congregations: More than 150

Beginnings

Once Polish immigrants arrived on American soil in the late nineteenth and early twentieth centuries, they found themselves dissatisfied with the Roman Catholic Church. One bone of contention was the absence of a bishop of Polish birth or descent in the American hierarchy. Another was the 1884 ruling that gave Roman Catholic bishops the title to all diocesan properties, including churches.

The Polish congregation of Sacred Hearts of Jesus and Mary parish in Scranton, Pennsylvania, had desired to retain ownership of its new church building. The Roman Catholic bishop, however, instructed that the deed be handed over to the diocese. This did not sit well with these Polish believers, so they began construction of another independent church, St. Stanislaus (1897). Francis Hodur (1866–1953), former curate and fellow native Pole, was called to be priest. Some 250 families formally united with the new parish. Their new constitution claimed the right for them to control their own properties, with elected administrators overseeing them. The constitution also stipulated that no non-Polish pastor could be appointed by a bishop without the consent of the parishioners.

The Roman Catholic Church promptly excommunicated Hodur and his new parish, but the parish quickly became the nucleus of a movement that would eventually become a synod in 1904. Some 147 delegates met in Scranton from two dozen parishes scattered across Pennsylvania, Maryland, Massachusetts, and New Jersey. Hodur was elected bishop and a new constitution was adopted.

In the early decades of the denomination, the Mass was celebrated in the Polish language. During the 1960s, however, English Masses became increasingly accepted among member churches. In 1922 the denomination abolished the requirement for celibacy among the clergy. As well, the denomination abolished the requirement of private confession for adults, allowing general confession for those who prefer it.

Beliefs

God. The one God includes three divine persons: the Father (the Creator of all things), the Son (who died for the sins of humankind and rose from the dead), and the Holy Spirit (who regenerates and sanctifies souls).

Jesus Christ. Jesus is the Son of God and is the second person of the Trinity. He is of the same divine substance as the Father. As Savior, He became a man to die for the sins of humankind. He resurrected from the dead on the third day. One of His ministries is that of Spiritual Regenerator of the world.

Holy Spirit. The Holy Spirit is the third person of the Trinity. He is the Ruler of the world and is the source of grace. He regenerates and sanctifies the souls of believers. He abides in the church to teach, govern, and sanctify its members.

Sin and Salvation. There is no original sin (that is, the sin of humankind's first parents does not pass to succeeding generations). Yet, individual human beings *do* sin and are in need of redemption. Jesus died on the cross for our salvation.

Church. The church is the body of Christ. It is made up of baptized Christians who worship together, partake of the sacraments, and hear and obey God's Word. The church is a steward of God's grace and is a light unto salvation.

Each parish owns, controls, and administers its own property and can select its own pastor. Each parish can elect one delegate for every 50 members to attend the General Synod, which is the church's main legislative body.

Sacraments. There are seven sacraments: baptism, penance, the Eucharist, confirmation, matrimony, holy orders, and the anointing of the sick. Each is said to convey grace to the participant. The Eucharist, or Mass, is considered by the church to be the central act of worship. The elements (the bread and wine) are administered via intinction, which involves the sacred Host (bread) being dipped into the consecrated wine and then being administered to church members at the altar. The Mass is celebrated in the language of the people.

End Times. A future judgment and immortality are affirmed by the denomination. There is life beyond the grave, and one's perfection and happiness in the next life is contingent upon one's present life—especially the state of the soul in the final hour before death.

Website

www.PNCC.org

5

CHRISTIAN CHURCHES

THE CHRISTIAN CHURCHES EMERGED out of the early nineteenth-century revivals in Pennsylvania and Kentucky. A primary goal of the group was to bring simple unity back to Christians.

Many people ventured westward after the American Revolution (1775–1783), and soon the frontier was filled with members of various denominations. People trying to survive on the frontier were less concerned about their neighbor's denomination than about working together in unity.

In the early 1800s, the Second Great Awakening (a wave of revivals) swept through America. Preachers in the movement were concerned about bringing unity to Christians because they believed denominations had a tendency to divide them. They wanted to restore the same kind of unity as that enjoyed by the first-century church. But they had no centralized coordination for these restoration efforts, and the restoration movement surfaced in several different locales under different leaders at about the same time.

Two important leaders of the movement were Thomas Campbell (1763–1854) and his son Alexander (1788–1866), both former Presbyterians who resided in western Pennsylvania. Their ultimate goal was to move Christianity back to its first-century roots.

Thomas had earlier been criticized by Pennsylvania church authorities for refusing to make Presbyterian creeds and confessions the basis for fellowship and communion (he committed the religious crime of serving communion to some non-Presbyterians). He felt that creeds led to divisions. He believed that the Bible was clear enough for anyone to understand, and such creeds were unnecessary. Church membership should be based solely on the beliefs and practices of New Testament Christianity.

He therefore decided to found a new group called the Christian Association of Washington County and had high hopes that this association would be the beginnings of a return to early Christianity. Instead of using creeds, the motto of the group was "Where the Scriptures speak, we speak; where the Scriptures are silent, we are silent." Thomas believed that unity should be sought under the lordship of Christ and the authority of Scripture.

A few years later, in 1811, Thomas and his son Alexander—less scholarly but more dynamic than his father—formed a new church at Brush Run, Pennsylvania. From there, the restoration movement started to spread west. Though their followers were sometimes called Campbellites, they preferred that members be simply designated "Disciples of Christ."

A third principal figure in the restoration movement was Barton Stone (1772–1844), who lived in Kentucky. Like the Campbells, Stone had broken away from the Presbyterian church and founded a separate church whose members were simply called "Christians" (which, he felt, all true believers should be called). He sought to break all denominational ties so that unity with the body of Christ at large could be fostered and enjoyed. Like the Campbells, he did not want to be bound by human creeds. Stone believed the Bible alone should be the rule of faith and practice.

In 1832 a historic union took place between Stone's 10,000 followers and the Campbells' 12,000 followers. They had agreed on basic beliefs and goals, and they united with a handshake in Lexington, Kentucky. Amusingly, however, they were unable to agree on a single name and thus decided to retain both names— "Christians" and "Disciples." This broad union functioned as a brotherhood of churches.

Following the Civil War (1861–1865), the movement grew rapidly—from its original 22,000 at its founding in 1832 to more than a million by 1900. Growth was especially heavy in Ohio, Illinois, Missouri, Indiana, and Tennessee.

CHRISTIAN CHURCH (DISCIPLES OF CHRIST)
Founded: 1832
Members: 518,434
Congregations: 3717

Beginnings

As noted previously, a historic union took place in 1832 between Barton Stone's 10,000 followers and Thomas and Alexander Campbell's 12,000 followers. The merged group was known as both "Christians" and "Disciples." In the latter part of the nineteenth century, however, a conflict between conservatives and progressives developed within the movement. The conservatives withdrew in protest against the development of missionary societies—a development interpreted as a step toward centralization, thus weakening the autonomy of the local church. The conservatives also opposed the use of instrumental music (organs) in church services. They felt that because neither of these was found within the pages of the New Testament, they should not be a part of the church. In 1906, the conservative dissenters thus formed a new denomination called the Churches of Christ, while the progressives who allowed instrumental music and missionary societies became known as Disciples of Christ.

In 1968, the Disciples of Christ strengthened their national outreach and framework, and formed a general assembly to coordinate missions and evangelism. At that time they reorganized as the Christian Church (Disciples of Christ).

Beliefs

Bible. The Bible is the sole ecclesiastical authority, providing guidance for worship, discipline, and church government. The motto is "No book but the Bible." It is the only basis for faith and conduct.

In interpreting the Bible, church members are free to follow their own consciences as guided by the Holy Spirit. Each person is granted the freedom to follow his or her own personal conviction on matters of theology. Most members hold to the following beliefs:

God. God is triune: The Father is the Maker of all things; the Son is a revelation of God's nature, will, and purpose; the Holy Spirit is the living presence of God among His people.

Jesus Christ. Jesus is the Christ, the Lord and Savior of the world, and the Son of the Living God. Belief in Jesus is required for church membership. However, in view of modern biblical criticism, the doctrines of Christ's absolute deity, preexistence, virgin birth, and sinlessness are not requirements for membership.

Holy Spirit. The Holy Spirit is the living presence of God among His people. It is by the fellowship and communion of the Holy Spirit that believers are joined to one another in brotherhood.

Sin and Salvation. The church does not believe in original sin, but it does recognize that people are sinful and are responsible for that sinfulness following the age of accountability. Salvation is God's unmerited gift of grace and love. Human beings are called to believe in Jesus, repent of sins, and be baptized by immersion. God will then grant the forgiveness of sins, eternal life, and the gift of the Holy Spirit.

Church. Belief in Jesus and baptism are required for church membership. Each local church manages its own affairs and determines its own worship style and programs. A general board meets annually to set general policies for all affiliate churches in the denomination.

Sacraments. Baptism is by immersion and is for adults only. The ritual follows one's confession of Jesus as Lord and Savior. Baptism brings remission of sins, is a condition of church membership, and enables one to enter into newness of life. Infant dedication is also practiced, whereby parents pledge to bring up their child in the love of Christ.

The Eucharist is served every Sunday as a memorial feast and is open to all who believe in Jesus (Christians of all persuasions). This open policy is in keeping with the church's goal of unity among Christians. The Eucharist is considered a celebration with thanksgiving of the saving acts and real presence of Jesus Christ.

End Times. Members are free to come up with their own views on such issues as the second coming, heaven, and hell. Most believe Christians will spend eternity with God in heaven.

Website

www.disciples.org

FAST FACTS ON
the Trinity

There is one God, and in the unity of the Godhead are three coequal and coeternal persons: the Father, the Son, and the Holy Spirit. This is based on three lines of biblical evidence:

1. There is one God.	This is the uniform testimony of the Bible (see John 5:44; 17:3; Romans 3:29-30; 16:27).
2. Three persons are called God in the Bible.	The Father is God (1 Peter 1:2). Jesus is God (Hebrews 1:8). The Holy Spirit is God (Acts 5:3-4).
3. There is three-in-oneness in the Godhead.	Matthew 28:19 tells us to baptize in the name of the Father, the Son, and the Holy Spirit. "Name" is singular, indicating one God. The definite articles before "Father," "Son," and "Holy Spirit" indicate distinct persons.

CHRISTIAN CHURCHES AND CHURCHES OF CHRIST

Founded: 1927
Members: 1,071,616
Congregations: 5579

Beginnings

A number of factors caused the conservatives in the Christian Church (Disciples of Christ) to break fellowship with their parent body and found a new convention. First was an increasing emphasis on the centralization of denominational authority among the Disciples of Christ (as opposed to the autonomy of the local church). Second, the Disciples of Christ were growing increasingly liberal in their theology and practice, including the acceptance of higher biblical criticism and a lower view of Jesus. Third, people who had not been baptized by immersion were allowed to transfer membership from another church. The conservatives believed this went against the goal of seeking to get back to a New Testament form of Christianity. Finally, the Disciples of Christ were becoming increasingly ecumenical.

The dissenting conservatives thus separated from the Disciples of Christ in 1927 and formed the North American Christian Convention, which constituted an entirely separate fellowship of Christian Churches and Churches of Christ. This convention had no creeds and no formal confessions of faith. The New Testament was viewed as the sole authority for faith. Moreover, the new convention was not to be a policy-making assembly that had authority over the local churches, but rather was a gathering for preaching, teaching, and good fellowship. The new convention took a strong stand against all forms of liberalism and sought to defend fundamentalist beliefs.

Beliefs

Bible. Both the Old and New Testaments are the Word of God, divinely inspired as God's full revelation for today. The New Testament is the primary authority for the Christian Churches and Churches of Christ, just as the Old Testament was authoritative for Jews in Old Testament times.

God. The one loving God is eternally manifest in three persons: the Father, the Son, and the Holy Spirit.

Jesus Christ. Jesus is the Christ, the Lord and Savior, and the Son of God. He is fully divine. In the Incarnation, He became fully man. He is the Mediator between the Father and humankind. His death on the cross was a redemptive sin offering. He was resurrected from the dead and ascended into heaven.

Holy Spirit. The Holy Spirit is the agent of conversion and indwells the hearts of all true believers.

Sin and Salvation. Sin is a human reality. Repentance and faith in Christ are necessary for salvation. Baptism by immersion brings penitent sinners remission of sins.

Church. Each church is autonomous. It is free to elect its own leaders, call and support its own ministers, and decide how its mission money is to be used. The church is congregational in polity, with no bishops and no superintendents. The North America Christian Convention meets annually but has no authority over local churches.

Sacraments. Baptism by immersion brings the remission of sins. Such baptism is a condition of church membership (see Acts 2:38). In a recent controversy, many have held to baptismal regeneration (baptism brings remission of sins). Others, while still holding a high view of baptism, do not believe baptism is in any way regenerative.

The Lord's Supper is observed weekly on each Lord's Day (Sunday). It is a simple memorial of Christ's death for the salvation of human beings.

End Times. The righteous will receive a future reward. The wicked will receive a future punishment.

Website

Unknown

CHRISTIAN CONGREGATION
Founded: 1887
Members: 119,391
Congregations: 1439

Beginnings

The Christian Congregation had its earliest beginnings in 1798 as an unincorporated religious society. During the early 1800s the group was loosely associated with the restoration movement led by Barton Stone, though an organic union with Stone's group never formally occurred. In 1887, the Christian Congregation incorporated as a distinct entity because these churches desired a closer, more formal association with each other. Today the Christian Congregation enjoys a strong presence in the Carolinas, Pennsylvania, Kentucky, Virginia, Ohio, Tennessee, and Texas.

The underlying philosophy of the Christian Congregation is based on John 13:34-35: "A new command I give you: Love one another. As I have loved you, so you must love one another. By this all men will know that you are my disciples, if you love one another." In keeping with this passage of Scripture, the Christian Congregation takes a strong stand against abortion, capital punishment, and all forms of warfare. Respect for all life is viewed as intrinsic to Christ's command. This "love one another" philosophy also necessitates that Christ's church transcend all racial and national boundaries.

This philosophy, moreover, has led to the policy that the basis of church unity is not doctrinal agreement but love. It is therefore not surprising that there is a wide range of doctrinal belief among members of the Christian Congregation. The spectrum includes fundamentalists and Pentecostals on one end and liberals and humanists on the other. But they all emphasize love.

Beliefs

In view of the wide diversity of beliefs in the Christian Congregation, no representative statements can be made on the doctrines of God, Jesus, sin, salvation, and the end times.

Website

www.netministries.org/see/churches/exe/ch10619

CHURCHES OF CHRIST
Founded: 1906
Members: 1,500,000
Congregations: 15,000

Beginnings

The Churches of Christ once existed as a part of the Christian Church (Disciples of Christ), and therefore originated in the restoration movement. In the latter part of the nineteenth century, however, a conflict emerged among members of the Christian Church (Disciples of Christ). The conservatives within the denomination were upset because of the move toward developing missionary societies. The conservatives believed this would lead to further centralization of the denomination, thus decreasing the autonomy of the local church. Further, many people in the denomination were open to the use of instrumental music (such as organs) in church services. Also, some people in the denomination were succumbing to theistic evolution, some were open to an increasing role for women in the church, and some were accepting higher critical theories of the Bible.

The motto of the church had always been "Where the Scriptures speak, we speak; where the Scriptures are silent, we are silent." Since missionary societies and instrumental music are not mentioned in the New Testament, the conservatives felt these should not be a part of the modern church. Further, the conservatives felt the Bible was clearly against such things as theistic evolution, women in leadership positions in the church, and biblical criticism.

In 1906, things came to a head. The conservative dissenters withdrew fellowship and formed a new denomination called the Churches of Christ. They are the most conservative in theology and practice among the churches that grew out of the restoration movement. The progressives who were in favor of instrumental music and missionary societies remained as the Disciples of Christ.

Today Churches of Christ exist in all 50 states in the United States, with the strongest concentration of churches in the South and Southwest. They consider themselves a brotherhood of churches with no overall formal organization (they reject denominational labels). Yet they cooperate in building and operating orphanages, homes for the aged, colleges, universities, and schools.

Beliefs

Bible. The Bible is inspired and inerrant and is the sole authority for faith and practice. Creeds are rejected because they are believed to generate schisms in the body of Christ. As well, theological paradigms (such as Calvinism and Arminianism) are avoided because the New Testament alone is the proper guide to doctrinal belief.

God. The one true God is eternally manifest in three persons: the Father, the Son, and the Holy Spirit.

Jesus Christ. Jesus is the Christ, the Lord and Savior, the divine Messiah, and the Son of God. Members affirm belief in the virgin birth, the Incarnation, the vicarious atonement wrought at the cross, and the bodily resurrection of Jesus.

Holy Spirit. The Holy Spirit is the third person of the Trinity.

Sin and Salvation. Members recognize a universality of sin among people after the age of accountability, at which point they become responsible to God for their sin. Christ's vicarious atonement wrought at the cross is the only remedy for this sin problem. To become saved, one must exercise faith in Christ, repent of sins, make a confession, and participate in believer's baptism by immersion in the name of the Father, the Son, and the Holy Spirit.

Church. The church is the body and bride of Christ. Joining the church is contingent on one's profession of faith in Jesus Christ, repentance from sin, and baptism by immersion for the remission of sins.

Each church is autonomous. The Churches of Christ have no central headquarters, no conventions or annual meetings, no central offices or officers, no general conference, no governing boards, and no official publications. They believe the early church in New Testament times made its own decisions autonomously, so the local churches of today must follow this example. The churches, however, voluntarily cooperate toward common goals.

Each local church is governed by a plurality of elders and deacons appointed by the local congregation. Traveling, non-salaried evangelists speak in the various churches.

Sacraments. Baptism is by immersion for believers only. Only adults are baptized, for only adults have a proper understanding and appreciation of penitence and faith. Infants cannot be baptized, for they have no sin (until the age of accountability) and cannot qualify as "believers." Baptism is necessary for salvation.

The Lord's Supper is observed on a weekly basis.

End Times. Church members have a strong hope of eternal life based on the grace of God in Jesus Christ. They believe there will be a final judgment. Most church members are either amillennial or postmillennial. Premillennialism is often viewed as a heresy that must be eradicated from the church.

Distinctives. Hymns are sung without instrumental accompaniment (*a cappella* singing).

Website

www.churchesofchrist.com

FAST FACTS ON
Music in the Bible

- God's victory over Egypt was celebrated with music (Exodus 15:3).

- Music was performed during pilgrimages (2 Samuel 6:5).

- Music aided prophets in receiving revelations (2 Kings 3:15).

- Music was performed at temple ceremonies (1 Chronicles 16:4-6).

- Israel's victory over Ammon and Moab was celebrated with music (2 Chronicles 20:27-28).

- Music was performed at the coronation of kings (2 Chronicles 23:11-13).

- Music was used at banquets and feasts (Isaiah 5:12; 24:8-9).

- Music was used at laments (Matthew 9:23).

- The homecoming of the prodigal son was celebrated with music (Luke 15:25).

6

CONGREGATIONAL CHURCHES

CONGREGATIONAL CHURCHES ARE SO named because each local congregation has full authority. It is believed that each congregation, made up of men and women devoted to the lordship of Jesus Christ, are fully capable to minister and govern among themselves through congregational vote. This is in obvious contrast to churches that have an episcopal government, with a hierarchy of bishops ruling over local churches.

Congregational churches emerged among individuals and congregations who escaped persecution from the religious authorities in England and who felt that the Church of England was desperately in need of purification. These Puritans believed the church needed reform not only in its worship but in its style of government as well. The Puritans made the dangerous choice of meeting in homes for Bible study and prayer, something that was illegal because of a state policy that religious meetings were not to take place without priests or bishops being present. Both religious and political authorities in England were displeased with these "separatists."

Among these separatist groups was one led by John Robinson (1575–1625). Because of escalating persecution, Robinson and his congregation of about 100 people fled England in 1609 and settled in the Netherlands. There he encountered another escapee from England's persecution, William Ames (1576–1633), a great Congregational theologian. Through Ames's influence, Robinson became a convert to Congregationalism.

In 1620 Robinson and a large company of his congregation set sail for the American colonies in the Mayflower. They made a covenant with each other as believers and as citizens of their new land—a spiritual and political covenant known as the Mayflower Compact. In this document we witness the seeds of a democratic government. Meanwhile, Puritans continued to immigrate into America, and the Massachusetts Bay Colony was eventually established in 1629. Congregational churches were planted and the movement grew rapidly.

One Congregationalist who impacted his own time and whose influence continues even today is Jonathan Edwards (1703–1758), the greatest intellect to ever emerge among Congregational churches. He played a leading role in the First Great Awakening in the 1730s and 1740s.

Congregationalists certainly played a major role in American history. Some of the New England Congregationalists were leaders in the American Revolution (1775–1783). As well, Congregationalists were involved in founding such influential schools as Harvard (1636), Yale (1707), and Dartmouth (1769).

In the 1800s the denomination suffered a theological split, rooted mainly in a debate over the Trinity. The conservatives in the group held strongly for the Trinity, while the liberals argued for a radical unity of God (Unitarianism). William Ellery Channing (1780–1842) preached a famous sermon entitled "Unitarian Christianity" in which he argued against the Trinity and sought to demonstrate how "irrational" the idea is. The sermon was published and reprinted seven times and became a popular pamphlet. This sermon affirmed the Unitarian belief that the ultimate authority is not the voice of the past as revealed in Scripture but the "living voice" of experience and reason. A division in the Congregational church was inevitable.

The American Unitarian Association was founded in 1825 by a dozen graduates of Harvard Divinity School. Most of the older Congregational churches in Massachusetts became Unitarian in theology. Yet traditional Congregational churches survived the split and have maintained steady growth through the years. Today Congregational churches continue to make a strong contribution to the religious life of America. Congregational autonomy certainly fits with American individualism.

CONGREGATIONAL CHRISTIAN CHURCHES (NATIONAL ASSOCIATION)

Founded: 1955
Members: 65,392
Congregations: 432

Beginnings

The Congregational Christian Churches (National Association) was founded in Detroit, Michigan, in 1955. Many congregationalists had become concerned about an upcoming 1957 merger of two denominations—the Evangelical and Reformed Church and the General Council of Congregational Christian Churches. This merger, which would become the United Church of Christ, caused concern because it was believed the new body would have a predominantly presbyterial form of church government. Therefore, instead of participating in the merger, those churches desiring to truly remain congregational founded the

Congregational Christian Churches (National Association). The association strongly emphasizes the autonomy of the local church.

The Congregational Christian Churches (National Association) is actually less a denomination and more a voluntary association—a "cooperative fellowship" of churches. Each church in the association fully retains its independence without infringement upon its self-government. The association has no binding ecclesiastical authority and no creed members must subscribe to.

The purpose of the association is to provide churches assistance, encouragement, inspiration, counsel on matters of common concern, and a broader fellowship with other like-minded congregations. Churches can enjoy these benefits without fear of their autonomy or freedom being threatened.

The denomination is heavily involved in social activism. Congregational minister Washington Gladden became famous for his emphasis on the social gospel. Broadly speaking, the association seeks to help the impoverished and disenfranchised around the world.

Beliefs

Church members are free to follow their own consciences regarding personal beliefs. For this reason, the doctrinal spectrum ranges from liberal to conservative in this denomination. Nevertheless, the association does commit to some basic doctrinal affirmations:

Bible. The Bible sets forth the duty of Christians. Christians can walk in the ways of the Lord by following its teachings.

God. God is loving and compassionate.

Jesus Christ. Jesus is the Lord and Savior of humankind. He was a perfect revelation of the love of God.

Holy Spirit. Church members seek to be led by the Holy Spirit, not by a man-made creed. The Holy Spirit guides each Christian in understanding the Scriptures.

Sin and Salvation. Salvation is based on a confession of faith in Jesus.

Church. Each church is autonomous and self-governing. Churches are free, however, to work together in associations and conferences. Representatives of all member churches participate in an annual meeting. Women can be ordained.

Sacraments. Baptism is for both infants and mature believers. In infant baptism, the Christian family commits to nurturing the child in the ways of the Lord. Baptism for mature believers is an outer, visible sign of one's desire for cleansing from sin. It is normally practiced when one joins the church. The method of baptism can be sprinkling, pouring, or immersion. The church allows people to opt out of baptism should they wish not to participate.

The Lord's Supper is observed either every month or every other month. All people are welcome to participate—whether church members, members of other churches, or members of no church at all. The sacrament serves as a memorial to Christ's life, death, and resurrection. It also serves to unite believers with both Christ and other church members.

Website

www.naccc.org

FAST FACTS ON
the Mode of Baptism

The Case for Sprinkling or Pouring	The Case for Immersion
A secondary meaning of the Greek word *baptizo* is "to bring under the influence of." This fits sprinkling or pouring better than immersion.	The primary meaning of the Greek word *baptizo* is "to immerse." Prepositions used in conjunction with *baptizo* ("into" and "out of") picture immersion.
Baptism by sprinkling or pouring better pictures the coming of the Holy Spirit upon a person.	Baptism by immersion best pictures death to the old life and resurrection to the new life in Christ (Romans 6:1-4).
The Ancient Near East probably did not have enough water or pools to baptize so many people in New Testament times (Acts 2:41; 8:38).	Archeologists have uncovered ancient pools all over the Jerusalem area.

CONSERVATIVE CONGREGATIONAL CHRISTIAN CONFERENCE
Founded: 1948
Members: 40,857
Congregations: 256

Beginnings

The early beginnings of this denomination date back to 1935 when Hilmer Sandine, a pastor in Hancock, Minnesota, started a monthly conservative publication called the *Congregational*

Beacon. It was essentially a platform for theologically conservative congregationalists. Sandine had become convinced that theological liberalism had penetrated Congregational and Christian churches' beliefs, policies, and practices.

In the following decade, evangelicals within the Congregational Christian churches sensed the need for fellowship and began to meet informally. This ultimately led to the formation of the Conservative Congregational Christian Fellowship in 1945 in Chicago. They reorganized in 1948 as the Conservative Congregational Christian Conference.

The purpose of the conference was to promote worship of God among the churches; deepen their fellowship with each other; facilitate their cooperation in evangelism, education, edification, stewardship, missions, and youth activities; and to promote the autonomy of the local church and freedom of the individual believer in Christ.

Beliefs

This denomination is theologically conservative but allows for diversity of opinion on peripheral issues.

Bible. Both the Old and New Testaments are inspired, inerrant, infallible, and authoritative as God's Word.

God. The one true God eternally exists in three persons: the Father, the Son, and the Holy Spirit. God is sovereign over all things.

Jesus Christ. Church members affirm Jesus' full deity, virgin birth, sinless life, miracles, substitutionary atonement, bodily resurrection from the dead, ascension into heaven to the right hand of the Father, and personal return in glory.

Holy Spirit. The Holy Spirit regenerates sinners, guides believers in understanding God's Word, indwells them, and enables them to live a godly life in an evil world.

Sin and Salvation. Man is fallen in sin. Redemption is available through faith in Christ.

Church. Membership in the church is restricted to those who profess regeneration. The task of the church is threefold: to worship God, edify the saints, and evangelize the world. Each local church is autonomous, and government is congregational. Churches join in fellowship with other churches for cooperative endeavors. This is facilitated through the Conservative Congregational Christian Conference. Each church makes its own policy regarding the role of women in the church.

Sacraments. The two sacraments are baptism (both children and adults) and the Lord's Supper.

End Times. Jesus will return in great power and glory. Members are free to believe as they wish regarding the specific sequence of events leading up to the second coming. All humanity will be resurrected—the saved (a "resurrection of life") and the lost (a "resurrection of damnation").

Website

www.ccccusa.org

FAST FACTS ON
Infant Baptism vs. Believer's Baptism

The Case for Infant Baptism	The Case for Believer's Baptism
Infant baptism is analogous to circumcision in the Old Testament, which was done to infant boys.	The New Testament pattern is that a person is baptized following his or her conversion experience (Acts 16:29-34).
Household baptisms in the New Testament must have included infants (Acts 16:33).	Household baptisms such as described in Acts 16:33 do not specify the presence of infants.

UNITED CHURCH OF CHRIST
Founded: 1957
Members: 1,359,105
Congregations: 5888

Beginnings

The United Church of Christ was founded in 1957 in Cleveland, Ohio, as a result of a merger between the General Council of Congregational Christian Churches and the Evangelical and Reformed Church. These two uniting bodies were themselves the results of former mergers that took place in the early twentieth century.

The denomination's name, the United Church of Christ, reflects their motto "That they may all be one." This motto is rooted in Jesus' prayer for the unity of the church (John 17:21). Church members believe that unity and fellowship do not depend on perfect doctrinal agreement but rather on the simple choice to maintain unity.

The doctrinal spectrum in the denomination ranges from liberal to moderately evangelical, though the conference leadership is predominantly liberal. The denomination is socially active, having been heavily influenced by the social gospel movement of the early twentieth century. Members work for peace, seek to reduce arms, stand for human rights (including those of homosexuals and bisexuals), oppose racism and sexism, and resist violence in all forms. The denomination ordains women to the ministry.

Beliefs

Bible. The Bible is the source for understanding the good news of the gospel and is the foundation for all statements of faith.

God. God is the Creator of man and the universe and exists eternally in three persons: the Father, the Son, and the Holy Spirit.

Jesus Christ. Jesus is the man of Nazareth who was crucified for our sins and rose from the dead, thereby conquering sin and death. By His death He has provided reconciliation of the world to Himself. Jesus is the sole head of the church.

Holy Spirit. The Holy Spirit is present among God's people, and He renews the church of Jesus Christ.

Sin and Salvation. God desires to save all human beings from aimlessness and sin. Justification is by grace through faith. Jesus promises all who trust in Him forgiveness of sins, eternal life in His eternal kingdom, and the fullness of His grace.

Church. The mission of the church is to follow the way of the risen Christ, to proclaim Christ's gospel to a fallen world, to embody the love of God to all humanity, to stand for justice and peace, to confront evil wherever it may be found, to minister to the oppressed and disenfranchised of the world, and to work for the healing and wholeness of life for all people.

Church polity involves a combination of congregational and presbyterial styles. Local churches are guaranteed the right to own their own property and call their own ministers, and they are free to withdraw from the denomination at any time. Most issues are decided at the local level. The national conference advises churches and individual members, but the advice is not binding.

Sacraments. The church practices infant baptism and believer's baptism, both normally done by sprinkling. Water is viewed as a symbol of washing, and washing represents renewal. Baptism thus symbolizes the believer being adopted into a new life that is hid with Christ.

The Lord's Supper is open to all baptized Christians. The bread and wine are symbols of the body and blood of Jesus. The Lord's Supper is a means of grace to those who partake.

End Times. Christ will come again to judge humanity. Views about heaven and hell vary.

Website

www.ucc.org

EPISCOPAL AND
ANGLICAN CHURCHES

CHRISTIANITY ARRIVED ON BRITISH soil long before the official Church of England was established. Christianity probably found its way to England in the second century, for there is historical evidence of an organized church there among the Celtic tribes by the third century.

The emergence of the Church of England has a rich and colorful history relating to King Henry VIII. Henry (1509–1547) took the throne at age 18 following the death of his father. One thing Henry wanted more than just about anything else was a male heir. His marriage to Catherine of Aragon was unable to produce this heir. She managed to give birth to a daughter, Mary, but also suffered through five miscarriages. This was not acceptable to Henry VIII. He wanted a son.

To remedy the situation, Henry sought a divorce from Catherine—something that Pope Clement VII was unwilling to grant. Henry promptly took matters into his own hands. He convinced the English Parliament to set statutes in place which denied the pope any authority or jurisdiction over the Church of England. In so doing, Henry followed the lead of earlier kings of England who exercised supreme authority over ecclesiastical affairs.

The Church of England thus became independent of the Roman Catholic Church, and Henry VIII declared himself its chief authority. To add insult to injury to the Roman church, Henry withheld the money England traditionally paid Rome on an annual basis.

Following the Church of England's break with Rome, Henry forced the selection of Thomas Cranmer (1489–1556) as the Archbishop of Canterbury, the most powerful church office in England. Cranmer then promptly granted an annulment of the marriage between Henry and Catherine. Problem solved!

Over time, Henry went through a series of marriages in hopes of fathering a male heir. Included among his wives were Anne Boleyn, Jane Seymour, Anne of Cleves, Catherine Howard, and Katharine Parr. Boleyn gave birth to a daughter, Elizabeth, while Seymour gave birth to a son, Edward. Seymour did not recover from the birth experience and died just two weeks after Edward was born. Nevertheless, Henry now had the male heir he was hoping for.

Following Henry's death, Edward VII took the throne at age nine. Because of his young age, his uncle Edward Seymour—Lord Protectorship and Duke of Somerset—guided the decisions of Edward's throne, taking the church in a distinctly Protestant direction in keeping with the theology of the Reformers. Through his influence, Thomas Cranmer's *The Book of Common Prayer* was made mandatory for all the churches in England. Neither the Catholics nor the Protestants appreciated this requirement. The Catholics did not like it because celebrating the Mass in Latin was abolished. The Protestants did not like it because of various shortcomings they perceived in the book. Tragically, King Edward died of consumption at age 16 (1553).

Upon Edward's death, his older sister Mary I assumed the throne at age 37. Mary was a devout, fervent Catholic, and she returned England to the Roman Catholic fold. She also restored the celebration of the Mass in Latin. Mary's claim to fame is that she burned at the stake more than 300 Protestants, including Thomas Cranmer. For this, she became widely known as Bloody Mary. England's recommitment to Roman Catholicism lasted until Mary's death in 1558 (she ruled a mere five years).

Elizabeth I, at 25 years of age, took the throne after Mary died. History looks favorably upon Elizabeth's reign, viewing her time on the throne as a truly great era. Seeking peace in her kingdom, Elizabeth sought a "middle way" between Roman Catholicism and Protestantism. She wanted a compromise between the two competing religious systems. Because most Englanders disliked the idea of having to bow before Rome, her middle-way approach for the Church of England was acceptable to most of England's churchgoers. Meanwhile, she was able to placate Catholics by saying that the worship in the Church of England could be considered a Mass. There were naysayers among the extremists in both camps, but she was able to satisfy the mainstream middle, whose members far outnumbered the extremists. The Church of England was here to stay and would eventually become an influential religious body in the world.

As will be seen below, the Anglican and Episcopal churches that emerged on American soil are rooted in the Church of England.

EPISCOPAL CHURCH USA
Founded: 1789
Members: 1,877,271
Congregations: 7364

Beginnings

The Episcopal church is so named because it is ruled by bishops. (The Greek word *episkopos* means "bishop" or "overseer.")

The Episcopal church is also an Anglican church because it has its roots in the Church of England. (*Anglican* literally means "English.")

Members of this denomination have included U.S. presidents, generals, and Supreme Court justices. Two-thirds of the signers of the Declaration of Independence were Episcopalians (Anglicans). Members of the church have included such luminaries as George Washington, Thomas Jefferson, and Patrick Henry.

The Episcopal church emerged on American soil as an extension of the Church of England, all the while remaining under its jurisdiction. The first Anglican church was founded by English settlers in 1607 in Jamestown, Virginia. As settlers continued to immigrate, Anglican churches continued to crop up around the American colonies, including such cities as Boston (1689), Philadelphia (1695), New York City (1697), and Newport, Rhode Island (1702). By the end of the colonial period, Anglican churches were in all 13 colonies. Indeed, by the time the American War of Independence began (1775), there were some 400 Anglican congregations in the colonies. This represents significant growth.

These Anglican churches experienced a major crisis related to the War of Independence. The problem was this: One simply cannot fight England for independence while at the same time maintaining allegiance to the English crown via submission to the Church of England through satellite Anglican churches on American soil. This predicament caused a split to emerge among Anglican clergy in America. Many Anglican clergymen in the North remained loyal to the English king. These would rather close down their parishes than remove prayer for the English king from the church's liturgy. These individuals eventually either returned to England, escaped to Canada, or were imprisoned in the colonies.

By contrast, many of the Anglican clergy in the south were colonial patriots, and they chose to withhold allegiance to the English church overseas. Their primary interest was independence from England and freedom for the American colonies. The result for Anglican churches in America was nothing short of catastrophic. By the end of the War of Independence, the church suffered a severe decline in membership. Those that survived were disorganized, and no formal association of churches survived. Everything was in utter disarray.

In keeping with the American spirit, however, the church survived and eventually even thrived. The Anglican clergy who remained in America decided to regroup and establish a denomination that was independent of the Church of England, just as the colonies were now independent from England. The goal was to form a church that would continue the spiritual legacy of the Church of England, which they liked, but at the same time would be completely autonomous. Preliminary steps were taken toward this end when clergy and laity met at the first general convention in Philadelphia in 1785.

The biggest problem the new denomination had to face was finding bishops. One result of the war with England was that England would no longer be sending any Church of England bishops to America. This meant that American churches had no way to ordain and consecrate new priests and bishops. With virtually all the church hierarchy residing in England, what were the churches in America to do? To make things even more difficult, English law stipulated that all bishops consecrated in the Church of England must swear allegiance to the British crown. No American clergy would be willing to do this, especially after the War of Independence.

By 1789 the problem was solved. Two American bishops, William White and Samuel Provost, sailed to England and were consecrated by the Archbishop of Canterbury. What made this possible is that the English Parliament met and rescinded the requirement that *all* bishops must swear allegiance to the British crown. This requirement was no longer enforced for bishops who resided in "foreign parts" (like America).

At a convention in 1789, the denomination adopted a constitution, ratified canons of the church, and revised *The Book of Common Prayer* for use in American Anglican churches. This represents the formal beginning of the Episcopal Church in America. It was initially called the Protestant Episcopal Church—*Protestant* to distinguish the church from Roman Catholicism, and *Episcopal* to reflect that the church is ruled by bishops.

Even though this was a new denomination, it nevertheless derived its basic doctrine, liturgy, and traditions from the Church of England. The denomination's convention was even careful to stipulate that it had no intention of departing from the Church of England in any essential point of doctrine, discipline, or worship.

In 1801 the church approved a revised version of the Thirty-Nine Articles of Religion, which is contained in *The Book of Common Prayer*. Later in the nineteenth century, the church expanded westward.

Unfortunately, all was not smooth sailing for the new denomination. A controversy erupted in the early 1800s related to the Oxford movement. In 1833, clerics at Oxford University launched a movement that sought a return to certain Catholic elements, such as elaborate rituals and ceremonies related to Catholic liturgy, adherence to the sacraments, and respect for Roman Catholic traditions. This movement resulted in the formation of the high-church party in the Episcopal church, which favored these Roman Catholic elements. In contrast to this party was the low-church party, which leaned more toward evangelical traditions and doctrine, Bible reading, and minimal ritual and ceremony. This controversy caused bitter differences among members of the Episcopal Church. Between these two groups was the broad-church party, which represented a middle-ground position. Episcopalians have since put a positive spin on this conflict by pointing to the great diversity and flexibility that exists within their denomination.

In more recent history, the Episcopal church has been heavily involved in the ecumenical movement. As a basis for ecumenism, the church says unity should be based on Scripture, the Apostles' and Nicene creeds, the sacraments of baptism and the Eucharist, and the episcopate. In the 1970s and beyond, the denomination has experienced conflict over certain social issues, such as the admission of women into the priesthood and the issue of homosexuality.

Beliefs

The standards of doctrine used in the Episcopal church include these:

1. The Apostles' Creed

2. The Nicene Creed

3. The Thirty-Nine Articles of Religion. (Note that these articles are not binding on clergy and are not to be considered rigid confessions.)

4. *The Book of Common Prayer.* This book constitutes a collection of worship services that Anglican worshippers around the world can use. The phrase "common prayer" points to the reality that *all* Anglicans pray these words together, all around the world. This book was initially compiled by Thomas Cranmer in the sixteenth century but has been revised a number of times to fit specific

needs among Anglican churches. The purpose has always remained the same: to provide a single book to guide Anglican Christians in proper worship. The book includes the Thirty-Nine Articles of Religion, ancient creeds, prayers, liturgies, a church calendar, a catechism, and a lectionary.

Rejection of Roman Catholic Doctrines. The Episcopal church rejects some of the distinctive Roman Catholic doctrines, including the jurisdiction of the pope over the church, the infallibility of the pope on Christian doctrine and moral truth, the doctrine of purgatory, and the doctrine of transubstantiation.

Diversity. The Episcopal church is diverse. Within the denomination one will find conservatives and liberals, fundamentalists and modernists, heterosexuals and homosexuals. What brings them unity is *The Book of Common Prayer.*

Bible. The Holy Scriptures, embodied in the Old and New Testaments, are the Word of God, containing all that is necessary for salvation. Yet the Bible must not be interpreted apart from tradition and human reason. Church tradition provides modern believers with the experience and understanding of Christians who have lived for the past two thousand years, and this collective wisdom provides a helpful starting point for proper interpretation. The process of weighing all this spiritual data is facilitated through the intelligence and reason God Himself has given humankind. In sum, then, the Bible is authoritative, but church tradition and human reason enables Christians to sort out their own understanding of it as it relates to their own lives.

God. The one true and living God is everlasting and is of infinite power, wisdom, and goodness. He is the Maker and Preserver of all things, visible and invisible. God is a Trinity: Father, Son, and Holy Spirit.

Jesus Christ. Jesus, the second person of the Trinity, is eternal and divine, being of the same substance as the Father and the Holy Spirit. Through His life, death, and resurrection, our sins are forgiven, and our lives are brought into fellowship with God.

Holy Spirit. The Holy Spirit, the third person of the Trinity, proceeds from the Father and the Son. He is of one substance, majesty, and glory with the Father and the Son.

Sin and Salvation. Human beings are very far gone from original righteousness and are naturally inclined to evil. Through the life, death, and resurrection of Jesus Christ, one's sins are forgiven and one's life is brought into fellowship with God. Nothing can separate the believer from the love of God.

Church. The one holy, catholic, and apostolic church is the body of Christ. In worship, the church follows the standards laid down in the revised *Book of Common Prayer*. The church emphasizes unity on the essentials and liberty on the nonessentials. It embraces independent thinking and religious liberty, allowing for a variety of viewpoints. Women are permitted to be ordained to the priesthood.

Church government is (obviously) episcopal in nature. The local parish is the basic unit of worship, and the bishop ordains all its priests and confirms all its members. A diocese is composed of not less than six parishes in a given geographical region, and each is overseen by a bishop. Each bishop is elected by a diocesan convention, subject to the approval of the majority of bishops of the church. The diocesan convention meets annually and is composed of all clergy and lay representatives of the parishes. It serves as the basic legislative body of the church.

Every three years, a General Convention meets to make broad decisions about policy and worship. It consists of a House of Bishops (composed of all diocesan bishops) and a House of Deputies (composed of four priests and four laymen from each diocese). All actions of the church must be passed by both houses.

Together, these two houses constitute the supreme legislative, executive, and judicial body of the church.

Sacraments. Two sacraments are ordained by Christ: baptism and the Eucharist. Baptism must be in the name of the Trinity and can be done by pouring, sprinkling, or immersion. Baptism is necessary for regeneration. Baptized persons are confirmed as members of the church by a bishop.

While transubstantiation is rejected, Christ is believed to reside in the elements in the Eucharist. *How* He is present is a holy mystery.

Confirmation, confession, anointing the sick, marriage, and ordination (accepted by the Roman Catholic Church as sacraments) are honored in the Episcopal church, but they are not universally accepted as divinely instituted sacraments in the New Testament.

End Times. The righteous will have eternal life and enjoy God forever. The unrighteous will experience eternal death in rejection of God.

Website

www.ecusa.anglican.org

REFORMED EPISCOPAL CHURCH IN AMERICA

Founded: 1873
Members: 6400
Congregations: 125

Beginnings

The Reformed Episcopal Church in America emerged in 1873 as a result of increased frustration among evangelicals in the denomination regarding its openness to the high-church group—that wing within the Episcopal church that utilizes Roman Catholic sacerdotal rituals, ornaments, and vestments. These evangelicals believed the Protestant character of the Anglican Church was becoming increasingly compromised.

Another cause of dissatisfaction was the Episcopal church's unwillingness to interact and fellowship with non-Episcopalians. In 1873, Reverend George Cummins (1822–1876), an assistant bishop of Kentucky in the Episcopal church, was publicly criticized by fellow Episcopalian bishops for participating in an interdenominational communion service sponsored by the Evangelical Alliance in New York City. He felt such criticism was unwarranted, uncharitable, and judgmental. He was not willing to go along with what he considered to be small-mindedness. He therefore resigned his position and, along with 28 other like-minded individuals, met in New York City to organize the Reformed Episcopal Church. At their meeting, they drew up The Declaration of Principles as a basis for their new denomination, a document based on the Thirty-Nine Articles of Religion.

Beliefs

In doctrine, the Reformed Episcopal Church is similar to the Episcopal Church USA with several notable exceptions. The Reformed believers reject the Episcopalian doctrine that Christ resides in the elements of the Eucharist, arguing instead that the Lord's Supper is symbolic of Christ. They reject the Episcopalian doctrine that baptism is necessary for regeneration, arguing instead that baptism is an outward expression of salvation. They reject the Episcopalian doctrine that the word "priest" is reserved for clergy alone, arguing instead that the word is applicable to all Christians, since the New Testament indicates that all Christians are a part of the priesthood (1 Peter 2:9).

Bible. Scripture as found in the Old and New Testaments is the written Word of God and contains all that is necessary for salvation. It is supreme in its authority to declare God's will. The church is not permitted to teach anything as necessary for salvation that is not found in Scripture.

Like the Episcopal Church USA, the Reformed Episcopal Church believes the Bible must not be interpreted apart from tradition and human reason. In tradition, the church possesses a universal consensus of what Christians have believed regarding faith and practice—as guided by the Holy Spirit—since the beginning of the church, in all parts of the world. Tradition includes the historic creeds, the first four ecumenical councils, the writings of the church Fathers, *The Book of Common Prayer*, and the Thirty-Nine Articles of Religion. Human beings should use their God-given reason to understand the Bible, along with the insights tradition gives us.

Note, however, that Scripture is the *highest* authority. Tradition is subordinate to Scripture in authority because tradition could be tainted by human error, historical prejudice, or individual shortcomings. Reason is the lowest authority, for the reasoning capability of a single Christian has less importance than the universal consensus of what Christians have believed and practiced for several thousand years.

God. The one true and living God is everlasting, without body, parts, or passions. He is of infinite power, wisdom, and goodness. He is the Creator and Preserver of all things visible and invisible. God is a Trinity, meaning that the one God is eternally manifest in three persons: Father, Son, and Holy Spirit. Each of the persons is distinct, yet they are equally divine in substance.

Jesus Christ. Jesus was begotten of everlasting from the Father and is very and eternal God. He is of one substance with the Father. In the Incarnation, He took on a human nature in the womb of the Virgin Mary so that two whole and perfect natures—God and man—were joined together in one person, never to be divided. Jesus suffered, was crucified, and was buried to reconcile us to the Father. His sacrifice was not only for original guilt but also for the actual sins of human beings. He was resurrected from the dead on the third day, ascended into heaven, and sits there until He returns to judge humanity at the last day.

Holy Spirit. The Holy Spirit is the third person of the Trinity. He is equal to the Father and Son in divine substance, majesty, and glory.

Sin and Salvation. Human beings are very far from original righteousness and are naturally inclined to evil. Every person born in the world is deserving of the wrath of God and eternal damnation.

Jesus came to be a holy Lamb without spot, by whose sacrifice the sins of the world are taken away. Human beings are accounted righteous before God only by the merit of Jesus Christ by faith, not by good works. Justification is by faith alone (though see "Sacraments" below).

Church. The church is the body of Christ, a congregation of faithful human beings, a royal priesthood. Through the sacrament of baptism, a person becomes a part of this priesthood. Within this priesthood are the various spiritual gifts and ministries conferred by Christ for the edification of the whole body of Christ, the household of God.

The church has three offices: bishop, elder, and deacon. The highest legislative body is the triennial General Council. Most authority, however, lies at the synodical and parish levels.

Sacraments. Sacraments are outward and visible signs of inward and spiritual grace given unto us, as ordained by Christ. Two sacraments are necessary for salvation: baptism and the Eucharist. Through water baptism in the name of the Trinity, an individual dies to sin and rises to new life in Christ. Through this regeneration, baptism washes away original sin and opens the door to God's grace. This baptism serves to graft a person into the church, the body of Christ. Baptism is a visible confirmation of one's forgiveness, one's adoption as a son of God, and one's status as an heir of salvation.

As mentioned earlier, members of the Reformed Episcopal Church reject the Episcopalian doctrine that Christ resides in the elements of the Eucharist, arguing instead that the Lord's Supper is symbolic of Christ. The Eucharist is a sacrament of the Christian's spiritual nourishment and growth in Christ. It is a pledge of the Christian's communion with Christ and with other Christians as members of His mystical body.

The Reformed Episcopal Church also permits confirmation, penance, matrimony, ordination, and unction as "minor or lesser sacraments."

End Times. Jesus will return again in the same manner that He ascended—bodily and visibly. He will come again as King and Judge. Eternal blessedness awaits the righteous, while divine judgment and condemnation await those who have rejected God's provision of redemption in Christ.

Website

www.recus.org

EPISCOPAL ORTHODOX CHRISTIAN ARCHDIOCESE OF AMERICA

Founded: 1963
Members: 6000
Congregations: 200

Beginnings

This recently formed denomination emerged in 1963 as a result of the protest Reverend James Dees led against the Episcopal church for its failure to firmly proclaim biblical doctrine. Dees felt the Episcopal church was more interested in the social gospel than in traditional Anglicanism. Himself a traditional Anglican, Dees grounded his new denomination in the 1928 (unrevised) version of *The Book of Common Prayer* and the unrevised Thirty-Nine Articles of Religion.

Beliefs

This denomination bases its doctrine on the Nicene Creed, the Apostles' Creed, and the Athanasian Creed.

Bible. The canonical books of the Old and New Testaments are viewed as Scripture and contain all things necessary for salvation. Whatever is not contained in the Bible is not to be required of any human being.

God. The one true and living God is everlasting, without body, parts, or passions. He is of infinite power, wisdom, and goodness. He is the Creator and Preserver of all things visible and invisible. In the unity of the Godhead are three Persons, of one substance, power, and eternity: Father, Son, and Holy Spirit.

Jesus Christ. Jesus was begotten of everlasting from the Father and is very and eternal God. He is of one substance with the Father. In the Incarnation, He took on a human nature in the womb of the Virgin Mary so that two whole and perfect natures—God and man—were joined together in one person, never to be divided. Jesus suffered, was crucified, and was buried to reconcile us to the Father. His sacrifice was not only for original guilt but also for the actual sins of human beings. He was resurrected from the dead on the third day, ascended into heaven, and sits there until He returns to judge humanity at the last day.

Holy Spirit. The Holy Spirit is the third person of the Trinity and is equal to the Father and Son in divine substance, majesty, and glory. He is very and eternal God.

Sin and Salvation. Human beings are very far gone from original righteousness and are naturally inclined to evil. Every person born into the world is deserving of God's wrath and eternal damnation.

Jesus came to be a holy Lamb without spot, by whose sacrifice the sins of the world are taken away. Human beings are accounted righteous before God only by the merit of Jesus Christ by faith and not by good works. Jesus is the only name by which a person can be saved. Justification is by faith alone. Good works are the fruit of faith and follow after justification.

The doctrine of election is affirmed. Before the foundation of the world, God decreed to deliver from curse and damnation those whom He chose in Christ out of humankind, to bring them by Christ to eternal life as vessels made to honor.

People who have received the Holy Spirit can depart from God's grace and fall into sin. However, by the grace of God, they can amend their lives and return to God.

Church. The visible church of Christ is a congregation of faithful human beings in which the pure Word of God is preached and the sacraments are duly administered.

Sacraments. The two sacraments are baptism and the Supper of the Lord. These sacraments must be received worthily. Those who receive them unworthily purchase for themselves damnation.

End Times. Jesus will one day return again to judge all human beings on the last day. All humans will be resurrected. Those who have lived virtuously will be resurrected unto reward. Those who have lived wickedly will be resurrected unto punishment. There is no purgatory.

Website

eoc.orthodoxanglican.net

ANGLICAN CATHOLIC CHURCH
Founded: 1977
Members: 12,000
Congregations: 200

Beginnings

The Anglican Catholic Church, founded in 1977, is catholic in the sense of "universal," or "what has been believed everywhere, always, and by all." It claims to be in concurrence with the great churches of Eastern Orthodoxy and Roman Catholicism.

The denomination grew out of the Congress of St. Louis, Missouri, held in 1977. Many members of the Episcopal Church USA felt the denomination was becoming increasingly liberal. Evidence for this liberalism included the ordination of women in the church and the denomination's choice to revise the 1928 version of *The Book of Common Prayer* (viewed as a departure from true Anglican orthodoxy). This called for a congress of Episcopalians to meet and consider alternatives to the Episcopal Church USA in order to preserve Anglican orthodoxy. Some 2000 Anglican bishops, clergy, and laypeople attended the congress.

The outcome of the conference was the formulation of the "Affirmation of St. Louis." This document specifically denounced the ordination of women, called for an allegiance to traditional Anglican doctrine as contained in the ancient creeds and church Fathers, and called for a return to the traditional practices of Anglicanism as set forth in the 1928 edition of *The Book of Common Prayer.*

The largest body that grew out of this conference was the Anglican Catholic Church, claiming over half its congregations and members. (Other groups formed as well.) The denomination describes itself as a continuation of traditional Anglicanism as expressed in the liturgy of the 1928 *Book of Common Prayer* and rooted in the Nicene, Apostles', and Athanasian Creeds. Today the denomination is found not only in North America but also in South America, the United Kingdom, New Zealand, Australia, and Spain.

Beliefs

Bible. The Holy Scriptures of the Old and New Testaments contain the authentic record of God's revelation to humanity and is valid for all people in all times. The Bible is inspired and contains God's revelation of Himself, His saving activity, and His moral demands. The denomination also honors tradition as set forth by the ancient catholic bishops and doctors, especially as defined by the seven ecumenical councils.

God. The one holy, almighty God is the Creator of all things. Within the unity of the Godhead are three persons: Father, Son, and Holy Spirit.

Jesus Christ. Jesus is Lord of heaven and earth. Through Him is the full revelation of God. He is the Redeemer of humankind. We are saved through the grace of Jesus Christ.

Holy Spirit. The Holy Spirit is the third person of the Trinity. At the sacrament of baptism, one receives the "seal of the Holy Spirit." The Holy Spirit enables Christians to walk in God's way.

Sin and Salvation. Human beings, having inherited original sin, are very far gone from original righteousness, are in rebellion against God's authority, and are thus liable to His righteous judgment. Humans cannot save themselves through their own self-efforts. Salvation is only by faith in Christ. There is no other name under heaven given among men by which we must be saved.

Church. The church, the body of Christ, bases its worship on the liturgy contained in *The Book of Common Prayer.* Knowing the liturgy enables each member of the church to pray as though it were his or her own personal prayer. The principle act of worship in each service is the celebration of the Eucharist, or Mass (see below).

To become a member of the church, one must make his or her desire known to the clergy and be baptized in water in the name of the Trinity. Baptism constitutes one's entrance into the Christian church. Most people attend an instruction class before being baptized.

Government in the church is by bishops in the apostolic succession. The three offices of the church are bishops, priests, and deacons.

Sacraments. The church holds to seven sacraments of grace: baptism, confirmation, holy Eucharist, holy matrimony, holy orders, penance, and unction of the sick. Each sacrament is an objective sign of Christ's continued presence and saving activity among us.

The most important sacrament is the Eucharist. This celebration of Christ's sacrifice is at the heart of all that church members are and do. In the Eucharist, Christ in His body and blood is truly and really present to each church member. The Eucharist should be celebrated every Sunday and Holy day, if not daily.

End Times. All people will one day appear before the judgment seat of Christ.

Website

www.anglicancatholic.org

FRIENDS (QUAKER) CHURCHES

THE EMERGENCE OF THE FRIENDS (or Quakers) is rooted in one man who lived in seventeenth-century England: the mystic preacher George Fox (1625–1691). According to his testimony, Fox had endured years of spiritual conflict during which he was seeking authentic Christian faith. He traveled throughout England speaking to priests and religious leaders, and he searched the Scriptures daily. He found no satisfying answers, however, and this was a great discouragement to him.

Fox was about to give up when he encountered a glimmer of hope. He recalls: "When all my hopes in men were gone, so that I had nothing outwardly to help me, nor could I tell what to do, then, oh! then I heard a voice which said, 'There is One, even Christ Jesus, that can speak to thy condition.' And when I heard it my heart did leap for joy."[1]

Through his direct experience with Christ, Fox came to believe that God gives every person a gift of divine Inner Light or Inner Voice. Every human heart is an altar or shrine of God. All one needs to do is wait upon God, and God will speak to the heart of the sincere seeker. Depending on how people respond to that Inner Light (God desires obedience), they can receive more light.

Fox's main message became "Christ is here among us, and He will directly teach our hearts if we are receptive to it."

Fox's belief that *every* person had this Inner Light affected his followers' interaction with those around them. They became very service-oriented and took a strong stand against slavery. (Even slaves had the Inner Light and therefore were equal with others.)

This Inner Light doctrine ultimately meant that revelation was no longer limited to the Scriptures. Even though the Bible is to be valued, its words should not be taken as God's final and definitive revelation. New revelations could come today just as they did in the days of the apostles. After all, the men who wrote the Bible did so under the power of the Holy Spirit. Since that same Holy Spirit works through us today, revelations can continue today. Even when we do read the Bible, we must depend on the Holy Spirit who wrote those Scriptures to guide us in our understanding of them.

Fox believed that people of his day could minister just as the first-century apostles did—teaching, prophesying, and healing, all under the same power of the Holy Spirit. He felt this was extremely important, for he believed that all this became lost when the church became institutionalized.

Because of the presence of the Inner Light in all people, Fox believed in the ministry of all believers. We do not need a hierarchical structure of priests and bishops, he said. We do not need mediators between God and us. Rather, each of us can have direct access to Jesus. One and one alone—Jesus Christ—can speak to each person's condition. And because all of us have access to Christ, we can all—both men and women—minister to others.

Fox had not intended to start a new sect or denomination. His goal had been to merely persuade the churches of his day that they needed to return to New Testament teachings. In 1667, however, a group of Fox's followers gathered and was organized into a system of monthly, quarterly, and yearly meetings. (A monthly meeting is a local congregation that meets weekly for worship and once a month for business.) By the time of his death in 1691, some 60,000 people had left their churches to become affiliated with Fox's movement.

Fox had consistently exhorted his followers not to become contaminated with the vanity that is part and parcel of this world. Simplicity in daily living became a part of his message. He believed people should dress in simple fashion, without adornments like wigs or jewelry. Moreover, his followers used the words "thy" and "thou" in daily life, though this is not practiced in modern times.

In seeming reaction against Anglican formality and liturgy, worship services were unprogrammed. Because of their belief in the Inner Light, church members typically sat in silence, waiting for the Spirit to prompt someone to speak, pray, or sing.

Fox's followers came to be known as Friends, based upon Jesus' comment to the disciples in John 15:14: "You are my friends if you do what I command." They also became known as Quakers. The term was first used when Fox was in a court of law, and he advised the judge to "tremble at the Word of God." The judge called him a "quaker." Before long, the Friends themselves embraced the term as a way to label their movement.

As the Quaker movement grew, so did resistance against them. They were persecuted—sometimes quite fiercely. Many were whipped, jailed, tortured, mutilated, and even murdered. Even Fox spent six years in jail.

The Quakers made their way to America in the mid-1600s. They did not find a hearty welcome at first. Some were accused of being witches, others were beaten on the whipping post, and some were even hanged. This persecution continued until the passage of the Act of Toleration of 1689.

One individual who was instrumental in the spread of the Friends movement in the colonies was William Penn. Penn had become a convert to the Quakers in 1667. In 1681, he was given a grant of land as a payment of a debt which King Charles II owed his father. The land became known as Pennsylvania.

Penn used his colony in Pennsylvania as a "holy experiment," allowing religious freedom to all and removing the government from interference. He attempted to apply Quaker principles to the running of his colony's government. The colony flourished for decades during this experiment. It became a haven for Quakers. In 1756, however, the Friends lost control of the Pennsylvania legislature over the issue of taxation.

In any event, Fox's efforts resulted in giving birth to a leading religious movement during the colonial period of America: the Religious Society of Friends. As history unfolded, a number of Friends affiliations emerged—including the Evangelical Friends International, the Friends General Conference, the Friends United Meeting, and the Religious Society of Friends (Conservative).

FRIENDS GENERAL CONFERENCE

Founded: 1900
Members: 34,000
Congregations: 650

Beginnings

The Friends General Conference is an association of 14 autonomous yearly meetings and seven monthly meetings. The association is open to all Friends who wish to affiliate with its programs. The association has no authority over member churches.

The Friends General Conference was established in 1900 and grew out of four previous Friends conferences: First-Day School General Conference (founded 1868), Friends Union for Philanthropic Labor (founded 1881), Friends Religious Conference (founded 1893), and Friends Education Conference (founded 1894). The present conference is governed by a central committee made up of 170 Friends.

Members prefer to think of the Friends General Conference as a service organization that seeks to nurture and enhance the spiritual life of affiliate churches and their members. Typical of Friends theology, the organization focuses on one's direct experience of God. All members are encouraged to experience God's living presence and discern God's leadings. Members are exhorted to share their experiences with each other.

The conference is open to theological diversity and is generally considered a more liberal group of Friends. They formally disavow creeds and believe each person must prayerfully seek guidance and follow his or her understanding of God's leading.

Beliefs

Bible. The Friends General Conference is less reliant on written Scripture than many groups. Heaviest emphasis is placed on the Inner Light that dwells in each person. This Inner Light includes continuing revelation. Whenever the Bible is read, it is to be understood through the same Holy Spirit who produced the Scriptures.

God. Emphasis is placed on a direct experience of God. God—or at least a spark of the divine—is found in every individual. Through the Inner Light within, human beings can experience God speaking to their condition.

Jesus Christ. There is a wide spectrum of beliefs regarding Jesus Christ.

Holy Spirit. The Holy Spirit is often spoken of as the Light of Christ, the Spirit of God, or the Inward Light. The Holy Spirit brings illumination. By virtue of the Holy Spirit, people can become centers of radiating love.

Sin and Salvation. Salvation involves a continuing process of spiritual renewal. It results from the power given to human beings to make correct choices under the guidance of the Inner Light.

Church. Worship services are unprogrammed (they have no set schedule). Members assemble and then worship in silence, fully expecting that someone will eventually speak as led by the Holy Spirit. Since any member is welcome to speak, the responsibilities normally handled by pastors are handled by church members. (No pastors are employed.) Women are as free as men to be involved in ministry. Homosexuals are also welcome.

Sacraments. No outward sacraments are observed.

Website

www.fgcquaker.org

FRIENDS UNITED MEETING

Founded: 1902
Members: 41,297
Congregations: 436

Beginnings

The Friends United Meeting seeks to provide a united Quaker witness in missions, Christian education, and the publication of Sunday school materials. Leadership development is also provided.

The goal is to energize and equip Friends through the power of the Holy Spirit and to gather people into fellowships that honor and obey Jesus Christ.

The roots of the Friends United Meeting go back to 1887, when delegates of Friends groups were called to a meeting in Richmond, Indiana. These delegates quickly discovered that they had a great deal in common in terms of missions, evangelism, Christian education, and the need for Bible schools. They decided that they could be much more effective in their overall goals if they undertook them together instead of individually. In 1902, a formal organization called the Five Years Meetings of Friends in America was founded in Indianapolis, Indiana. In 1963, the name of the organization was changed to Friends United Meeting after the decision was made to meet every three years instead of every five years. The Friends United Meeting sponsors both local monthly meetings and regional yearly meetings.

Beliefs

Bible. All Scripture is inspired by God. The Bible contains a divinely authorized record of the doctrines that are binding on Christians. The Bible must be read in dependence upon the same Holy Spirit who inspired it.

The Bible is not God's only revelation. Through the Inner Light, people receive continuing revelations today. All revelations received through this Inner Light are checked against Scripture, for the Holy Spirit will never lead a person to believe something that is contrary to the Word, which He inspired.

God. The one true God is all-wise and everlasting. He is the Creator and Preserver of the universe. He is eternally manifest in three persons: the Father, the Son, and the Holy Spirit. True religion involves a direct encounter with this living God.

Jesus Christ. Jesus is fully God. He is Lord and Savior, the eternal Word, and Redeemer. In the Incarnation, He was the fullness of the Godhead bodily. His death on the cross brought redemption and the remission of sins. He was buried and rose again the third day, after which He ascended into heaven.

Holy Spirit. The Holy Spirit convinces the world of sin, righteousness, and judgment. He witnesses to and glorifies Jesus. He is a teacher and guide of believers. He quickens and sanctifies them, indwells their hearts, and enables them to understand Scripture.

Sin and Salvation. Humankind fell into transgression and thereby lost the spiritual life of righteousness in which it was created. Sin is not imputed to specific human beings, however, until they individually transgress God's divine law, having understood its moral consequences.

Salvation is a gift that is received by God's grace. Upon repentance and faith, a person is justified, pardoned of sins, and given a new life. Guilt is taken away, and one is reconciled to God. Believers who backslide can repent and receive forgiveness.

Church. The church is a company of people in whom Christ dwells. About one-fifth of the church services are unprogrammed, in which church members wait in silence for God to inspire someone to speak, sing, or pray. The remaining services are programmed, utilizing pastors to provide preaching, teaching, and pastoral care. Women are included among those who can become pastors.

Sacraments. The denomination does not celebrate outward rituals or sacraments. Inward attitudes are much more important than outward rites. Church members believe the one true baptism is spiritual and inward and involves one's yielding to God's will. Likewise, they believe the one true Lord's Supper involves inward attention to and communion with God.

End Times. Jesus will come again to render final judgment. The righteous will be resurrected unto eternal life; the unrighteous will be resurrected unto eternal punishment.

Distinctives. The Friends United Meeting is a peace-loving denomination. Service in the military, however, is a matter of individual conscience.

Website

www.fum.org

FAST FACTS ON
Salvation Words

Born Again	Literally means to be "born from above." It refers to God's giving of eternal life to the one who believes in Christ (Titus 3:5).
Justified	God declares righteous all those who believe in Jesus. He acquits them and pronounces a verdict of not guilty.
Reconciled	For the one who believes in Jesus, the alienation and estrangement that formerly existed between oneself and God is eradicated (2 Corinthians 5:19).
Forgiven	God said, "Their sins and lawless acts I will remember no more" (Hebrews 10:17). This is forgiveness.
Adopted	Believers are adopted into God's forever family (Romans 8:14).

THE RELIGIOUS SOCIETY OF FRIENDS (CONSERVATIVE)

Founded: 1904
Members: 1500 (estimate)
Congregations: Unknown

Beginnings

The Religious Society of Friends (Conservative) emerged in 1904 as a result of several divisions that occurred among the Friends. In England, a Friends leader named Joseph John Gurney (1788–1847) influenced Quakers toward evangelical beliefs, including the authority of the Bible. Meanwhile, Elias Hicks (1748–1830), a New York Friends leader, opposed Gurney's evangelicalism as being inconsistent with the Quaker emphasis on the Inner Light. This led to a division in 1827 between those who followed Gurney's evangelical lead and those who followed Hicks with his traditional emphasis on the Inner Light.

In 1837, Gurney relocated from England to the United States and was involved in yet another division. This time the division was between followers of Gurney (who stressed the authority of the Bible) and those who were loyal to John Wilbur (1774–1856), a Rhode Island Friends leader who placed heavy emphasis on the Inner Light. Wilbur did not deny the authority of the Bible, but he felt Gurney tended to substitute a creed for immediate and direct revelation from the Holy Spirit.

Those who followed Wilbur's traditional Quakerism became the Religious Society of Friends (Conservative). They were called "conservative" not because of conservative theology but because they chose to continue and preserve traditional Friends beliefs (especially belief in the Inner Light).

Beliefs

Substantial theological diversity exists among the Religious Society of Friends (Conservative), so making representative statements about theological beliefs is difficult. The society agrees on these points:

Jesus Christ. Believers are to experience the living Christ.

Holy Spirit. Believers are to experience the Holy Spirit.

Church. The style of church worship is unprogrammed. The service begins with silent, expectant waiting upon God. All church members can directly commune with God, so all members are welcome to share in ministry to others during the service.

Website

www.quaker.org/friends

FAST FACTS ON
Worship

Key Word	Meaning
Old Testament Hebrew word: *Shaha*	Means "to bow down" or "to prostrate oneself" (see Genesis 22:5; 42:6).
New Testament Greek word: *Proskuneo*	Means "to prostrate oneself" (see Matthew 2:2,8,11).
English word: *Worship*	In Old English, "worship" was rendered "worthship," pointing to the worthiness of God. Such worship is the proper response of a creature to his Creator (Psalm 95:6). Worship can be congregational (1 Corinthians 11–14) or individual (Romans 12:1).

EVANGELICAL FRIENDS INTERNATIONAL
Founded: 1990
Members: 27,057
Congregations: 278

Beginnings

The Evangelical Friends Alliance was formed in 1965. The alliance involved an association of four autonomous Quaker groups: the Evangelical Friends Church (Eastern Division), the Rocky Mountain Yearly Meeting of Friends, the Mid-America Yearly Meeting of Friends, and the Northwest Yearly Meeting of Friends. These four groups were among the most theologically conservative among the Friends. The alliance was founded to bring about denominational unity and an evangelical emphasis. In 1990 the alliance was formally restructured to become the Evangelical Friends International. (The organization now has an international outreach into Africa, Asia, Europe, and Latin America.)

Beliefs

The denomination is generally conservative in theology.

Bible. The Bible is God's Word. It is inspired, infallible, and authoritative. Humans can understand Scripture through the illumination of the Holy Spirit.

God. The one true God is the Creator and Sustainer of the universe. He is the Judge of humankind. He is eternally manifest in three persons: Father, Son, and Holy Spirit.

Jesus Christ. Jesus is the Son of God. In the Incarnation, He was full deity and full humanity. He was virgin-born, lived a sinless life, engaged in miracles, was crucified to bring redemption through His blood, was resurrected, and then ascended to the right hand of the Father. It is in our living union with Jesus that we find our true identity.

Holy Spirit. The Holy Spirit lives within every believer. He satisfies the human need for grace, truth, love, and righteousness. He is a comforter and counselor to Christians and gives them spiritual gifts so they can engage in service to the Lord.

Sin and Salvation. As a result of the fall, the perfect image of God in man was warped, marred, stained, and corrupted. Since then all people have inherited a pervasive sinfulness that invades every aspect of their being. All people are thus separated from God. God imputes sin to specific humans, however, only when they personally transgress the divine law after having received sufficient capacity to understand it.

Salvation is received by grace through faith in Jesus, not by good works. To those who repent and trust in Christ, God grants the forgiveness of sins, eternal life, regeneration, and the promise of a resurrection body. Those who fall away can lose their salvation.

Church. The church is composed of all those who have repented and exercised faith in Jesus Christ as Lord and Savior. The church is universal, uniting all Christians everywhere. The church also has local expressions in individual congregations and in families of churches (denominations).

Sunday worship is programmed and includes Scripture reading, hymns, and a sermon by a pastor. Women have been involved in ministry leadership throughout the denomination's history. Church government is congregational.

Sacraments. Church members are granted liberty regarding the observance or nonobservance of the external ordinances of baptism and the Lord's Supper. Baptism in the Holy Spirit is more important than water baptism. The baptism in the Holy Spirit occurs when a believer submits his life to the Lord.

End Times. Jesus will return in glory. There will be a pretribulational rapture of the church. The second coming will be followed by a 1000-year millennial reign of Christ. Believers will live eternally in heaven by God's grace; unbelievers will suffer eternally in hell. Church members do not divide over eschatology.

Website

www.evangelical-friends.org

FUNDAMENTALIST AND BIBLE CHURCHES

IN THE LATE NINETEENTH CENTURY, the attack on historic Christianity by German rationalism and theological liberalism was pervasive. Scholars in this tradition taught that the Bible is a fallible human document, approached Scripture with an antisupernatural bias, and dismissed miracles as the fantasies of ignorant people in biblical times who did not understand the laws of nature. They viewed humanity as fundamentally good with no real sin problem. They saw Jesus not as God incarnate nor as a divine Savior but rather as a man supremely full of God who lived with ethical and moral excellence. Jesus was portrayed as an example to the human race, a mere moral teacher. He did not die on the cross for our sins, but His death nevertheless has an uplifting moral influence on people, setting an example of sacrifice.

The fundamentalist movement emerged largely in reaction to this tidal wave of modernism and theological liberalism. Fundamentalists are conservative Christians who hold to the fundamental doctrines of Christianity and not to liberal interpretations. These doctrines include the inspiration and infallibility of the Bible, the Trinity, creationism (as opposed to evolution), human depravity, salvation by faith in Christ, the full deity of Christ, His virgin birth, His miracle-working power, His substitutionary atonement, His resurrection from the dead, His ascension into heaven, His premillennial second coming, and the resurrection of every human being with an ultimate destiny in heaven or hell, depending on whether one has placed faith in Christ. Fundamentalists ultimately took their name from a series of widely distributed small books called *The Fundamentals: A Testimony of Truth,* published from 1910 to 1912. These books, published by two wealthy Presbyterians, were distributed freely and contained nearly 100 articles defending the doctrines listed above (and others).

Though ascribing the emergence of fundamentalism to a few key conservative Christians would be a gross oversimplification, these names are worthy of mention:

Dwight L. Moody (1837–1899). Moody was a powerful evangelist whose voice shook a nation for the cause of Christ. He was the founder of the Moody Bible Institute. His influence survives to the present day.

John Nelson Darby (1800–1882). Darby was a dispensationalist whose emphasis on biblical prophecy touched a nerve among American and British Christians. He was instrumental in popularizing belief in a coming rapture of the church, followed by a seven-year tribulation period, the second coming of Christ, and the establishment of the millennial kingdom. He was also instrumental in causing an increasing number of people to reject the idea of a state church (such as the Church of England) and pursue a nondenominational approach to church life.

Cyrus Scofield (1843–1921). Scofield, also a dispensationalist, edited the *Scofield Reference Bible,* which became wildly popular among American Christians. It too served to focus attention on biblical prophecy. The formation of a Jewish state in 1948 gave a stamp of approval to fundamentalist teaching because fundamentalists had long taught that the prophetic Scriptures indicated that Israel would come back to her homeland.

Because of the influence of these and other Christians, the fundamentalist movement emerged and forever changed the religious landscape. Today virtually thousands of fundamentalist bodies exist in the United States.

FAST FACTS ON
the End Times

Rapture	The dead in Christ are instantly raised from the dead, and living Christians are instantly translated into their resurrection bodies. Both groups meet Christ in the air (1 Thessalonians 4:13-17).
Tribulation Period	A seven-year period during which God will pour out His judgments on earth (Revelation 4–18). Many believe it follows the rapture.
Second Coming	Following the tribulation period, Christ will come again in glory and majesty as King of kings and Lord of lords (Revelation 19:16).
Millennial Kingdom	Following the second coming, Christ will rule on earth for a 1000-year period (Revelation 20:2-3).
Eternal State	After the millennial kingdom, believers will dwell forever in heaven. Unbelievers are forever consigned to hell (Revelation 20:11–21:27).

AMERICAN EVANGELICAL CHRISTIAN CHURCHES

Founded: 1944
Members: 15,470
Congregations: 180

Beginnings

The American Evangelical Christian Churches were founded by G.W. Hyatt in Chicago, Illinois, in 1944. This association is made up of churches and individuals who accept a doctrinal statement called the "Seven Articles of Faith" (the Bible as God's Word, the virgin birth, the deity of Christ, salvation through the atonement, guidance through prayer, the second coming, and the establishment of the millennial kingdom). The association is dedicated to the spread of the gospel at home and in foreign lands through churches, ministers, and missionaries.

The association also seeks to provide an alternative ministerial track for those who have not been formally trained at a seminary but who sense the call of God on their lives to the work of ministry. This ministerial track is also appropriate for those who have chosen not to go through their own denomination's ministerial track. The association operates a college where members can pursue educational needs. Following training, ministerial students receive licenses qualifying them to perform the various functions of ministry.

Beliefs

This denomination has very brief doctrinal requirements.

Bible. The Bible is the written and verbally inspired Word of God. It contains the revealed will of God. It is the all-sufficient rule for faith and practice and has final authority.

God. There is one true God.

Jesus Christ. Jesus is full deity. He took on human flesh without giving up His deity, having been born of the Virgin Mary. His death on the cross was an atonement for sin. He will one day return.

Holy Spirit. The Holy Spirit guides believers throughout their lives.

Sin and Salvation. Salvation is made possible by the atonement wrought by Christ at the cross.

Church. Each local church is independent and autonomous. Polity is congregational. Women are welcome in ministry.

End Times. The rapture is an imminent event in which Christ will meet all believers (dead and alive) in the air and take them back to heaven. The second coming of Christ will occur after the tribulation period. Following this, Christ will set up His millennial kingdom.

Website

www.aeccministries.com

BAPTIST BIBLE FELLOWSHIP INTERNATIONAL

Founded: 1950
Members: 1,200,000
Congregations: 4500

Beginnings

In 1950 Baptist pastor G.B. Vick was asked by certain Baptist leaders to become the president of the Bible Baptist Seminary in Fort Worth, Texas, a school affiliated with the World Fundamental

Baptist Missionary Fellowship, run by John F. Norris. Without warning, a Baptist feud erupted. Before Vick even arrived to begin his job, the dictatorial and militant Norris opposed him, had him ousted, and managed to have a man of his own choosing installed as president. Vigorous debate erupted, Norris' actions were challenged by many, an impasse was reached, and Vick decided to resign.

Vick promptly met with 120 pastors and sympathizing lay people to consider a new organization. The Baptist Bible Fellowship International emerged out of the dissatisfaction these Baptists felt toward Norris and his organization. In addition to the Baptist Bible Fellowship, the Baptist Bible College was also founded. Vick became the head of this school, and another Baptist leader, W.E. Dowell, became the first president of the Baptist Bible Fellowship International.

Beliefs

Bible. The Bible is inspired by the Holy Spirit and contains truth without any mixture of error. It is infallible. It contains the complete and final revelation of God's will for humankind. It constitutes the supreme standard for human conduct, creeds, and opinions.

God. The one true living God is an infinite, intelligent Spirit. He is glorious in holiness. He is the Maker and supreme Ruler of heaven and earth. Within the unity of the Godhead are three persons who are equal in every divine perfection: the Father, the Son, and the Holy Spirit.

Jesus Christ. Jesus is both the Son of God and God the Son. He is the Savior of humankind. In the Incarnation, He was conceived by the Holy Spirit and born of the Virgin Mary. He wrought salvation at the cross. He rose from the dead and ascended into heaven, where He is now enthroned.

Holy Spirit. The Holy Spirit is equal in nature to the Father and the Son. He was active in creation, restrains evil, convicts men of sin, bears witness to the truth, and is the agent of the new birth. He also seals, endues with power, guides, teaches, and sanctifies believers.

Sin and Salvation. Adam and Eve voluntarily sinned against God and fell from their happy estate. Now all human beings are sinners, not by constraint but by choice, and are therefore under God's just condemnation.

Salvation is wholly of God's grace and is a free gift, made possible by the vicarious sacrifice of Jesus on the cross. To be saved, sinners must be born again. Those who repent and believe in Christ are justified, which means God pardons their sin, gives them eternal life, and imputes the very righteousness of Christ to them. True believers in Christ will endure to the end and not lose their salvation. A special providence of God watches over their welfare.

Church. The church is a congregation of baptized believers who are associated by a covenant of faith and fellowship of the gospel. The mission of the church is found in the Great Commission: to make disciples, to build up the church, and to teach and instruct as He has commanded.

Every church is autonomous, free from the interference of any hierarchy of individuals or organizations. The officers of the church are pastors/elders and deacons, whose qualifications and duties are clearly delineated in Scripture. Only men are eligible for leadership positions. The one Superintendent of the church is Jesus Christ through the Holy Spirit. Churches cooperate with each other in contending for the faith and for the furtherance of the gospel. Each church is free to determine the measure and method of its cooperation.

Sacraments. Baptism is by immersion in the name of the Father, Son, and Holy Spirit. It points to our faith in the crucified, buried, and risen Savior, and it pictures our own death to sin and resurrection to new life. It is a prerequisite to participation in the Lord's Supper. The Lord's Supper is to be preceded by a solemn self-examination and commemorates the dying love of Christ. Only members of the church can participate in the sacrament.

End Times. Jesus is coming again personally, bodily, and visibly. He will rule during the millennial kingdom for 1000 years, putting all enemies under His feet. There will be a final judgment. The saved will enjoy everlasting blessedness in heaven, and the wicked will experience everlasting conscious suffering.

Distinctives. Scriptural giving (tithing) is considered one of the fundamentals of the faith. Only the King James Version is used in English-speaking congregations. Jesus is viewed as a Baptist in His thinking and work.

Website

www.bbfi.org

FAST FACTS ON
Church Officers

Officers	Role
Elders	These leaders of the church oversee (1 Timothy 3:1), rule (1 Timothy 5:17), and guard right doctrine (Titus 1:9).
Deacons	These male leaders serve the elders and the congregation in various capacities (Acts 6:1-6).
Deaconesses	These female leaders serve the elders and the congregation in various capacities (Romans 16:1). (Many churches do not accept deaconesses as legitimate church officers.)

BAPTIST MISSIONARY ASSOCIATION OF AMERICA

Founded: 1950
Members: 234,732
Congregations: 1525

Beginnings

Originally called the North American Baptist Association (Little Rock, Arkansas, 1950), this association of independent conservative Baptist churches adopted its present name in 1968. The churches associated with the group cooperate on missions work, a worldwide radio outreach, and a publications department that publishes Sunday school curricula and other kinds of religious materials. The local church is primary; the association exists only to expedite the ministries of the church.

The association only cooperates with other Christian groups that hold to the same fundamentalist doctrines they do. They encourage a separation from all churches and church alliances that uphold heresies and ideas not in keeping with God's Word.

Beliefs

Bible. The Bible—both the Old Testament and the New Testament—is verbally inspired and infallible. It is the final standard for the believer's faith. It is to be interpreted literally.

God. The one true God is the Creator of the universe. He is eternally manifest in three persons: the Father, the Son, and the Holy Spirit. The three persons are equal in the divine attributes.

Jesus Christ. Jesus is full deity. He is the Son of God and the Savior of the world. He was virgin-born. He died for human sin, was buried, and rose from the dead. He then ascended back to heaven, where He is seated at the right hand of the Father, interceding for us.

Holy Spirit. The personhood and work of the Holy Spirit are affirmed.

Sin and Salvation. Human beings are totally depraved—a result of the fall. Salvation is based entirely on the blood atonement wrought by Christ on the cross. Believers are justified by faith alone and not by any works. Believers are eternally secure in their salvation.

Church. All churches in the association must subscribe to the fundamentalist interpretation of Christian doctrine. Churches are autonomous, each choosing its own officers, directors, and missionaries. Pastors and deacons are the permanent offices of the church (pastors do the teaching; deacons assist the pastor). The denomination does not endorse women in the ministry. Churches share equally in the cooperative activities of the association. Such cooperation is entirely voluntary.

Sacraments. Baptism is for believers only. The proper mode is immersion. It represents a confession of faith in Jesus Christ. Only baptisms administered by the authority of a scriptural Missionary Baptist church are valid. Such baptism is a prerequisite for partaking of the Lord's Supper. The Lord's Supper is a memorial to be observed within the context of the church, celebrated only by baptized believers. It is a memorial to the crucified body and shed blood of Christ.

End Times. Christ will come again personally and bodily. This event is imminent. Following His coming, He will reign on earth for 1000 years. There will be two resurrections. The first is the resurrection of the righteous, which takes place at Christ's second coming. The second is the resurrection of the wicked, which takes place at the end of the millennial kingdom. There will be a judgment of all humankind. True believers will experience everlasting happiness in heaven. Unbelievers will suffer everlasting punishment in hell.

Distinctives. Members recognize a perpetuity of independent Baptist churches from Christ's day until His second coming.

Website

www.bmaam.com

CHRISTIAN AND MISSIONARY ALLIANCE

Founded: 1897
Members: 191,318
Congregations: 1727

Beginnings

The Christian and Missionary Alliance was founded in 1897 as a result of a merger of two societies established a decade earlier by Dr. Albert Simpson (1843–1919), a Presbyterian minister. These two societies were the Christian Alliance, involved in home missions, and the Evangelical Missionary Alliance, involved in missions abroad. The Christian and Missionary Alliance seeks to exalt Christ as Savior, Sanctifier, Healer, and coming King. It also seeks to complete Christ's Great Commission, evangelizing and discipling people throughout the United States.

Beliefs

Bible. The Old and New Testaments are verbally inspired and are inerrant as originally given. The Bible is the only rule of Christian faith and practice.

God. The one true God is infinitely perfect. He eternally exists in three persons: the Father, the Son, and the Holy Spirit.

Jesus Christ. In the Incarnation, Jesus was true God and true man. He was conceived by the Holy Spirit and born of the Virgin Mary. He died on the cross—the just for the unjust—as a substitutionary sacrifice for the sins of humanity. He rose from the dead and ascended to heaven, where He is now at the right hand of Majesty as our great High Priest.

Holy Spirit. The Holy Spirit convinces the world of sin, righteousness, and judgment. He indwells, guides, teaches, and empowers believers. God desires all believers to be filled with the Holy Spirit and be sanctified wholly, separated from sin and the world.

Sin and Salvation. Adam and Eve fell through disobedience to God, thereby incurring both spiritual and physical death. Since then all human beings have been born with a sin nature, separated from God. Those who repent and believe in Jesus Christ are born again of the Holy Spirit, receive the gift of eternal life, and become the children of God.

Church. The church is composed of all who believe in the Lord Jesus Christ, are redeemed through His blood, and are born again of the Holy Spirit. Christ is the head of the church. Local churches meet together for the worship of God, edification through God's Word, prayer, fellowship, the proclamation of the gospel, and observance of the ordinances. Christ commissions the church to go into the entire world as His witness, preaching the gospel to all nations. Women can be credentialed but not ordained for ministry.

Local churches develop their own bylaws, but they adhere to a common constitution set by the denomination. Local churches are part of geographical districts, and a national office oversees all ministry in the United States.

Sacraments. Baptism is for believers, and the proper mode is immersion. The Lord's Supper is open to all professing to be born-again Christians.

End Times. Jesus will come again to establish His kingdom of righteousness and peace. This coming is imminent and will be personal, visible, and premillennial. The just will be resurrected unto life, and the unjust will be resurrected unto judgment. The saved will have everlasting joy and bliss in heaven. The unsaved will live forever in conscious torment.

Distinctives. Christ's atonement provides for the healing of the mortal body. Prayer for the sick and anointing with oil are Scriptural teachings.

Website

www.cmalliance.org

CONSERVATIVE BAPTIST ASSOCIATION OF AMERICA

Founded: 1947
Members: 200,000
Congregations: 1800

Beginnings

The Conservative Baptist Association of America was founded in 1947 at Atlantic City, New Jersey. It emerged from the fundamentalist-modernist controversy that afflicted the Northern Baptist Convention. The conservatives at the convention attempted to alter its liberal course, but to no avail. They finally broke away and formed a new conservative body—the Conservative Baptist Association of America.

This association considers itself as a loose affiliation or cooperative agency that equips like-minded churches and facilitates missions. The ultimate goal is to fulfill the Great Commission. Toward this end, the association throughout the 1950s, 60s, and 70s was involved in planting hundreds of churches throughout America. In the 1980s this church planting continued, but the association was also involved in training congregations for evangelism and discipleship.

A wide range of services is offered to affiliate churches. This includes conflict resolution, financial analysis, retirement planning, referrals for counseling, help on church growth, assistance on women's and youth ministry, ministry placement, and more. A national conference is held annually.

Beliefs

Bible. The Bible is the divinely inspired Word of God. It is inerrant and infallible in the original manuscripts. It is the supreme and final authority on all matters of which it speaks.

God. The one true God is the Creator and Sustainer of all things. He is perfect in holiness, wisdom, power, and love. He eternally exists in three persons: the Father, the Son, and the Holy Spirit. Though they are equal in the divine perfections, they have distinct but harmonious offices in the work of creation, providence, and redemption.

Jesus Christ. Jesus is God's eternal Son and has the same divine nature as the Father and Holy Spirit. In the Incarnation, He was very God and very man, having been born of a virgin. He lived a sinless life, died as a substitutionary sacrifice on the cross, rose from the dead, and ascended into heaven. He now engages in priestly intercession on behalf of believers.

Holy Spirit. The Holy Spirit is engaged in the ministries of regeneration, sanctification, and preservation. He glorifies Jesus and empowers believers for godly living.

Sin and Salvation. All people are sinners by nature and by choice. They are spiritually dead and separated from God. Salvation is by grace through faith and is based entirely on the work of Christ at the cross. Those who repent of sin and believe in Jesus as Savior are regenerated by the Holy Spirit. Salvation results in righteous living and good works.

Church. The church is Christ's spiritual body, of which He is the head. It is composed of all who have been born again by the Holy Spirit. Local churches are made up of believers baptized by immersion after their confession of faith in Jesus. The church gathers for the purpose of worship, instruction, evangelism, and service.

Each local church is self-governing, free from any interference by ecclesiastical authorities. These churches nevertheless work interdependently to enhance their effectiveness.

Sacraments. The two ordinances are baptism and the Lord's Supper. Baptism is by immersion.

End Times. The second coming of Christ will be personal, visible, and premillennial. There will be a bodily resurrection of the saved and the lost. All humans will be judged. The saved will enjoy eternal life in heaven, while the unsaved will be consigned eternally to hell.

Website

www.cbamerica.org

IFCA INTERNATIONAL

Founded: 1930
Members: 61,655
Congregations: 659

Beginnings

IFCA International is the new name of the former Independent Fundamentalist Churches of America. The name was changed because it was felt that *fundamentalist* was no longer a suitable term because of undesirable radical and militant nuances.

The Independent Fundamentalist Churches of America joined together in 1930 in Cicero, Illinois, as an association of Bible-believing churches and organizations whose goal was to safeguard fundamental doctrine. The founders—from denominations including the Presbyterians, Congregationalists, and Baptists—include such well-known Christian personalities as theologian J. Oliver Buswell and Radio Bible Class personality M.R. DeHaan. Members have included such influential leaders as Charles Ryrie, John Walvoord, J. Vernon McGee, and John MacArthur.

The bylaws of the association state that its purpose is to unify those who have separated from denominations that harbor unbelievers and liberal teachers, and to encourage one another in world evangelism. The association also provides a united front in defending the fundamental teachings of Scripture. The unity of affiliate churches is based on acceptance of a sixteen-article doctrinal statement.

The association coordinates and facilitates joint participation without in any way infringing upon each church's autonomy. Membership is voluntary and is reaffirmed annually.

Beliefs

Bible. The Bible is the verbally inspired Word of God. It is infallible and God-breathed, inerrant in the words of the original manuscripts. It is the final authority for life and faith.

God. The one true God eternally exists in three persons: the Father, the Son, and the Holy Spirit. These three are eternal in being, identical in nature, and equal in power and glory.

Jesus Christ. Jesus is the eternal Son of God. In the Incarnation, He became a man without ceasing to be God, having been born of a virgin. He lived a sinless life and died as a substitutionary atonement for the sins of humanity. He physically rose from the dead, ascended into heaven, was exalted to the right hand of the Father, and is now our intercessor and advocate.

Holy Spirit. The Holy Spirit convinces the world of sin, righteousness, and judgment. He regenerates believers, baptizes them into the body of Christ, indwells and seals them, and guides them into the truth.

Sin and Salvation. In Adam's sin all humanity fell, inherited a sinful nature, and became alienated from God. Salvation is a free gift that people receive through personal faith in the Lord Jesus. This gift is based entirely on the blood Jesus shed at the cross of Calvary. Once saved, believers are secure in their salvation.

Church. The universal church is the body and bride of Christ. It is a spiritual organism composed of all born-again persons of the present age. Each local church is autonomous and independent, free from any external authority or control. Each church chooses its own name, sets up its own government, calls its own pastor, and invites into the pulpit any speakers it deems sound in the faith. As well, each church is free to determine which missionaries it will support. Yet, "independent" does not mean "isolated."

Churches voluntarily associate to network in accomplishing common goals.

Sacraments. All believers are encouraged to be baptized in water as a testimony of their faith in Christ. All born-again persons are invited to celebrate the Lord's Supper regardless of church membership.

End Times. Jesus will rapture the church prior to the tribulation period. This event is imminent. Following the tribulation, the second coming of Christ will occur, after which He will set up His millennial kingdom. At the bodily resurrection of all human beings, the saved will inherit eternal life, and the unsaved will go to everlasting punishment. Heaven and hell are literal places.

Distinctives. IFCA International has two distinctives:

First, IFCA International espouses dispensationalism. The different dispensations are not different ways of salvation but rather different divinely ordered stewardships by which God directs humankind according to His purpose. Three of these dispensations are the focus of much Scripture: the age of the law, the age of the church, and the age of the millennial kingdom.

Second, IFCA International takes a stand against movements that are contrary to historic Christianity. These include ecumenism (which promotes the organizational unity of all Christianity and ultimately all religions), neoorthodoxy (a movement that often uses evangelical terminology but in fact seriously departs from orthodoxy), and neoevangelicalism (a movement within evangelicalism characterized by a toleration of and dialogue with theological liberalism).

Website

www.ifca.org

FAST FACTS ON
the Rapture Debate

Pretribulational View	Christ will rapture the entire church before any part of the tribulation period begins.
Midtribulational View	Christ will rapture the church in the middle of the tribulation period.
Posttribulational View	Christ will rapture the church after the tribulation period.
Partial Rapture View	Only spiritual Christians are raptured throughout the tribulation period.

PLYMOUTH BRETHREN
Founded: 1820
Members: 100,000
Congregations: 1150

Beginnings

In the early 1800s, many Christians in the British Isles were uncomfortable with the formalism, clericalism, and spiritual dryness of churches run by a denominational hierarchy. These Christians sought a simpler form of Christianity where they could read Scripture and worship the Lord in small gatherings like those of the early church. They met together for communion, prayer, and Bible teaching, using a simple New Testament pattern. Eventually, large gatherings were established in Dublin and Plymouth. The movement as a whole ultimately took on the name Plymouth

Brethren* because the gathering in Plymouth was so large and influential. Soon, through steady evangelism and church planting, churches began cropping up all over England, Scotland, Europe, and North America. Famous Plymouth Brethren include George Mueller, John Nelson Darby, Sir Robert Anderson, F.F. Bruce, Jim Elliot, H.A. Ironside, William Kelly, C.H. Mackintosh, W.E. Vine, and G.V. Wigram.

Beliefs

Bible. The Bible is verbally and fully inspired in the words of the original manuscripts.

God. The one true God is eternally manifest in three persons: the Father, the Son, and the Holy Spirit (there is a Trinity in unity).

Jesus Christ. Jesus is the eternal Son of God.

Holy Spirit. The Holy Spirit is the third person of the Trinity.

Sin and Salvation. Salvation is based entirely on the work of Christ at the cross. Those who believe in Christ are eternally secure in their salvation.

Church. Church gatherings are often unstructured. This is especially true of the hour-long Remembrance Meeting (communion service). There are no salaried ministers. There is no distinction between the clergy and the laity. Generally, gifted brothers in the congregation minister as they are able. These individuals are often supported in their work of ministry, but they are not in authority over the congregation. Gifted sisters minister at women's Bible studies.

A distinction exists between Open Brethren and Exclusive Brethren churches. Open Brethren churches are completely independent and autonomous. Church government is by a plurality of

---

* This group's use of "brethren" should not be taken to mean that it is affiliated with the Brethren churches associated with the Pietist movement.

elders who meet the qualifications delineated in 1 Timothy 3 and Titus 1. Some churches have deacons to take care of physical needs.

Exclusive Brethren churches are not independent and prefer to be part of a "Circle of Fellowship." This circle is an association of like-minded churches. Often "leading brothers" in each congregation take the responsibilities of elders.

Sacraments. Baptism is for believers only (not infants), and the proper mode is immersion. The Lord's Supper is celebrated weekly at Remembrance Meetings. It is for all believers who have separated themselves from evil.

End Times. Plymouth Brethren are pretribulational, premillennial, and dispensational. Christ's rapture of the church is considered imminent. The saved will experience eternal bliss in heaven. The unsaved will suffer eternal torment in hell.

Distinctives. Many women wear head coverings during the church service.

Website

www.brethrenonline.org

10

HOLINESS CHURCHES

THE EMERGENCE OF THE HOLINESS churches was inspired by Christ's injunction to His followers: "Be ye therefore perfect, even as your Father which is in heaven is perfect" (Matthew 5:48 KJV). The goal of being perfect led to the doctrine of perfectionism and entire sanctification in the theology of John Wesley (1703–1791), the founder of Methodism, and this, in turn, contributed to the rise of the Holiness churches.

As Wesley preached from town to town, he urged his listeners to practice holiness and ethics in day-to-day living. He encouraged them to seek perfection—that is, the absence of sin. Before long, Wesley came under criticism from his contemporaries who noticed that people in Wesley's movement continued to manifest various imperfections. Wesley responded by saying that perfectionism does not exempt one from making mistakes or erroneous judgments, nor does it exempt one from experiencing temptation. He was also careful to emphasize that the doctrine of perfectionism does not mean a particular person is incapable of further progress on the road to holiness. Later, Wesley began to back off the idea that perfectionism involved the absence of sin, instead suggesting that perfectionism should be understood in terms of one's love for others and for God (a perfection of love).

In the late 1800s, many Holiness groups who strongly held on to the idea of perfection from sin in this life broke away from the Methodists. These groups viewed this perfectionism—also known as entire sanctification—as a "second blessing" or "second work of grace" in the life of the believer.

In this line of thinking, a person is first saved, at which point he is justified and born-again. Following this, he experiences a period of growth in which he progressively becomes more holy in daily living. This ultimately culminates in a second work of grace whereby the Holy Spirit cleanses his heart of original sin, literally eradicating all inbred sin. The Holy Spirit then imparts His indwelling presence, empowering the believer to live the Christian life in perfection. This is the baptism of the Holy Spirit. It happens instantaneously as the believer presents him- or herself as a living sacrifice to God with an attitude of full consecration.

This doctrine of entire sanctification is precisely what many people in the Holiness movement felt was lacking in many Methodist churches. These individuals therefore split off from the Methodists and founded smaller independent Holiness churches. Eventually many of these small congregations joined to form denominations, some of which are discussed in this chapter.

A female evangelist who was instrumental in the growth of Holiness churches was Phoebe Palmer (1807–1874), who claimed to have experienced entire sanctification in 1837. After having this experience, her goal was to travel and help others make the same discovery she had made. She taught that any person could experience entire sanctification, even near the beginning of his or her Christian life. She viewed it as an immediate possibility for any believer in Christ. The doctrine caught on, and through the influence of Palmer and a number of Holiness preachers, Holiness churches starting cropping up all over the country.

Holiness churches have been distinguished from other churches by their more strict standards of holiness. Those who join a Holiness church are expected not to smoke, drink, go dancing, go to movies, listen to inappropriate worldly music, or wear makeup or flashy clothes. The goal of being perfect as the heavenly Father is perfect requires such commitment.

Fast Facts on
the Perfectionism Debate

Perfection *Is* Possible	Perfection *Is Not* Possible
Believers can be enabled by the Holy Spirit to consistently say no to sin if they surrender to God (Titus 2:11-12).	If we claim to be without sin, we deceive ourselves (1 John 1:8).
In entire sanctification, the heart can be cleansed from all inherited sin (1 John 1:9).	The sin nature remains with us until we die (Ephesians 2:3).
Though a perfect, sinless life has never actually been attained, never-theless such a life is possible through God's grace (Romans 6:1-18).	Great saints of the Bible consistently recognized their sinfulness (Isaiah 6:5; Daniel 9:4-19; Ephesians 3:8).

CHURCH OF CHRIST (HOLINESS) USA

Founded: 1894
Members: 10,475
Congregations: 191

Beginnings

The Church of Christ (Holiness) USA grew out of the holiness movement that emerged in the closing decade of the nineteenth century. A Baptist preacher in Alabama and Mississippi, Charles Price Jones, was the key figure in this denomination's emergence. Jones had sought God with his whole heart, mind, and soul. He desired that his life be entirely in God's hands with no compromise. He had been utterly unsatisfied with a faith that yielded no fruit. According to his testimony, the Holy Spirit promised him and his associates that if they fasted for three days, God would sanctify them. They did as God requested, and they became filled with light, joy, and the Holy Spirit.

Jones and his associates began to spread their ideas in the late 1800s. At first Jones' emphasis and *modus operandi* were nondenominational (he believed denominations were "slavery"). But because of the persecution from other Christians that soon surfaced against him and his followers, they decided to establish their own denomination in 1894. This represents the beginnings of the Church of Christ (Holiness) USA.

Theologically the denomination is close to the Church of the Nazarene (see below). They follow the Methodist Articles of Religion (a doctrinal statement). Their goal is to spread the gospel worldwide, convert sinners, reclaim backsliders, help people understand the reality of divine healing, and promote the teaching that the Lord is returning.

Beliefs

Bible. The Bible—including the Old and New Testaments—is the inerrant Word of God. All the books contained therein are inspired by the Holy Spirit. The Bible contains all necessary truth pertaining to salvation and to living the Christian life.

God. The one true God is eternal, invisible, all-wise, all-good, merciful, loving, and full of grace. He is the Maker of heaven and earth. He is eternally manifest in three persons: the Father, the Son, and the Holy Spirit.

Jesus Christ. Jesus is the Son of God and is coequal and coeternal with the Father and the Holy Spirit. He became incarnate by the power of the Holy Spirit and was born of a virgin. Following His death on the cross, where He attained human salvation, He rose from the dead, ascended to heaven, and now sits at the right hand of the Father, making intercession for us.

Holy Spirit. The Holy Spirit is ever present and ever active in the church. He convicts and regenerates those who believe in Jesus. He indwells believers, teaches them, comforts them, guides them into truth, and empowers them to obey God.

Sin and Salvation. Original sin involves the corruption of the nature of Adam and all his offspring such that they are now sinners by nature. They have no righteousness in them. This sin renders human beings unfit to enter God's presence and incapacitated for serving Him. They are under the just penalty of death and are "children of wrath." This original sin cannot be overcome by mere human efforts but can only be eradicated by the Holy Spirit through the blood of Jesus Christ.

The atonement wrought by Christ at the cross involved the shedding of His blood for the remission of sins for all humankind. Whoever repents and believes in the Lord Jesus Christ is justified, regenerated, and saved from the dominion of sin. A person can fall from grace and lose his or her salvation. Such is unlikely, however, for one who abides in Christ.

Church. The church has a representative form of government. Each local church has pastors who have divine oversight over the body of believers in that church. Bishops are delegated the power to speak on their behalf, and the senior bishop is the highest official in the church. The final authority rests in the national convention, which is made up of church elders, clergy, and local lay leaders.

Women who are gifted in teaching are given the opportunity to teach in the church, but only under the direct supervision of the pastor. The church does not ordain women to preach.

Sacraments. Baptism is an ordinance that is for believers only (not infants). The proper mode is immersion. The Lord's Supper is an ordinance that points toward the Lord's death and is to be celebrated until He comes again. The bread and wine represent the body and blood of Christ. Foot washing should be practiced as an act of obedience in following our Lord's act of humility with the disciples (see John 13:1-18). Note, however, that foot washing is not viewed as an ordinance.

End Times. Christ will one day rapture the church. Following the second coming will be a resurrection of the dead—the just to eternal life and the unjust to eternal damnation. Christ will judge all human beings. Heaven will be the final eternal home for the Christian, while hell will be the final eternal home of the unbeliever.

Distinctives. Believers must become sanctified. Sanctification involves an act of divine grace in which human beings become freed from original sin and are made holy. In sanctification, the actual inclination toward practicing sin is removed from the believer. Sanctification must be experienced by believers to make them fit to see God.

The denomination also affirms all the spiritual gifts (including speaking in tongues) listed in 1 Corinthians 12–14 and Romans 12:3-4. No particular gift, however, is a final determinative evidence of the Holy Spirit's presence in the life of the believer. True evidences of the Spirit-filled life are faith, hope, and love.

Website

www.cochusa.com

FAST FACTS ON

the Role of Women in the Church

The Case for Women in Leadership	The Case Against Women in Leadership
Jesus considered men and women equal (Luke 10:38-42).	Men and women are equal in worth, but there is still a male-female authority structure (1 Corinthians 11:3).
Jesus first appeared to a woman after the resurrection (Mark 16:9).	Jesus called only males as apostles. Paul instituted only male elders in the church.
Female subordination is a result of the fall. Christ ended the curse brought by sin.	Male headship is established in Genesis 2—before the fall ever occurred.
Galatians 3:28 speaks of the equality of men and women.	Positional equality does not negate the male-female authority structure.
Ephesians 5:21-24 instructs both men and women to submit to each other.	Other verses give additional information: • The woman was created from Adam's rib to be his helper (Genesis 2:18). • Adam named the woman, showing his authority over her (Genesis 2:23). • God gave instructions to Adam alone, showing his headship (Genesis 2:16-17).
Verses about women not being in authority over men reflect only a first-century culture.	The apostle Paul argued theologically, not culturally, for male leadership.

CHURCH OF GOD (HOLINESS)
Founded: 1886
Members: 8000
Congregations: 140

Beginnings

The Church of God (Holiness) is an association of autonomous congregations united by common beliefs. It began in 1886 when some former Methodists founded a holiness church in Centralia, Missouri. These individuals left the Methodist church because they believed it was neglecting to teach the doctrine of entire sanctification (see "Distinctives" below).

The founding members of the denomination were part of the "come out" movement that surfaced in the late 1800s. This was a movement of people leaving mainline denominations in order to establish new independent churches because of a disagreement over some issue. In a way, the entire holiness movement was a "come out" movement, emerging from the Methodist church.

Beliefs

Bible. The Bible is inspired Scripture. It is infallibly true and constitutes our only divinely authorized rule of faith and practice.

God. The one true God is infinite, eternal, and holy. He is the sovereign Creator and Ruler of the universe. He is triune in nature, meaning that within the unity of the Godhead there are three coeternal persons: the Father, the Son, and the Holy Spirit.

Jesus Christ. Jesus is the Son of God. In the Incarnation, He was very God and very man, having been conceived of the Holy Spirit and born of a virgin. He died on the cross, the just for the unjust, and His complete and final sacrifice wrought salvation for those who would believe in Him. He rose from the dead and ascended into heaven.

Holy Spirit. The Holy Spirit convinces the world of sin, righteousness, and judgment. He also indwells believers, guides them, teaches them, empowers them, and represents God on earth.

Sin and Salvation. Human beings have willfully sinned against God and separated themselves from Him. They can do nothing to overcome this chasm. The only hope for humankind is to turn to God through Jesus Christ and seek redemption. Justification is provided solely on the merit of His shed blood.

To be saved, one must repent of personal sin, be converted, believe in Jesus, and confess Him publicly. Holiness in life is the clear evidence of the Holy Spirit's presence in one's life.

A person can fall from grace. However, one can live a victorious life so long as he or she is obedient to the Bible.

Church. The one true church is composed of those who have become saved by believing in the Lord Jesus Christ, and who willingly submit to His divine program in the church. Christ is the supreme head of the church.

Churches are autonomous, and government is congregational. Each church sends delegates to an annual convention. Women have a place in the ministry of the church.

Sacraments. Baptism is an outward sign of an inward work of grace in the human heart through the Holy Spirit. All believers should be baptized. The Lord's Supper represents the redemption we have in Jesus. The ordinance should be observed with great reverence.

End Times. All people will one day die, and death seals the final destiny of people. People have no second chance after death. The second coming will be a visible event and will be followed by the establishment of a literal millennium. Christ will judge all human beings. The saved will be assigned to eternal life. The unsaved will be assigned to suffer eternal separation from God.

Distinctives. Entire sanctification includes deliverance from inbred sin (original sin) and the complete moral purification of one's nature from depravity. Human nature is renewed in holiness, and believers are empowered by the Holy Spirit for Christian service and a perfect love for God and human beings. Entire sanctification is accomplished instantaneously when the believer consecrates his entire being to God. It takes place subsequent to one's regeneration and is preceded by a conviction of one's remaining inbred sin and one's desire to be finally rid of it. It includes no accompanying signs (such as speaking in tongues).

Website

www.cogh.net

Church of the Nazarene
Founded: 1908
Members: 633,264
Congregations: 4504

Beginnings

In the late 1800s and early 1900s, a number of splits and mergers took place among various Christian denominations. The Church of the Nazarene, the largest of the Holiness bodies, grew out of a merger of three independent regional Holiness groups in the early 1900s. The Association of Pentecostal Churches in America, a regional group with strong representation in New England and New York, merged in 1907 with a California group called the Church of the Nazarene, founded by Phineas Bresee, a former

Methodist pastor. The merged group took the name Pentecostal Church of the Nazarene.

A year later, in 1908, a southern group called the Holiness Church of Christ united with the Pentecostal Church of the Nazarene at Pilot Point, Texas. About a decade later, in 1919, the term "Pentecostal" was dropped from the denomination name so it would not be confused with tongues-speaking groups. Since 1919, a number of other churches and associations have merged with the Church of the Nazarene.

Beliefs

Bible. The entire Bible is inspired. It inerrantly reveals the will of God, containing all necessary truth for Christian faith and living.

God. The one true God is eternal, infinite, and holy in nature and attributes. He is the Sovereign of the universe and is eternally manifest as the Father, Son, and Holy Spirit.

Jesus Christ. Jesus is eternally one with the Father and Holy Spirit. He became incarnate through a miracle of the Holy Spirit, was born of a virgin, and was very man and very God in one person. He died for our sins, rose from the dead, ascended into heaven, and now intercedes to the Father for us.

Holy Spirit. The Holy Spirit is "another Counselor" and is ever present and ever active with believers. He convinces the world of sin, regenerates those who repent and believe, sanctifies believers, and guides them into all truth. His presence among humans is equivalent to God's presence.

Sin and Salvation. Original sin is the corruption of one's nature, due to Adam's sin, such that we are averse to God, without spiritual life, and inclined toward evil continually. It continues to exist in the life of the believer until it is eradicated by the baptism of the Holy Spirit. Because of original sin, people are so depraved that they cannot turn in their own strength to call upon God for salvation.

This necessitates the bestowing of the grace of God through Jesus Christ, which enables people to turn to righteousness, believe on Jesus Christ for salvation, and follow after good works that are pleasing in His sight. This grace is given to all people, but people must repent and believe in order for it to become effective. Whoever repents and believes in Jesus is justified, regenerated, adopted into God's family, and saved from the dominion of sin.

People can fall from grace and apostatize. Unless they repent and turn back to God, they will be hopelessly and eternally lost.

Church. The church is a community of people that confesses Jesus as Lord, and a covenant people of God made new in Christ. It is composed of all spiritually regenerated persons whose names are written in the book of life in heaven. Local churches are localized expressions of specific members of this universal body. The mission of the church is to promote the redemptive work of Christ. This is done in the power of the Holy Spirit through holy living, evangelism, discipleship, and service. All clergy in the local church must profess that they have experienced entire sanctification.

Church government is a combination of congregational, presbyterian, and episcopal. Local churches retain autonomy while at the same time submitting to the oversight of both district and general superintendents. Churches maintain the freedom to call their own pastors, under the supervision of their district superintendent. The General Assembly is the highest legislative body, and its policies are binding on congregations.

Women can be ordained to ministry and are welcome to be elected and appointed at all levels of leadership.

Sacraments. Baptism signifies the acceptance of the benefits of the atoning work of Christ on the cross. It symbolizes death to the old way of life and the new life that God provides. It is administered only to believers by immersion, sprinkling, or pouring.

The denomination prefers to dedicate infants rather than baptize them. But church members have the option of having infants baptized if they commit to giving the child Christian training with the hope that the child will grow up to follow Christ.

The Lord's Supper symbolizes the body and blood that Jesus gave in redeeming humankind. It is a celebration of Christ's death until He comes again. All believers are invited to share in the sacrament whether or not they are members of the church. The sacrament is not appropriate for unbelievers.

End Times. Jesus is coming again. The just will be resurrected to life; the unjust will be resurrected to damnation. God will judge every person and hold each one accountable for his or her deeds. Heaven is the final destiny of the saved; hell is the final destiny of the unsaved. The denomination takes no official stand on millennial views.

Distinctives. Like other Holiness churches, the Church of the Nazarene is distinguished by its belief in entire sanctification. It is considered a second work of grace and takes place at the baptism of the Holy Spirit. Believers are made free from original sin, renewed in the image of God, brought into a state of entire devotion to God, and empowered by the Holy Spirit to love God with their whole heart, soul, mind, and strength. Entire sanctification is wrought instantaneously by faith and is preceded by entire consecration to God.

Website

www.nazarene.org

CHURCHES OF CHRIST IN CHRISTIAN UNION

Founded: 1909
Members: 10,104
Congregations: 208

Beginnings

The Churches of Christ in Christian Union began in 1909 in Marshall, Ohio. Some ministers and laymen of the Christian Union (founded 1864) disagreed with this union's increasingly negative stance on John Wesley's holiness and sanctification message. When the union voted to censure any minister that preached the Wesleyan holiness doctrine, a number of ministers and lay people withdrew from the union. The Churches of Christ in Christian Union formed to allow complete freedom in preaching and teaching the salvation and sanctification message of John Wesley.

Beliefs

Bible. The Bible is inspired by the Holy Spirit and is inerrant. It is accurate in every detail in the words of the original manuscripts. It is a fully sufficient rule of faith and practice.

God. The one true God is eternally manifest in three persons: the Father, the Son, and the Holy Spirit.

Jesus Christ. Jesus is one with the Father and the Holy Spirit. In the Incarnation, He was conceived by the Holy Spirit and born of a virgin. He was entirely without sin. He died on the cross to save us, rose from the dead, and ascended to the right hand of the Father, where He now intercedes to the Father on our behalf.

Holy Spirit. The Holy Spirit is one with the Father and Jesus. He is God's agent for convicting sinners of sin. He regenerates sinners and sanctifies consecrated Christians. He magnifies Christ in the lives of believers and energizes them to live victoriously.

Sin and Salvation. Humanity broke fellowship with God by choosing to disobey Him. This broken fellowship resulted in an impassible chasm between God and human beings. All humans are now sinful by nature and by practice.

Salvation has been made possible through Christ's atoning death on the cross. To receive this salvation, one must repent (turn away from sin) and accept Christ as Lord and Savior. Those who repent and believe experience a fourfold salvation: regeneration (believers are forgiven and baptized *by* the Holy Spirit into the body of Christ), entire sanctification (a baptism *with* the Holy Spirit such that we are cleansed from the carnal mind), growth in grace after sanctification (in which we are made more and more like Jesus), and immortality of the soul. People can choose to sever their saving relationship with Jesus Christ, thereby losing salvation.

Church. The church is composed of all true believers in Jesus Christ. The purpose of the church is to worship God and enjoy Christian fellowship. Christ is the head of the church. He commissions the church to take the gospel to every creature.

Every church is self-governing, though this governing must be within the guidelines set by the denomination manual. Polity is congregational within the limits set by the denomination. Each local church cooperates with the district and general authorities of the denomination.

Women are welcome in all forms of ministry.

Sacraments. Baptism is an outward testimony of the inward work of saving grace in one's life. There is no one exclusive mode of baptism ("let each be fully persuaded in his own mind"). The Lord's Supper is a memorial of Christ's sacrificial death on our behalf. It is open to all persons who have trusted in Christ for salvation.

End Times. The second coming of Christ includes two phases:

- the rapture, in which the church is taken to heaven prior to the tribulation period

- the second coming, in which Christ comes to judge the nations

Heaven and hell are literal places. Believers will spend eternity with Christ in heaven. Unbelievers will be consigned to judgment and sentenced to eternity in perdition.

Website

www.cccuhq.org

WESLEYAN CHURCH
Founded: 1968
Members: 114,211
Congregations: 1887

Beginnings

The Wesleyan Methodist Church of America was founded in Utica, New York, in 1843. This group's emergence was rooted in the abolitionist movement. Earlier, some Methodists had protested the tolerance of slavery by the Methodist Episcopal Church. Members of that church tried to silence the protesters, so 22 ministers and 6000 lay people left and formed the Wesleyan Methodist Connection of America. A century later (1947) the group was renamed the Wesleyan Methodist Church.

Meanwhile, the Pilgrim Holiness Church was founded in 1897 in Cincinnati, Ohio, during the holiness revival that emerged in the late nineteenth century. This church and the Wesleyan Methodist Church had a theological kinship because they both believed in the holiness doctrines taught by Wesley. They merged in 1968 to form the Wesleyan Church.

Beliefs

Bible. The Bible constitutes the Word of God. It is inspired, infallible, and inerrant in the words of the original manuscripts. It has been transmitted to the present day without corruption of any essential doctrine. It is authoritative and supersedes all human authority.

God. The one true God is holy, loving, eternal, almighty, all-wise, and all-good. He is the Creator and Preserver of the universe. In the unity of the Godhead are three coeternal persons: the Father, the Son, and the Holy Spirit.

Jesus Christ. Jesus is the Son of God and Savior of all humanity. In the Incarnation, He was very God and very man, having been conceived by the Holy Spirit and born of a virgin. He died on the cross for human sin, rose bodily from the dead, ascended into heaven, and now intercedes to the Father on our behalf.

Holy Spirit. The Holy Spirit proceeds from the Father and the Son and is of the same essential nature as the Father and the Son. He is the effective agent in the conviction of sin, regeneration, and sanctification. He is ever present with believers, preserving, guiding, and enabling them to live the Christian life. Christians can be holy in character and conduct only by being filled with the Holy Spirit.

Sin and Salvation. Adam and Eve sinned against God. Because of original sin, all of Adam's descendants are unable in their own strength to do what is right. They are all naturally inclined to evil continually. Because of the effects of original sin, humans cannot of themselves call upon God or exercise faith for salvation.

There is no other ground of salvation other than Jesus Christ. Through Jesus, God's prevenient grace empowers humans to do what they could not do in their own self-effort. This prevenient grace is bestowed on all people, enabling all who respond to be saved. To appropriate what God's prevenient grace has made possible, people must respond in repentance and faith. When they do so, they are justified, regenerated, and adopted into God's family.

Church. The church is the entire body of believers in Jesus Christ, the founder and head of the church. The universal church includes believers who have died and those still in mortality on earth. The purpose of the local church is to tell the world about Jesus through its worship, witness, and loving deeds. The church is called to make disciples, which involves training in spiritual growth and holy living.

This denomination has a modified episcopal form of church government headed by a Board of General Superintendents. Women can be ordained to the ministry.

Sacraments. Baptism is a symbol of the new covenant of grace and signifies one's acceptance of the benefits of Christ's atonement. By participating, the believer openly declares his faith in Jesus as Savior. The Lord's Supper is a sacrament that points to our redemption by Christ's death as we await His return. It is also a sign of the love Christians have for each other.

End Times. Jesus will one day come again personally and visibly. At His second coming, Jesus will triumph over evil and judge all humanity on the last day. At the resurrection of the dead, the just will be raised to eternal life and the unjust to eternal damnation. Heaven is the final abode of the saved; hell is the final abode of the unsaved.

Distinctives. Like other Holiness churches, the Wesleyan Church emphasizes the doctrine of entire sanctification. It is wrought instantaneously at the moment of full consecration to God and results in a full cleansing of the heart from all inbred sin.

Website

www.wesleyan.org

11

LUTHERAN CHURCHES

LUTHERAN CHURCHES EMERGED from the lectures, teachings, and writings of Martin Luther (1483–1546), who is sometimes called the father of Protestantism. This appellation is understandable in view of the fact that his work motivated many to "protest" against key teachings and rituals of the Roman Catholic Church.

Luther was a man who could not be ignored. He was a fierce defender of his beliefs and was not afraid to confront the powerful religious authorities of his day. He followed his convictions without flinching and became the most influential person involved in the Reformation.

Luther's spiritual journey was fascinating. This young German had studied to be a lawyer, but one day a bolt of lightning struck right next to him, and this terrified him so horribly that he cried out to Saint Anna, promising her that if she delivered him to safety, he would become a monk. The rest is history. True to his word, Luther became an Augustinian monk in 1505, and two years later he was ordained as a priest.

Luther took his spirituality seriously. He agonized daily over the perpetual presence of sin in his life and was acutely aware of the magnitude of his own personal failings. For a time he engaged in the impossible task of meriting salvation through ascetic practices. As time passed, he perceived the futility of his efforts. He found no personal satisfaction or deliverance from his condition by participating in Catholic rituals. Even though he went through all the right religious motions as prescribed by the Roman Catholic Church, he did not feel he had been made right with God.

Luther threw himself into theological studies. During his doctoral work, he began to uncover significant differences between teachings of the Bible and those of Roman Catholicism. Most importantly, he discovered that salvation is not something that can be attained by human effort but rather is God's gift to be received by faith.

Completing his doctoral work at age 28, Luther took a teaching position at the University of Wittenberg. In 1517, he posted his famous 95 Theses on the door of Wittenberg Castle Church. His goal was to motivate the Roman Catholic Church to reform some of its theology and practices so that the church was more in keeping with the Word of God. His concerns included...

- *The power of the pope.* Luther saw virtually no scriptural authority for it.

- *The abuse involved in the sale of indulgences.* Luther had noticed that an increasing number of people were failing to show up at church for confession, and the reason became clear to him. Why go to confession when you can purchase indulgences to cover the sins you are going to commit? The profits the Roman Catholic Church made from the sale of indulgences financed the building of Saint Peter's Basilica in Rome. All this was repugnant to Luther.

- *The teaching that souls are in purgatory.* Either Christ's atonement is sufficient or it is not. If it is fully sufficient, then those who trust in Christ go to heaven because they are justified. They need no further purging in purgatory.

Luther's 95 Theses caused a firestorm. The Roman Catholic pope and religious authorities pressured Luther to repent and recant his views, but he refused, taking an ever-stronger stance against these and other theological errors. Luther argued against the idea that one must confess sins to a priest. He argued from the Bible that Christians confess directly to God and do not need an earthly priest. Luther's position obviously threatened the very heart of Roman Catholic ritual.

Luther hoped to bring reformation to the church, but he ended up bringing division to the church. The Roman Catholic Church refused to change its ways. Both the pope and Luther were unbending. The pope excommunicated Luther and Luther refused to recognize the authority of the pope.

Luther himself did not coin the term "Lutheran." Rather, Luther's enemies used the term in derision. Before long, however, Luther's followers used the term as a badge of honor.

Eventually, Luther and some of his associates encapsulated their doctrine in a codified form. In 1529 he wrote both his Large Catechism and his Small Catechism. Then, in 1537, in association with Philipp Melanchthon (1497–1560) and some other German reformers, he wrote the Smalcald Articles of Faith. Luther also wrote great hymns, such as "A Mighty Fortress Is Our God."

Lutheran beliefs first widely penetrated Germany and Scandinavia but soon enough spread throughout the world. Luther translated the Bible from Latin into German, and because of the recent invention of Gutenberg's printing press, he was able to make this translation widely available to the common people. Luther had struck a match, and a wildfire was spreading.

When Luther died, some of his followers debated some of the finer points of theology. However, Lutheran orthodoxy was quickly consolidated in a single book entitled *The Book of Concord* (*concord* means "agreement" or "unity of mind"). This book contains the

Apostles' Creed, the Nicene Creed, the Athanasian Creed, the Augsburg Confession, Luther's Small Catechism, Luther's Large Catechism, and the Smalcald Articles of Faith. Understandably, since many Lutheran churches utilize *The Book of Concord*, many are similar in their theology. Some Lutheran churches, however, have departed from this book and have grown more liberal in theology.

The first Lutherans to migrate to America in colonial days were from Germany and Sweden. They poured into the colonies, most initially settling in Pennsylvania but eventually also settling in New York, North Carolina, Maryland, and Ohio. Eventually Lutheranism penetrated the rest of the country.

The local church is the basic unit of Lutheran government. Churches own their own property and select their own pastors. On a broader level, synods are composed of pastors and lay representatives who are elected by the congregations. (The word *synod* literally means "walking together." A synod is a group of church representatives who "walk together" in governing the church.) Synods only have power as local churches delegate it to them. Sometimes these synods are subsumed under a larger general body called a conference.

The American Association of Lutheran Churches

Founded: 1987
Members: 14,095
Congregations: 91

Beginnings

The American Association of Lutheran Churches emerged when some theologically conservative Lutherans did not want to participate in the American Lutheran Church's merger with the more theologically liberal Lutheran Church in America and the Association of Evangelical Lutheran Churches. These conservatives wanted to uphold the doctrine of inerrancy and infallibility of the Bible, which they felt was being threatened by the merger. They began the American Association of Lutheran Churches in 1987 in Bloomington, Minnesota. They hold to the ecumenical creeds and Lutheran confessions found in *The Book of Concord*. The agenda of the denomination is broad.

- They establish new congregations throughout North America that will faithfully preach God's Word and properly administer the sacraments.

- They assist congregations in their ministries to children, youth, and adults.

- They utilize the media to communicate the gospel to the masses.

- They set up pension, medical, and disability plans for church pastors and their families.

- They work in cooperation with other churches that are in doctrinal agreement with them.

The primary decision-making body of the denomination is the General Convention, to which each church sends delegates. Policy decisions made at the convention are referred to the local churches for final approval.

Beliefs

Bible. The Bible is divinely inspired (God-breathed). Since it is inspired, God is the true author of every word of Scripture, and all of Scripture has a basic unity. The Bible is inerrant and contains no ultimate contradictions. It is an infallible authority in all matters of life and faith and is the only rule and norm by which teachers and teachings are to be judged.

God. God is the divine Creator of the universe. He is triune in nature, eternally manifest in three persons: the Father, the Son, and the Holy Spirit.

Jesus Christ. Jesus is the Son of God, the eternal Word of God, the divine Savior, and the Redeemer of humankind. In the Incarnation, He was true God and true man. He died upon the cross for human sin, rose from the dead, ascended into heaven, and was exalted on high.

Holy Spirit. The Holy Spirit empowers believers to grow in faith, inspires love among them, works to produce holiness in them, produces fruit in them, and gives spiritual gifts to them for the purpose of ministry. He seeks to glorify and exalt Christ, and He works through the means of grace (the Word of God and the sacraments) to call unbelievers into saving faith in Jesus.

Sin and Salvation. Adam and Eve were born in a state of righteousness, innocence, and blessedness. Following the fall, all humans are born into the world with a sin nature.

Lutherans place a heavy emphasis on law and gospel. The law is used by God to bring human beings into an awareness of their sin. The gospel teaches that through faith in Jesus alone human beings can receive forgiveness of sins, eternal life, and salvation (though see the section on sacraments below). Believers can fall away from God and lose their salvation.

Church. Wherever God's Word is faithfully preached and the sacraments rightly administered, the one, holy, Christian, apostolic church exists. Jesus is the head of the church. The mission of the church is to make disciples of every nation, bearing witness to Jesus through the preaching of God's Word and the proper administration of the sacraments. The church also seeks to nurture and spiritually renew members of the congregation.

Each local church is autonomous, making their own decisions, managing their own property, and calling their own pastors. God uses both men and women in ministry, but the church ordains men alone for the pastorate.

Sacraments. Through baptism, God forgives original sin, He bridges the chasm between God and man, and new life begins. The Holy Spirit generates new life through baptism. The mode of baptism can be sprinkling, pouring, or immersion. Baptism is in the name of the Father, the Son, and the Holy Spirit.

In the Lord's Supper, participants receive the true body and blood of Jesus, and the repentant believer receives the forgiveness of sins. The Lord's Supper is a means by which a believer becomes assured of his salvation.

End Times. Christ will one day return and judge all humanity following the resurrection. Believers will enjoy a blissful relationship with Jesus forever in heaven. Unbelievers are eternally damned and will suffer eternal separation from God in hell.

Website

www.taalc.com

FAST FACTS ON
the Lord's Supper

Roman Catholic View	The bread and wine actually change into the body and blood of Jesus at the prayer of the priest. Jesus is literally present. The sacrament imparts grace to the recipient.
Lutheran View	Christ is present *in, with,* and *under* the bread and wine. Christ's presence is real, but the elements do not change. God communicates grace through them.

Reformed View	Christ is spiritually present at the Lord's Supper, and it is a means of grace.
Memorial View	The elements do not change, and they do not communicate grace to the participant. The bread and wine are symbols and reminders of Jesus in His death and resurrection, our anticipation of the second coming, and our oneness as the body of Christ.

ASSOCIATION OF FREE LUTHERAN CONGREGATIONS

Founded: 1962
Members: 28,060
Congregations: 145

Beginnings

The Association of Free Lutheran Congregations was organized in 1962 by 42 conservative congregations who opposed the merger of the Lutheran Free Church with the American Lutheran Church. These congregations felt that the American Lutheran Church was more liberal in its theology, held to a deficient view of the Bible, and compromised on the issue of congregational government. Instead of participating in the merger, these congregations established a new association that took a strong stand on conservative theology, the inspiration and inerrancy of the Bible, and the autonomy of the local church. The association holds to the creeds and confessions in *The Book of Concord*.

Presently the Association of Free Lutheran Congregations is the fourth-largest Lutheran body in the United States, with congregations in 27 states—most in the upper Midwest. The association holds an annual conference where delegates report on various ministries and make recommendations.

Beliefs

Bible. The Bible is the Word of God and is the only authentic, infallible, and inerrant record of God's revelation to us. It has been preserved by the Holy Spirit for our salvation and instruction. It is the only norm for Christian doctrine and life.

God. The one true God is eternally manifest in three persons: the Father, the Son, and the Holy Spirit.

Jesus Christ. Jesus is the Son of God. In the Incarnation, He was true God and true man, having been conceived of the Holy Spirit and born of a virgin. He died for human sin, rose from the dead, and ascended into heaven. He is the Lord of humankind.

Holy Spirit. The Holy Spirit guides the church and individual Christians. His ministries include the regeneration and sanctification of believers.

Sin and Salvation. Because of the sin of Adam and Eve, all human beings are now fallen in sin. Salvation is found only through personal faith in Jesus Christ. "Once saved, always saved" is rejected, for apostasy is always possible.

Church. The church consists of all those who in their hearts truly believe in Jesus as Lord and Savior. Each church is fully autonomous, calling its own pastor, conducting its own program of worship, and maintaining its own property. The Association of Free Lutheran Churches is a *free* association. It imposes no bonds of compulsion. Conferences do not enact any laws or rules that the churches must follow, but rather make recommendations regarding actions and practices that the churches are free to accept or reject. Church polity is congregational. The denomination does not ordain women to ministry.

Sacraments. The two sacraments are baptism and the Lord's Supper. Each is a means of grace but must be met with a response of faith in the heart in order to be efficacious. The mode of baptism is generally sprinkling. The Lord's Supper is celebrated monthly and is only for those who confess Jesus as Lord and Savior.

End Times. Following the future judgment, Christians will spend eternity in heaven, while unbelievers will spend eternity in hell.

Website

www.aflc.org

FAST FACTS ON
Famous Christian Creeds

- Throughout church history, a number of important creeds—formal, authoritative statements of belief based on Holy Scripture—have been formulated as statements of orthodoxy.

- The word "creed" derives from the Latin word *credo*, which means "I believe."

Nicene Creed	A.D. 325	Affirms belief that Jesus eternally preexisted and is of the same divine substance as the Father.
Athanasian Creed	Date unknown	Affirms three distinct persons in the Trinity, noting that they are equal in glory and majesty.
Chalcedonian Creed	A.D. 451	Affirms that Jesus in the Incarnation was perfect God and perfect man—one person with two distinct natures.
Westminster Confession	A.D. 1646	A strongly Calvinistic confession that emphasizes the sovereignty of God.

CHURCH OF THE LUTHERAN BRETHREN OF AMERICA

Founded: 1900
Members: 8194
Congregations: 145

Beginnings

The Church of the Lutheran Brethren of America was founded in 1900 by five independent Lutheran congregations who met in Milwaukee, Wisconsin. Their primary goal was to unite for the purpose of facilitating home and world missions and Christian education. For the first 50 years of the organization, more than 50 percent of denominational funds were dedicated to missions around the world. Presently, about 40 percent of denominational funds are so directed.

The denomination serves local churches only in an advisory and cooperative capacity. It seeks to help churches in their local, national, and international missionary outreaches. All this is done with a view to being obedient to the Great Commission. The denomination adheres to the creeds and confessions in *The Book of Concord*.

Beliefs

Bible. The Bible is verbally and entirely inspired and is free from error in whole and in part. It is the supreme and finally authoritative guide for Christian faith and conduct. It is a means of grace.

God. The one true God is the Creator and Preserver of the universe. In the one essence of the divine Godhead are three distinct persons: the Father, the Son, and the Holy Spirit.

Jesus Christ. Jesus is the eternal Son of God. In the Incarnation, He was true man and true God, having been conceived by the

Holy Spirit and born of a virgin. By His perfect obedience to God's law and His substitutionary death on the cross, He purchased human redemption. He rose from the dead for our justification and ascended to the right hand of the Father in heaven. He now lives to make intercession for us as our High Priest.

Holy Spirit. The Holy Spirit is a divine person who is eternally one with the Father and Jesus. He convicts people of sin, righteousness, and judgment. His ministries include regeneration, sanctification, and preserving believers. He comforts, equips, directs, and empowers the church to fulfill the Great Commission.

Sin and Salvation. Adam and Eve fell into sin and lost their fellowship with God. Through their disobedience, the entire human race became totally depraved. It is therefore under God's just condemnation. In their fallen nature, people are unable to trust, fear, or love God.

Through the law, God brings sinners into an awareness of their lost condition and their need to repent. Through the gospel, God brings sinners into an awareness that only by faith in Jesus Christ can one be saved, be justified, receive eternal life, and enter the ongoing process of sanctification. Utilizing the gospel, the Holy Spirit awakens sinners to their sin, convicts them of personal guilt, calls them to repent and believe in Jesus, and enables them to accept God's grace in Jesus Christ. Those who so believe are instantly forgiven and justified, being credited with the very righteousness of Christ.

Christians are secure in their salvation. However, if they cease to live in a relationship of faith with Jesus, they will perish.

Church. The universal church is comprised of all people who truly believe in Jesus as Savior. The local church is a local assembly of believers in which leaders teach the Word of God and properly administer the sacraments. Personal profession of faith is the primary criterion for church membership.

Church government is congregational. The church is overseen by a board of elders elected by the congregation. Each church is autonomous. The denomination only advises churches. The office of the pastor is filled by men only.

Sacraments. The sacraments are means of grace. Baptism offers the washing of regeneration and newness of life to all who believe. Baptism is also for infants because they too are fallen in sin and need to become members of Christ's believing church. As adults, they will need to confess their faith in Jesus. By so doing, they are led from the faith received in infant baptism into a conscious faith in Christ as Lord and Savior.

The Lord's Supper is only for those who profess personal faith in Jesus as Savior. In the sacrament, Christ gives to participants His body and blood *in*, *with*, and *under* the elements of bread and wine. The sacrament serves to declare the forgiveness of sins to believers and strengthens their faith.

End Times. Jesus will come again personally, bodily, and visibly, and will establish His millennial kingdom. He will judge the living and the dead. Heaven is reserved for all who believe in Jesus as Savior. Hell is the destiny of all who do not believe in Jesus.

Website

www.clba.org

EVANGELICAL LUTHERAN CHURCH IN AMERICA

Founded: 1987
Members: 3,794,969
Congregations: 9379

Beginnings

During colonial days, Lutherans migrated to the United States and retained their original languages and cultures. America became the new home for German Lutheran churches, Dutch Lutheran churches, Scandinavian Lutheran churches, Danish Lutheran churches, and the like. Eventually, the people in these churches began to speak English and became assimilated into American culture. As this happened, these churches had little reason to remain separate and distinct from each other. In time, many of them merged.

- In 1962, some German, Danish, Slovak, Swedish, and Icelandic Lutheran congregations merged to form the Lutheran Church in America.

- In 1963, other German, Danish, and Norwegian Lutheran congregations merged to form the American Lutheran Church.

- In 1976, the Lutheran Church—Missouri Synod suffered a split. The conservatives remained the Lutheran Church—Missouri Synod, and the moderates formed the Association of Evangelical Lutheran Churches.

All this leads up to the founding of the Evangelical Lutheran Church in America. In 1987, three of the above denominations—the Lutheran Church in America, the American Lutheran Church, and the Association of Evangelical Lutheran Churches—merged to form the Evangelical Lutheran Church of America in Columbus, Ohio. This brought together over five million Lutherans (members and non-communicant attenders) into a single body to form the largest Lutheran denomination. The denomination holds to the creeds and confessions in *The Book of Concord.*

Beliefs

Bible. The Bible is the primary authoritative witness to the church's faith. The New Testament in particular is the authority for Christian faith and practice. The Bible is not intended to be a definitive record of history or science but is rather a record of the drama of God's saving care for the creation throughout history.

God. The one true God is the Creator of the universe. He is eternally manifest in three persons: the Father, the Son, and the Holy Spirit.

Jesus Christ. Jesus is the Son of God and the divine Messiah. In the Incarnation, He was truly God and truly man, having been conceived by the power of the Holy Spirit and born of a virgin. He perfectly obeyed the Father's will and died as a perfect sacrifice on the cross, thereby redeeming humanity from sin. He rose from the dead, ascended into heaven, and continues as the living Lord.

Holy Spirit. The Holy Spirit is God's presence with His people. He is active in the church, guiding its faith, giving spiritual gifts, and empowering church members to engage in various ministries.

Sin and Salvation. Sin involves humankind's inability to live up to God's expectations as expressed in His law (including the Ten Commandments). To become saved, human beings must place personal faith in Jesus Christ.

Church. The church is made up of those who have trusted in Jesus Christ as Savior and have been baptized in the church. As a community of faith, the church began on the day of Pentecost, and Lutherans see themselves as part of that community.

The church exists for the hearing and doing of God's Word. It fulfills its God-ordained mission when it preaches the living word of Christ, administers the sacraments, and engages in good deeds in the world. Women can be involved in various ministries in the church, including being ordained.

Each local church has representatives at one of 65 synods. More broadly, churches are represented at the biennial church-wide Assembly.

Sacraments. Baptism can be administered to either adults or infants in the name of the Father, the Son, and the Holy Spirit. In baptism, participants are united with Christ in His death and resurrection, and they receive the promise of forgiveness and eternal life. By it, people become members of Christ's body on earth, the church.

In the Lord's Supper, Jesus is *in*, *with*, and *under* the elements of bread and wine. Those who partake thus receive in the elements the body and blood of Jesus Christ, and they receive the gifts of forgiveness and salvation.

End Times. Jesus will one day come again and judge the just and the unjust. Believers will live eternally in the new heavens and new earth. Unbelievers will experience eternal separation from God.

Website

www.elca.org

EVANGELICAL LUTHERAN SYNOD
Founded: 1918
Members: 16,815
Congregations: 139

Beginnings

In 1917, various Norwegian churches merged into a new church body called The Norwegian Lutheran Church. About a year later, 13 conservative pastors and their congregations—a minority in the overall group—expressed concern that some of those who participated in the merger held to the "false teaching" that a person could cooperate in his conversion. These conservatives believed that conversion is due to God's grace alone, and the merger compromised this pivotal doctrine.

In 1918, with a view to remaining faithful to God's Word on this issue, these conservatives met at Lime Creek Lutheran Church near Lake Mills, Iowa, and reorganized as the Norwegian Synod of the American Evangelical Lutheran Church. The name was later changed to the Evangelical Lutheran Synod (1957).

The denomination represents conservative and confessional Lutheranism. Members avow total allegiance to the inspired and inerrant Word of God. They hold to the creeds and confessions in *The Book of Concord*. They now have congregations in some 20 states in America.

Beliefs

Bible. The Bible is inspired and inerrant in the words of the original manuscripts. It is without error in all that it teaches, including matters of geography, science, history, and the miraculous. It is the only infallible rule and norm for Christian doctrine and practice.

God. There is one true God, and in the unity of the divine essence, there are three eternal persons: the Father, the Son, and the Holy Spirit. Only those who believe in the Trinity can be saved.

Jesus Christ. Jesus is the Son of God. In the Incarnation, He was conceived by the Holy Spirit and born of the Virgin Mary. He was thus true God and true man in one person. Because Jesus was fully God, He was able to save us by His divine power. Because He was fully man, He was able to die as our substitute under God's holy law.

Holy Spirit. The Holy Spirit works through the gospel to bring about a person's conversion to faith in Christ. He spiritually renews people in the sacrament of baptism.

Sin and Salvation. Adam and Eve were morally righteous and were in perfect harmony with God, but they fell into sin. They and their descendants thereby lost their righteousness and became sinful and corrupt by nature. Because of original sin, no one is able in his or her own strength to earn favor with God or avoid eternal condemnation.

By Jesus' perfect life and perfect sacrifice on the cross, He provided redemption for the world. A person becomes justified—declared righteous—when he is brought to faith in Jesus as Savior.

A person's conversion to faith in Jesus is accomplished entirely by the Holy Spirit working through the gospel. This is necessary because fallen sinners are unable to cooperate in conversion.

Those who convert and are preserved in the true faith have, from eternity, been elected according to God's unmerited love to an adoption in His family. Christians should therefore be sure of their salvation because God's election to salvation stands firm.

Church. The one holy Christian church is composed of all who truly believe in Jesus as Lord and Savior. Local churches are to be found wherever the Word of God is faithfully preached and the sacraments are properly administered. Jesus is the head of the church. Government is congregational. Only qualified men are eligible for the pastoral office. Women should not exercise authority over men in the congregation's decision-making process (for example, by having a vote in an assembly that makes final decisions for a church).

Local churches are part of a synod, but the synod functions only in an advisory capacity. Its resolutions may be accepted or rejected by local congregations.

Sacraments. Baptism involves a washing of regeneration and renewing of the Holy Spirit. The sacrament is for all people, including infants and children.

In the Lord's Supper, communicants receive the true body and blood of Jesus (*in, with,* and *under* the elements). When combined with faith in the Word of God, the sacrament brings the remission of sins and strengthens one's faith. It is intended for Christians alone. Christians should engage in a spiritual self-examination and repent of known sin before partaking of the elements.

End Times. Christ will one day come again and resurrect the bodies of all the dead. There will be a judgment. Believers will spend eternity in a new heavens and a new earth. Unbelievers will spend eternity in the lake of fire. All forms of millennialism are rejected.

Website

www.EvLuthSyn.org

THE LUTHERAN CHURCH— MISSOURI SYNOD

Founded: 1847
Members: 1,920,949
Congregations: 5204

Beginnings

In 1838 some German Lutheran immigrants migrated to America, seeking to escape the rationalism that had invaded Lutheran churches in their homeland. They settled in Perry County, Missouri, just south of Saint Louis. C.F.W. Walther became their primary leader.

Together they founded the German Evangelical Lutheran Synod of Missouri, Ohio, and Other States, starting with just 14 congregations and 22 ministers. They were committed to confessional Lutheranism, the inerrancy of the Bible, conservative theology, and a strong world missions program. They held their first convention in 1847.

The denomination name was eventually shortened to The Lutheran Church—Missouri Synod, but its influence now extends far beyond the borders of Missouri. Indeed, it is now the second-largest Lutheran denomination and has churches in some 74 countries around the world. As well, the denomination operates the largest elementary and secondary school system in Protestantism in the United States, and it operates the third-largest Protestant publisher, Concordia Publishing House.

The Lutheran Church—Missouri Synod is a voluntary association of churches. They are united by their shared confession of Jesus Christ as taught in the Bible and the Lutheran confessions. The synod is divided into 35 districts. Synod meetings take place in three-year cycles, with a different aspect of denominational business addressed during each successive yearly meeting. The cycle then repeats itself.

Beliefs

Bible. The Bible is the Word of God and is verbally inspired by the Holy Spirit. It is inerrant, containing no errors or contradictions, and is infallible in all its parts and words. It is the sole source for Christian doctrine in the church and is the rule and norm against which all teachers and teachings must be measured.

God. The one true God is the Creator of all that exists. Within the unity of the one Godhead are three persons: the Father, the Son, and the Holy Spirit. Each of the three persons is of the same divine essence, equal in power, equal in eternity, and equal in majesty. A denial of the Trinity places one outside the pale of historic Christianity.

Jesus Christ. Jesus is the Son of God. When the proper time came in God's plan, He became a man, born of a virgin through a divine operation of the Holy Spirit. Jesus was thus true God and true man in one undivided and indivisible person. As the God-man, His death on the cross constituted a fully sufficient ransom for the sins of humanity, thereby enabling human beings to be reconciled to God. Three days after His death, He rose from the dead, thereby attaining victory over death and Satan.

Holy Spirit. The Holy Spirit is eternally one with the Father and Jesus. He creates faith in peoples' hearts through the Word of God and the sacraments. His goal is to edify the church and glorify Christ. He gives spiritual gifts to believers to equip them for ministry.

Sin and Salvation. Sin entered the world through Adam. Since then, all Adam's natural offspring lost their original righteousness and holiness and are born in sin, inclined to evil perpetually, and thereby subject to the wrath of God. Humans are unable, through their own self-efforts, to remedy this situation.

Salvation is a work of God and not of human effort. Faith in the gospel is a work of God's grace and power alone. It does not involve man's cooperation with God, as if man had some role to play. A person's *non*-conversion, however, is due to his or her own stubbornness and resistance to the work of the Holy Spirit.

Those who respond to the gospel in faith, as enabled by the Holy Spirit, are justified—meaning that God acquits them of their sins and accounts them as righteous. Following justification, good works naturally emerge in the Christian's life. Good works never precede faith, but they are the result of faith.

Those who have responded to the gospel in faith are among the elect of God. This election of grace embraces a limited number of people, whom God has chosen from the beginning to be saved. Note, however, that there is no accompanying election to damnation (double predestination). Christians should be assured of their election, for they are called "chosen ones" in Scripture.

Church. There is one holy Christian church on earth, of which Christ is the head. It is made up of all those who have trusted in Christ for the forgiveness of sins. Because only those who have exercised faith in Christ are a part of this body, and because no human being has the capacity to perceive true faith in the hearts of other human beings, the Christian church on earth is invisible until the future day of judgment, when all will be made clear.

Local churches affiliated with the Lutheran Church—Missouri Synod have the primary officer of pastor, whose business is to faithfully preach the gospel and properly administer the sacraments. Worship is liturgical in style. God's call on the church is to go into the entire world, preaching the gospel and administering the sacraments.

Women are permitted to hold some offices in the church—such as teachers, deaconesses, and social workers. But they are not permitted to hold the office of the pastorate.

Sacraments. The sacraments are considered means of grace that communicate to human beings the forgiveness of sins and other blessings. Baptism, when combined with God's Word, works the forgiveness of sins and salvation in a person. It involves a washing of regeneration and a renewing by the Holy Spirit. Infants can also be baptized.

The Lord's Supper is only for those who share the church's confession of faith. This is called "closed communion." As a means of grace, the Lord's Supper communicates salvation and the forgiveness of sins.

End Times. Jesus will one day come again. All human beings will be resurrected and experience a judgment. Believers will enjoy everlasting joy and eternal life in heaven. Unbelievers will suffer everlasting punishment in hell.

Website

www.lcms.org

WISCONSIN EVANGELICAL LUTHERAN SYNOD

Founded: 1850
Members: 314,750
Congregations: 1243

Beginnings

The Wisconsin Evangelical Lutheran Synod was organized in 1850 in Milwaukee, Wisconsin. Many of the new German Lutheran immigrants to America were in need of pastors. Three pastors who were sent to America by a German mission society organized the First German Evangelical Lutheran Synod. The organization took place under the direction of John Muelhaeuser at Salem Evangelical Lutheran Church in Milwaukee.

More than 40 years later, in 1892, the synod federated with two other synods—the Michigan Synod and the Minnesota Synod. They joined forces to facilitate a higher level of effectiveness in educational and missionary outreach. Some 25 years after that, in 1917, they formally merged to give the Wisconsin Evangelical Lutheran Synod its present form.

The synod is conservative in theology and is committed to the inerrancy and infallibility of the Bible. It subscribes to the creeds and confessions in *The Book of Concord.*

Beliefs

Bible. The Bible is verbally inspired in the words of the original manuscripts. It is true and without error in all it says. It is an infallible authority and guide for everything Christians believe and do. The Lord has providentially preserved the Hebrew and Greek texts through many hand-copied manuscripts.

God. The one true God is holy and eternal, possessing infinite power and wisdom. He is triune: In the unity of the one God are three persons who are equal in power, glory, and attributes—the Father, the Son, and the Holy Spirit. Whoever does not worship the triune God worships a false god.

Jesus Christ. Jesus is the eternal Son of God. He is one with the Father and the Holy Spirit from all eternity. In the Incarnation, He took on a human nature, having been conceived by the Holy Spirit and born of a virgin. His perfect righteousness in life is accepted by the Father as our righteousness, and His death for sin as our death for sin. Three days after His death, Jesus rose from the dead and ascended into heaven, where He is now exalted on high.

Holy Spirit. The Holy Spirit is the third person of the Trinity. One of His main ministries is working faith in the hearts of people through the Word of God. He enables people to have faith to recognize Jesus as Lord and Savior.

Sin and Salvation. When Adam and Eve sinned, they lost their divine image and suffered judgment under God. Since then all people have been conceived in a sinful condition and are inclined continually toward evil. They are unable in their own self-efforts to reconcile themselves to God.

The Holy Spirit enables people to have faith to recognize that Jesus is Savior and Lord. He works this faith by means of the gospel. Ultimately, a person's conversion is entirely the work of God's grace. However, a person who remains unconverted finds only himself to blame inasmuch as he has resisted the grace given through the Holy Spirit.

Those who exercise faith in Christ, as enabled by the Holy Spirit, are justified, acquitted of all guilt, and declared righteous. This gift of justification can only be received by faith, and works play no role.

Scripture teaches that before God created the world, He sovereignly elected or chose certain individuals whom He would in time convert through the gospel of Jesus Christ and preserve in faith to eternal life. This is in keeping with salvation being entirely the work of God and not of human effort.

Believers can fall away from faith. The idea of "once saved, always saved" is rejected. Those who remain in faith until the end of life are eternally saved.

Church. The one holy Christian church is the body of Christ. Its members are those who have placed personal faith in Jesus. Because only the Lord knows who are truly His, finite humans cannot distinguish true believers from hypocrites. Only God knows the true membership of His church.

Church members affirm that wherever the gospel is faithfully preached and the sacraments are properly administered, the holy Christian church is present. In this sense, the sacraments are the *mark* of the church.

A woman may not serve as the pastor of a local church. However, women are welcomed to participate in other offices and activities that do not involve authority over men.

Sacraments. The sacraments are means of grace, and when connected with the Word of God, they give the forgiveness of sins. Through baptism, in combination with the Word of God, the Holy Spirit applies the gospel to sinners, cleansing them from all sin and giving them new life. Baptism is not just for adults but also for infants because they are born sinful and need to be brought to faith through baptism. In the Lord's Supper, participants experience the forgiveness of sins, and their faith is strengthened. *End Times.* Jesus will one day come again visibly and physically. At the resurrection, the souls of all the dead will be reunited with their bodies. The resurrected will appear before the throne of judgment. Unbelievers will be condemned to an eternity in hell. Believers will be glorified and spend eternity in heaven with Jesus Christ.

There is no rapture of the church, no future millennial kingdom, and no Antichrist who will emerge on the world scene. Rather, all characteristics of the Antichrist are fulfilled in the papacy in the Roman Catholic Church.

Website

www.wels.net

12

MENNONITE CHURCHES

MEMBERS OF TRADITIONAL MENNONITE churches are notable for their lifestyle. They typically lead quiet lives, uninvolved with secular society, and consider themselves a "called out" fellowship of believers—that is, "called out" from involvement with the secular world. Their interest is in godly living. Members of some contemporary Mennonite churches are more integrated with mainstream society, but they do tend to maintain the historic Mennonite tendency toward nonviolence.

The Mennonites originated in Switzerland and the Netherlands during the time of the Protestant Reformation. They emerged out of the "radical reformer" movement of the 1520s, which involved a number of individuals who went far beyond the teachings of Swiss Reformer Ulrich Zwingli (1484–1531).

These radical reformers—including the likes of Konrad Grebel, of Zurich, Hans Denck, of Bavaria, and Balthasar Hubmaier, of Germany—disagreed with Zwingli on a number of issues, not the least of which was the issue of infant baptism. Zwingli allowed infant baptism, but the radical reformers argued staunchly for believer's baptism. They felt that if a person was baptized as an infant in the Roman Catholic Church, he or she needed to be rebaptized with a valid baptism. Moreover, they disagreed with Zwingli's openness to a union of church and state.

Because of the emphasis on rebaptism, these individuals came to be known as Anabaptists, from the Greek word *anabaptizein,* meaning "to rebaptize." The first Anabaptist congregation was organized at Zurich, Switzerland, right on Zwingli's home turf. Despite the doctrinal sincerity of the Anabaptists, they soon found themselves on the receiving end of criticism and persecution. Because they were not Roman Catholics, the Roman Catholic Church was against them. Because they took a stand against Zwingli, the Protestants were against them. Because they advocated a separation of church and state, the state was against them. After being accused of heresy and sedition, many Anabaptists were persecuted and even martyred. History records over 1500 Anabaptists being martyred during these tumultuous years.

Enter Menno Simons (1496–1561), an influential Dutch leader of the radical reformation. Simons was born in 1496 in Witmarsum in the Netherlands. He was educated for the Roman Catholic priesthood and ordained in 1524, but he converted to the Anabaptist movement in 1536. The previous year, in 1535, his brother—an Anabaptist—was martyred for his beliefs.

As Simons studied Scripture, he came to believe that some of his previous convictions were wrong. He felt that Scripture everywhere speaks of believer's baptism but nowhere speaks of infant baptism. He saw that the bread and wine used in communion were not the real body and blood of Christ, as Roman Catholicism taught. He also came to believe that biblical Christians were supposed to share their resources with each other, live in simplicity, care for the poor and widows, and refuse violence in all circumstances. Because Simons planted so many Anabaptist congregations, and because he was so active in promoting Anabaptist doctrine, the movement came to be associated with his first name, Menno. Hence, Anabaptists soon came to be known as Mennonites. Their basic theological beliefs are based on the Dordrecht Confession of Faith, composed in 1632 in the Netherlands.

Because persecution and harassment continued against the Anabaptists or Mennonites, many fled to America—more specifically, to Pennsylvania. Quaker William Penn (1644–1718) offered them a safe haven, and the Mennonites were among the first to settle in Germantown, Pennsylvania, in 1683. Thousands of Mennonites from various countries—including Germany and Switzerland—eventually immigrated to America. They settled not only in Pennsylvania but also spread out to Ohio, Virginia, Indiana, Illinois, Missouri, Kansas, Nebraska, South Dakota, and the far western United States.

Distinctive among the Mennonites were the followers of a seventeenth-century Swiss Mennonite bishop named Jakob Amman (1656–1730), after whom the Amish are named. Amman was a rather strict fellow, and his strictness on the issue of excommunication and shunning led him and his followers to split off from mainstream Mennonites, even though they share a common heritage and some common beliefs. Amman's teachings include these:

- Men ought to wear untrimmed beards and modest attire (that is, very plain clothing), including broad-brimmed hats.

- Women ought also to wear modest attire, including bonnets and aprons.

- Discipline against a sinner should include the practice of shunning. Shunning prohibits one from engaging in conventional social relationships with the sinning brother or sister. One should not eat at the same table with this person. One should not buy or sell from this person. A person who is married to such a person must not engage in marital relations with him or her. By such treatment, the person will be brought to repentance.

In the latter 1800s, many Amish met at a formal conference to address some of the differences they had with each other. Not finding full agreement, a schism developed. One group, the Old Order Amish, held on to the old ways. The other group—New Order Amish—were open to a more progressive lifestyle, accepting social change and technological innovation.

BEACHY AMISH MENNONITE CHURCHES

Founded: 1927
Members: More than 10,000
Congregations: 435

Beginnings

The Beachy Amish Mennonite Church split off from the Old Order Amish in 1927 in Somerset County, Pennsylvania, under the leadership of Bishop Moses M. Beachy (1874–1946). The Old Order Amish churches were very strict on the issue of church discipline, including banning and shunning. Bishop Beachy, while still supporting the basic practice, believed in a kinder and gentler version. Beachy was also more open to new technology than those of the old school.

Beachy had been an Old Order Amish bishop from 1916 to 1927. Even then, he held to a more moderate view of banning and shunning. A situation developed in which some members of the Old Order Amish departed to join a Conservative Mennonite congregation in Maryland, and some of the Old Order Amish leaders wanted them to be banned and shunned. Beachy would not go along with this. Old Order loyalists promptly withdrew fellowship from Beachy, after which Beachy and his remaining supporters founded a new association—the Beachy Amish Mennonite Churches.

Today those affiliated with the Beachy Amish Mennonite Churches have a less strict view of banning and shunning. Unlike the Old Order Amish, they are allowed to use electricity, alarm clocks, motorized vehicles, telephones, mirrors, and the like. Further, they have distinct church buildings and Sunday schools, they operate a Bible school, and they support missionary work. (Old Order Amish churches meet in homes or barns, do not have Sunday school or a Bible school, and do not support missionaries.) However, their dress code is still similar to the Old Order Amish code.

Beliefs

The Beachy Amish Mennonite Churches subscribe to the Dordrecht Confession of Faith (1632).

Bible. The Scriptures are inspired and are God's infallible source for all Christian beliefs and practice.

God. The one true God is eternal, almighty, and incomprehensible. He is the Creator of all things, visible and invisible. He is the Sustainer of the universe. Within the unity of the one God are three eternal persons: the Father, the Son, and the Holy Spirit.

Jesus Christ. Jesus is eternal God. He is the Alpha and Omega, the first and the last. At the appointed time, He became flesh, being born of a virgin. In His own body, He yielded up a sacrifice, thereby providing redemption and salvation for humankind. He was crucified and buried, and He rose from the dead, ascended into heaven, and now sits at the right hand of God.

Holy Spirit. The Holy Spirit is the third person of the Trinity. In salvation, believers experience regeneration and the "renewing of the Holy Ghost."

Sin and Salvation. Adam and Eve were disobedient to the Creator, bringing sin into the world and to all human beings. All humans are thus under the wrath of God, separated and estranged from Him.

Those who repent and believe in Jesus will be saved. Human beings must go to God with an upright heart and in perfect faith believe in Jesus to obtain the forgiveness of sins, become sanctified, experience justification, and be made children of God.

Church. The visible church of God is composed of those who have truly repented and believed, are rightly baptized, are one with God in heaven, and are rightly incorporated into the communion of the saints here on earth. The church is the bride of Christ, purchased by the blood of the Redeemer.

Churches are semiautonomous. Though not controlled by an external hierarchy, the churches are committed to each other with an unspoken but very real loyalty and accountability. The "bench" (that is, the ministerial team) includes a bishop, one or two ministers, and a deacon in each congregation. Other than the office of deaconess, women are not permitted to hold offices in the church.

Sacraments. All true believers, upon confession of faith and a renewing of life, are to be baptized with water to bury their sins and be incorporated into the communion of saints. The Lord's Supper is to be observed in remembrance of His suffering and death in providing our salvation. The elements point to the brokenness of His body and shedding of His blood in making redemption possible. Church members also engage in the practice of foot washing. Christ enjoined and practiced it as a sign of humility. The practice also serves to remind believers that they are washed through the precious blood of Jesus.

End Times. Jesus will one day come again to judge the quick and the dead. In the last day, all human beings will be resurrected and stand before God in judgment. Believers will enter into eternal life and obtain joy in heaven. The wicked shall be cast into outer darkness and experience the everlasting pains of hell, having no further hope, comfort, or redemption.

Distinctives. Regarding the practice of banning, the Beachy Amish denomination holds to the Dordrecht Confession on this issue. Therein we read:

> We also believe in, and confess, a ban, separation, and Christian correction in the church, for amendment, and not for destruction, in order to distinguish that which is pure from the impure: namely, when any one, after he is enlightened, has accepted the knowledge of the truth, and been incorporated into the communion of the saints, sins again unto death, either through willfulness, or through presumption against God, or through some other cause, and falls into the unfruitful works of darkness, thereby becoming separated from God, and forfeiting the kingdom of God, that such a one, after the deed is manifest and sufficiently known to the church, may not remain in the congregation of the righteous, but, as an offensive member and open sinner, shall and must be separated, put away, reproved before all, and purged out as leaven; and this for his amendment, as an example, that others may fear, and to keep the church pure, by cleansing her from such spots, lest, in default of this, the name of the Lord be blasphemed, the church dishonored, and offense given to them that are without; and finally, that the sinner may not be condemned with the world, but become convinced in his mind, and be moved to sorrow, repentance, and reformation.[1]

Yet in shunning, the denomination also believes that discretion must be used so that the shunning will not destroy the person but rather lead him or her to repentance and restoration. If the person being shunned is needy, hungry, thirsty, sick, or is in other distress, then the body of believers must respond by helping him or her. The offender is not an enemy, but a brother or sister in need of correction.

Website

Unknown

CHURCH OF GOD IN CHRIST, MENNONITE

Founded: 1859
Members: 12,754
Congregations: 458

Beginnings

In the middle of the nineteenth century, some within the Mennonite movement felt their denomination had drifted away from sound doctrine and experienced a general spiritual decline. They sought to contend earnestly for the faith that was once for all entrusted to the saints (Jude 3). One of these was John Holdeman (1832–1900), born in Wayne County, Ohio, to Mennonite parents. Though baptized in a Mennonite church at age 12, he reconsecrated his life to the Lord at age 21. He poured himself into the study of God's Word and early Mennonite literature, and he developed a number of concerns about the Mennonites of his day:

- Individuals were being baptized whose personal conversions were in serious doubt. In many cases, their lives gave little evidence of true conversion.

- Children were not being trained properly.

- The church had fallen away from a strong stand on church discipline of erring members.

- Church members were not making enough effort to avoid apostates.

- Church members were participating in political elections.

- There was a lack of true spirituality in general.

Holdeman became an evangelist for the true Mennonite faith. He, along with some like-minded sympathizers, began meeting separately from the Mennonite church in 1859. This move resulted in the eventual organization of the Church of God in Christ, Mennonite. They are sometimes called Holdeman Mennonites.

Members of these churches believe in simple homes, simple and modest clothing, devotional head coverings for women (symbolizing submission to man), and beards for men. Christians are not to participate in politics or hold government offices. They practice nonresistance—meaning there should be no quarrels with other people and no lawsuits. Evil should not be returned for evil, and one should not participate in civil law enforcement or the armed forces. The church and the state should be clearly separate.

Church members believe Christians are to be a separate people, not conformed to the world. This means that such things as fashion, pleasure and entertainment, professional sports, idolatrous art, television, radio, movies, popular music, dancing, alcohol, illicit drugs, and smoking (among other things) must be avoided.

The denomination has a General Conference that is composed of ministers, deacons, and other delegates. The conference meets every five years for decision making.

Beliefs

The denomination accepts the Dordrecht Confession of Faith of 1632.

Bible. The Scriptures are inspired and are God's infallible source for all Christian beliefs and practice.

God. The one true God is eternal, almighty, and incomprehensible. He is the Creator of all things, visible and invisible. He is the Sustainer of the universe. Within the unity of the one God are three eternal persons: the Father, the Son, and the Holy Spirit.

Jesus Christ. Jesus is eternal God. He is the Alpha and Omega, the first and the last. At the appointed time, He became flesh, being born of a virgin. In His own body, He yielded up a sacrifice, thereby providing redemption and salvation for humankind. He was crucified and buried, and He rose from the dead, ascended into heaven, and now sits at the right hand of God.

Holy Spirit. The Holy Spirit is the third person of the Trinity. In salvation, believers experience regeneration and the "renewing of the Holy Ghost."

Sin and Salvation. Adam and Eve were disobedient to the Creator, bringing sin into the world and to all human beings. Mankind is therefore under the wrath of God, separated and estranged from Him.

Human beings are saved by God's grace through the atoning sacrifice of Christ. The new birth involves faith in Jesus, repentance, the forsaking of sins, and service to Christ. This new birth makes the believer a child of God, saves him from the condemnation of sin, and gives him eternal life. Those who are faithfully obedient can be assured of salvation.

Church. The church is the visible representative of Christ's spiritual kingdom on earth and is comprised of all who are regenerated and baptized into its fellowship. Christ Himself established the church, and through it has preserved His faith and doctrine through the ages.

The church's divinely appointed mission is to proclaim the gospel to the world, nurture Christians by teaching them to obey Christ's commands, and display a pattern of good works for the glory of God. The church is also called to regulate the observance of the ordinances, to exercise discipline when necessary (including excommunication), and to shun those who are excommunicated for the sake of the purity of the church.

Worship and Sunday school take place on Sunday mornings in plain buildings. Musical instruments are not used—all singing is *a cappella*. Teaching, fellowship, and singing take place on Sunday and Wednesday evenings. Ministers are chosen from within their own ranks and are not salaried. Formal training of ministers is not required. Ministers do not deliver prepared sermons but rather preach extemporaneously. Women are not ordained for the ministry.

Sacraments. Baptism is to be administered only upon a confession of faith. It is an outward sign of an inward cleansing and infilling of the Holy Spirit. It is to be observed by pouring water on the believer's head.

Closed communion is held with unleavened bread and unfermented juice of grapes. It is observed as a memorial of Christ's death, symbolizing the blood and body of Christ. It is to be preceded by self-examination, and is observed about once a year.

Foot washing is observed, with male ministers washing the brethren's feet and the wives of ministers or deacons washing the sister's feet. It symbolizes a cleansed walk of life and humility in serving one another.

End Times. Members subscribe to amillennialism. The present world will end with the glorious appearing of Jesus Christ. Jesus will judge humankind. Heaven is the final resting place of the righteous, where they will enjoy the fullness of joy with God forever. Hell is a place of everlasting punishment prepared for those who reject Christ.

Website

Unknown

FAST FACTS ON
Millennial Views

Premillennialism	Following the second coming, Christ will institute a literal kingdom of perfect peace and righteousness on earth that will last for 1000 years.
Amillennialism	When Christ comes, eternity will begin with no prior 1000-year (millennial) reign on earth. The 1000-year reign metaphorically refers to Christ's present (spiritual) rule from heaven.
Postmillennialism	Through the church's progressive influence, the world will be "Christianized" before Christ returns. Immediately following this return, eternity will begin.

CONSERVATIVE
MENNONITE CONFERENCE
Founded: 1910
Members: 10,334
Congregations: 102

Beginnings

The Conservative Mennonite Conference had humble beginnings. It emerged from a meeting of just five ministers at the site of the present Pigeon River Mennonite Church (Pigeon, Michigan) on November 24–25, 1910. The meeting was called by

Bishop S.J. Schwartzendruber and the Reverend M.S. Zehr. They were reluctant to adopt the Old Order Amish Mennonite approach to cultural expressions (such as the forbidding of meeting houses and Sunday schools). Yet they were more conservative than the dominant Mennonite and Amish Mennonite approaches of the time. They began the Conservative Mennonite Conference as a means of attaining the balance they were seeking. At first they were called the Conservative Amish Mennonite Conference. In 1954, however, the adjective "Amish" was dropped from its official name.

Like other Mennonites, members of this denomination follow a policy of nonresistance and decline participation in any government function that requires the use of force (whether police or military). They prohibit fashionable attire, worldly business associations, the holding of political office, gambling, the swearing of oaths, and the use of tobacco (smoking or chewing) and intoxicating beverages.

The Minister's Business Meeting is the highest decision-making body in the denomination. An executive board and general secretary oversee the day-to-day operations of the denomination.

Beliefs

The denomination subscribes to the Dordrecht Confession of Faith (1632), the Mennonite Confession of Faith (1963), and the Conservative Mennonite Statement of Theology (1991).

Bible. The Bible is the Word of God, verbally inspired by the Holy Spirit and without error in the original manuscripts. It is the final authority for faith and practice.

God. The one true God is eternal, perfect, infinite, holy, loving, all-wise, merciful, righteous, and powerful. He is the Creator and Preserver of all things in the universe. He is self-existent and is eternally manifest in three divine persons: the Father, the Son, and the Holy Spirit. These persons are distinct in function but equal in power and glory.

Jesus Christ. Jesus is one with the Father and the Holy Spirit in the triune Godhead. He is the divine Son of God. Prior to the Incarnation, He was eternally with God and was God. In the fullness of time, He became a human being, conceived by the Holy Spirit, born of the Virgin Mary, and thus was fully God and fully man. He lived a perfect life on earth and revealed God perfectly. He gave His life as a substitutionary atonement on the cross, thereby paying the price of redemption. He then rose from the dead and ascended into heaven to the right hand of the Father, where He now makes intercession for us.

Holy Spirit. The Holy Spirit is one with the Father and the Son in the triune Godhead. He has all the attributes of deity. He is God, present and active in the world. He convicts sinners of sin and regenerates penitents. He gives comfort, assurance, guidance, and victory to believers. He is the agent of sanctification and produces spiritual fruit in the believer's life. He gives spiritual gifts to believers.

Sin and Salvation. Human beings willfully disobeyed God, thereby causing alienation between themselves and God. As a result, all humankind is born in a state of depravity, death, and eternal lostness.

God sent Jesus into the world to attain the salvation of the world. Salvation is a free gift of God's grace and is based on Jesus' blood, shed upon the cross. Those who receive God's gift of salvation through repentance and faith become children of God, are justified, and become sanctified in their walk. Believers are secure in their salvation through ongoing obedience to Christ. Security is conditional rather than unconditional.

Church. The church is the universal body of redeemed believers, committed to Jesus as Lord. It finds expression in the local church in worship, fellowship, holiness, discipline, the teaching and preaching of God's Word, prayer, the exercise of spiritual gifts, and the administering of the New Testament ordinances. The church is a visible representation of God on earth.

Church government is primarily congregational, with all major decisions being subject to church approval. Churches also have a board of elders comprised of clergy and laymen who are involved in running the church.

Women are permitted to be involved in a variety of ministries, but leadership, governance, teaching, and ordination are for men only.

Sacraments. Baptism is for believers only. It symbolizes cleansing through the blood of Christ in regeneration. The mode can be either pouring or immersion. Communion commemorates the body and blood Jesus sacrificed for human salvation. It also points to the spiritual unity in the body of Christ. Foot washing is also practiced.

End Times. Jesus will one day personally return again. All the dead will be resurrected, the unjust to everlasting punishment and the just to eternal glory and bliss in heaven. Then the glorious reign of the kingdom of God will be eternally fulfilled.

Website

www.cmcrosedale.org

GENERAL CONFERENCE OF MENNONITE BRETHREN CHURCHES

Founded: 1860
Members: 50,915
Congregations: 590

Beginnings

In 1860, some Mennonites in Russia—heavily influenced by German pietism—left the established Mennonite Church and organized the Mennonite Brethren Church to pay greater attention to Bible study, a consistent biblical lifestyle, and prayer.

Fifteen years later, many of these believers (about 200 families) left Russia and found their way to Kansas, where they established a congregation. Eventually, new congregations sprang up in Nebraska, Minnesota, the Dakotas, and Mississippi. In 1879 these various congregations organized themselves as a General Conference. Eventually the movement spread all the way to California. In 1960 the Krimmer Mennonite Brethren merged with the General Conference of Mennonite Brethren Churches, adding 1600 new members to the conference.

Today the denomination embraces five district conferences in the United States and six provincial conferences in Canada. The highest authoritative body is the General Conference, which meets biennially. Delegates from the United States and Canada participate.

Beliefs

Bible. God has revealed Himself in both the Old and New Testaments. All Scripture is inspired by God and is the authoritative guide for faith and practice.

God. The one true God is the source of all life. He created the heavens and the earth. He is the Preserver and Ruler of the entire universe. Within the unity of the Godhead are three persons: the Father, the Son, and the Holy Spirit.

Jesus Christ. Jesus is Lord and Savior. He triumphed over sin through His obedient life, sacrificial death, and victorious resurrection.

Holy Spirit. The Holy Spirit empowers believers with new life, indwells them, and unites them into one body. He transforms believers from the unrighteous pattern of the present age into a life of joyful obedience. He also guides people in understanding the Scriptures.

Sin and Salvation. Sin has alienated human beings from the Creator and the creation. Sin is individual and corporate opposition to God's good purposes and leads to physical and spiritual death. God offers redemption and reconciliation through Jesus, the Savior of the world. Those who trust in Jesus, He delivers from the tyranny of sin and death, and He redeems them for the eternal life that is to come.

Church. The church is a covenant community called by God through Jesus Christ to live a life of discipleship and be His witnesses as empowered by the Holy Spirit. The local church gathers to facilitate worship, fellowship, and accountability. The mission of the church is to fulfill the Great Commission by making disciples of all nations, calling people to repent, baptizing them, and encouraging them to love God and neighbor.

Sacraments. Baptism is a public sign that a person has repented of sin, received forgiveness, died with Christ, and been raised to new life through the power of the Holy Spirit. It is also a public declaration of a believer's inclusion in the body of Christ. The Lord's Supper is a remembrance of Christ's atoning death. It is a celebration of the forgiveness and new life we have in Christ and points to the fellowship and unity of all believers.

End Times. Jesus will one day triumphantly return and destroy all evil powers. Those who have rejected Him will be consigned to everlasting punishment. Believers will reign with Christ forever in glory.

Website

Unknown

MENNONITE CHURCH

Founded: 1725
Members: 118,070
Congregations: 1202

Beginnings

In the late 1600s, Dutch and German immigrants found their way to Germantown, Pennsylvania, and set up their congregation—the Mennonite Church. The Dordrecht Confession of Faith (1632) became their statement of faith at a conference of Pennsylvania Mennonite ministers in 1725. This represents the beginning of the denomination on American soil. A primary emphasis of the denomination is that loyalty should be to God alone and not one's nation.

One of their distinctives is their freedom from traditional Mennonite regulations on attire. They have become known as liberal-minded Mennonites (though not liberal in theology). They continue to hold to the traditional Mennonite emphasis on nonresistance and peacemaking as a way of life.

Beliefs

The denomination holds to the Dordrecht Confession of Faith (1632) and the Confession of Faith in a Mennonite Perspective (1995).

Bible. Scripture is inspired by the Holy Spirit and is the fully reliable and trustworthy standard for Christian faith and life. The Bible is the Word of God written. It provides us with all we need to know for salvation. It enables us to distinguish truth from error, helps us discern between good and evil, and guides us in prayer and worship.

God. The one true God is the Creator and Preserver of the universe. He is sovereign, full of mercy, and characterized by unlimited justice. He eternally exists as the Father, the Son, and the Holy Spirit, with each of the three persons being equally divine.

Jesus Christ. Jesus is the Son of God and is fully divine. He is the Messiah, the head of the church, and the exalted Lord over all. He is the Word of God made flesh, being conceived of the Holy Spirit and born of the Virgin Mary. He is the Savior of the world who has delivered us from the dominion of sin and reconciled us to God.

Holy Spirit. The Holy Spirit is fully divine and is God's presence and power active in the world. He convicts people of sin, calls them to repentance, and leads them into the way of righteousness. He indwells children of God, teaches them, reminds them of the words of Jesus, empowers them to speak the Word of God with boldness, and gives them spiritual gifts for ministry. He comforts believers in their suffering and intercedes for them in their weakness.

Sin and Salvation. Beginning with Adam and Eve, humanity has continually disobeyed God and chosen to sin. All have fallen short of the Creator's intent. The image of God, in which they were created, has become marred. Because of sin, human beings are enslaved to evil and death. We are separated from God and in need of redemption.

Through the life, death, and resurrection of Jesus, God offers salvation from sin and a new way of life to all people. One receives God's salvation by repenting of sin and accepting Jesus as Lord and Savior. By His death and resurrection, Jesus has broken the power of sin and death and has opened the way to new life.

Church. The church is the assembly of those who have accepted God's offer of salvation through faith in Jesus Christ. It is a household or family of God. It is a society of those committed to following Christ, accountable to one another and to God.

Each local church is part of an area conference. The highest legislative body is the General Assembly, which meets every two years. Churches formulate their own policies regarding the role of women in ministry.

Sacraments. Baptism is a sign that a person has repented, received forgiveness, renounced evil, and died to sin. It is a public pledge of the believer's covenant with God to walk in newness of life through the power of the Holy Spirit. It is for believers only.

The Lord's Supper is a sign by which the church remembers the new covenant Jesus established by His death on the cross. It points to Jesus, whose body was given for us and whose blood was shed to establish the new covenant. By participating, members renew their covenant with God. It is for believers only.

Many churches in the denomination practice foot washing. In this ritual, believers acknowledge their frequent need of cleansing, renew their willingness to let go of pride and a self-focused life, and recommit to humble service and sacrificial love.

End Times. Jesus will one day come again in glory to judge the living and the dead. All people will be resurrected—those who have done good to the resurrection of life, and those who have done evil to the resurrection of condemnation. The righteous will experience eternal life with God, while the unrighteous suffer eternally in hell, separated forever from God.

Website

www.MennoniteChurchUSA.org

MISSIONARY CHURCH

Founded: 1969
Members: 33,249
Congregations: 610

Beginnings

The Missionary Church emerged in 1969 as a result of a merger between the Missionary Church Association (founded at Berne, Indiana, in 1889) and the United Missionary Church (founded at Englewood, Ohio, in 1883). Both these denominations find their roots in Mennonite history. The denomination is conservative and evangelical in its theology. A central goal is to fulfill Christ's Great Commission.

Beliefs

Bible. The Bible is the Word of God given by divine inspiration. It is inerrant in the words of the original manuscripts. It remains our unchanging authority in matters of Christian faith and practice.

God. The one true God is Spirit, self-existent, infinite, personal, unchangeable, and eternal. He is perfect in holiness, love, justice, goodness, wisdom, and truth, and is omnipotent, omniscient, and omnipresent. He is the Creator and Sustainer of all things and eternally exists in three persons who are coequal in power and glory: the Father, the Son, and the Holy Spirit.

Jesus Christ. Jesus is full deity and is eternally generated from the Father. In the Incarnation, He was conceived by the Holy Spirit and born of the Virgin Mary, thus uniting in one person the divine and human natures in their completeness. He lived a sinless life. His vicarious death made atonement for the sins of the world. He bodily rose from the dead, ascended to the right hand of the Father, and is presently the believer's Advocate before the Father.

Holy Spirit. The Holy Spirit proceeds from the Father and is sent by the Son. He is one in substance with the Father and Son. He convicts the world of sin and regenerates penitent sinners. His ministry to believers includes enduing them with power, teaching them, guiding them, and comforting them. He gives believers spiritual gifts for ministry.

Sin and Salvation. Through sin, the first couple became alienated from God and incurred upon themselves and their posterity the sentence of death, both spiritually and physically. The entire human race has thus become corrupt. Humans are now born with an evil disposition that leads to acts of sin, and they are therefore under just condemnation from God.

God, in His infinite love, has provided salvation in Jesus Christ. Receiving this salvation necessitates both repentance and faith. Genuine repentance involves a change of mind toward and a godly sorrow for sin. Faith must be active throughout the life of the believer and must show itself by good works. God justifies and regenerates the sinner who meets the requirements of repentance and faith.

Church. The invisible and universal church is an organism made up of all believers in Jesus Christ who have been called out from the world, are separated from sin, and are vitally united to

Christ by faith. The visible and local church is an organized body of believers in Christ who voluntarily join together at regular times for the teaching of God's Word, fellowship of the saints, observance of the ordinances, the administration of discipline, engaging in prayer, and participation in public worship and evangelism.

Local churches handle their own affairs, but they also adhere to a hierarchical system of government involving district conferences and a General Conference. Women are not permitted to fill the roles of elder, overseer, or pastor.

Sacraments. Baptism is a symbol of one's union by faith with Christ in death, burial, and resurrection. It is by immersion and is only for those who have been born again. The Lord's Supper is a memorial of Christ's death for the remission of our sins. It is to be observed only by Christians. It should be preceded by a time of self-examination.

End Times. Prior to the tribulation judgments, Christ will descend into the clouds, the church will be caught up to Him (raptured), and He will take the church back to heaven. Following the tribulation judgments, Christ will return with His church to judge the nations and set up His millennial kingdom, over which He will rule for 1000 years. All human beings will be judged. Believers have an ultimate destiny in heaven. Unbelievers will be consigned to the lake of fire, where they will suffer for all eternity.

Website

www.mcusa.org

OLD ORDER AMISH CHURCHES

Founded: 1720s
Members: 80,820
Congregations: 3592

Beginnings

Amish churches emerged in the 1720s out of the teachings of the seventeenth-century Mennonite bishop Jakob Amman (1656–1730). In the latter 1800s, many of the Amish met at a formal conference to address some of the differences they had with each other. Not finding full agreement, a schism developed. One group, the New Order Amish, was open to a more progressive lifestyle, accepting social change and technological innovation. The other group, the Old Order Amish, held on to the old ways (see "Distinctives" below).

Beliefs

The denomination subscribes to the Dordrecht Confession of Faith of 1632.

Bible. The Scriptures are inspired and are God's infallible source for all Christian beliefs and practice.

God. The one true God is eternal, almighty, and incomprehensible. He is the Creator of all things, visible and invisible. He is the Sustainer of the universe. Within the unity of the one God are three eternal persons: the Father, the Son, and the Holy Spirit.

Jesus Christ. Jesus is eternal God. He is the Alpha and Omega, the first and the last. At the appointed time, He became flesh, being born of a virgin. In His own body at the cross, He yielded up a sacrifice, thereby providing redemption and salvation for humankind. He was buried, rose from the dead, ascended into heaven, and now sits at the right hand of God.

Holy Spirit. The Holy Spirit is the third person of the Trinity. In salvation believers experience regeneration and the "renewing of the Holy Ghost."

Sin and Salvation. Humanity is fallen in sin and is therefore under the wrath of God. Not willing for people to be lost forever, God sent His Son, Jesus Christ, to shed His blood for the remission of sins. Those who repent and believe in Jesus will be saved. There is no assurance of salvation. One becomes guilty of pride by claiming a certainty of salvation. A believer's focus should be on living a righteous life.

Church. Religious services are held in homes or barns, not in church buildings. Sometimes the Old Order Amish are referred to as the "House Amish" because their worship services take place in private homes. This is in distinction to the "Church Amish"— the New Order Amish—who worship in meeting houses. Most forms of organized church activity are rejected. Formal missionary work and evangelistic services are rejected. Church services are every other Sunday. (On alternate Sundays, when there are no services, families stay home or visit relatives.) Services generally last three hours. The congregation is divided according to sex and marital status.

Amish settlements are divided into autonomous church districts, each having 15 to 30 families, totaling about 75 baptized members. Each district has a bishop, two to four preachers, and an elder. If a district gets too large, it is geographically divided. There is no general conference, missionary agency, or any kind of cooperative agency.

Sacraments. All true believers, upon a confession of faith and a renewing of life, are baptized with water in the name of the Father, the Son, and the Holy Spirit, for the burying of their sins and their incorporation into the communion of saints. The Lord's Supper is observed twice a year in remembrance of Jesus' suffering and death in providing our salvation. The elements point to the brokenness of His body and shedding of His blood in making redemption possible. Foot washing is often practiced in connection with the communion service.

End Times. Jesus will one day come again to judge the quick and the dead. In the last day, all human beings will be resurrected and stand before God in judgment. Believers will then enter into eternal life and obtain joy in heaven. The wicked shall be cast into outer darkness and experience the everlasting pains of hell, having no further hope, comfort, or redemption.

Distinctives. The Old Order Amish are the most conservative among the Amish in beliefs and practices. They cling to a seventeenth-century way of life, rejecting many modern conveniences. They dress very plainly (most clothing is self-made). Adult males wear beards (no mustaches), dark suits, suspenders, solid-colored shirts, dark socks and shoes, and broad-brimmed black hats. Coats fasten with hooks and eyes. Females wear bonnets, long dresses, shawls, black shoes, and stockings. Their hair—never cut—is worn in a bun. Jewelry is not allowed. They refuse to use electricity (they run appliances with bottled gas). They refuse to use personal telephones (sometimes they use a communal phone). They refuse to use automobiles, instead using horse-drawn buggies and bicycles (though cars are permitted in emergencies). They discipline by shunning. Marriage with outsiders is condemned.

Website
Unknown

13

METHODIST CHURCHES

JOHN WESLEY (1703–1791), THE FOUNDER of Methodism, was born in a rectory at Epworth, Lincolnshire. He was the son—the fifteenth child—of an Anglican rector. He was trained at Oxford University. While there, around 1729, he and his younger brother Charles (1707–1788) began methodically meeting with a group at a stated time for "prayer and religious exercises." They were quite serious about their spirituality. Because they were so methodical—meeting precisely on time and systematically engaging in a strict regimen of prayer, fasting, Bible reading, and ministry—they soon acquired the name "Methodists." In jest, some referred to them as "Bible bigots," "Bible moths," and the "Holy Club." With this humble beginning, John and Charles would soon cause a spiritual revolution—John by preaching evangelistic sermons and Charles by writing hymns.

John was ordained a deacon in the Church of England in 1728 and even served at his father's church for a few years before his father passed away. Following this, he returned to Oxford and was ordained a priest in 1735.

Later that year, John and Charles visited America as missionaries—a mission trip destined to become a failure. Nevertheless, while on the ship to Savannah (a port in the colony of Georgia), he met some Moravian Christians whose simple piety and morality greatly impressed him. He continued his association with them in Georgia, and upon his return to England in 1738, he again sought them out.

On May 24 of that same year, John attended a Moravian service on Aldersgate Street in London. During the meeting, he experienced a religious awakening that would change the course of his life. He came to understand the revolutionary concept of justification by faith alone and became convinced that salvation was possible for every person who exercised faith in Jesus. He recalls his response after a person at the meeting read from Martin Luther's Preface to the Epistle to the Romans:

> About a quarter before nine, while he was describing the change which God works in the heart through faith in Christ, I felt my heart strangely warmed. I felt I did trust in Christ; Christ alone, for salvation; and an assurance was given me, that he had taken away my sins, even mine, and saved me from the law of sin and death.[1]

Wesley was revitalized. He was finally at peace with God. His religion was no longer just an intellectual faith but rather a personal relationship with God. He soon sought the revitalization of church life in England. He was enthusiastic about his work, but because his methods seemed somewhat unorthodox, he did not find a welcoming hand from Anglican pulpits. After some encouragement from evangelist George Whitefield, he decided to preach in the open air. The response was so enthusiastic that he decided this was the best method for reaching the masses. He preached to the poor, the downtrodden, and the dispossessed—anyone who would listen to him. He preached in open fields, on street corners, and at town squares, often to very large crowds. He preached on repentance, regeneration, and justification by faith. He preached on sanctification and the need for holiness. His meetings led to a revival of religious fervor throughout England, especially among the poor. He also wrote books that were sold cheaply—so cheap that even the poor could afford them.

Wesley's converts organized not into distinct churches but into "societies" that generally met in private homes. In these small societies, members supported each other and were accountable to each other. Members were honest in sharing their weaknesses and failings, and they encouraged one another to stay true to the faith. They also prayed for each other and sang hymns.

In the latter half of the eighteenth century, early Methodist societies began to take root in the American colonies. In 1766, minister Philip Embury organized a "Connection" of Methodist societies in New York—the first organized Methodist group in America. Societies quickly formed in other states, including Philadelphia and Maryland. In 1769, Wesley sent his first missionaries to America, the greatest of these being the dynamic Francis Asbury (1745–1816), who was instrumental in establishing the American Methodist church.

In 1773, the first annual Methodist conference was held in Philadelphia. Methodism was on the rise! At a conference in Baltimore, Maryland, in 1784, the Methodist Episcopal Church was formally organized as a body separate from the English Methodist structure. Asbury and an associate, Thomas Coke (1747–1814), became bishops in authority over the new church. Wesley then sent to the new church his 25 Articles of Religion, adapted from the 39 Articles of the Church of England. This document served as the statement of faith for the church.

Under Asbury's capable leadership and the ministry of circuit riders, Methodism expanded across America. Circuit riders traveled from one location to another across the American frontier, preaching distinctively Methodist sermons with an emphasis on the need for conversion and regeneration. Camp revival meetings happened everywhere. Sometimes thousands of people attended. The Methodist emphasis on personal religious experience and practical ethics attracted large numbers of people. By the mid-1800s, there were about 1.3 million Methodists in the United States.

After Wesley died in 1791, his followers eventually divided into a number of separate church bodies. During the nineteenth century, various Methodist denominations emerged in Britain and the United States, each holding to its own version of the Wesleyan tradition.

Methodists follow Wesley's lead in rejecting the Calvinist emphasis on predestination and instead opt for Arminianism, which emphasizes human free will and the belief that the death of Christ provided an atonement for *all* human beings. (Calvinism taught that Christ died only for the elect.) Methodists also advocate belief in God's "prevenient grace." This is the idea that God reaches out to every person, providing each person with prevenient (anticipatory) grace, offering him or her salvation through faith in Jesus Christ. Those who use their free wills as empowered by God's grace to positively respond by faith in Jesus become justified (acquitted of the guilt of sin and declared righteous by God).

Regarding other issues, Methodist bodies tend to have varying beliefs today. Most Methodist churches pay more attention to quality of life than to defending specific doctrines. Many, however, subscribe to some form of Wesley's doctrine of perfectionism—the idea that believers can be enabled by the Holy Spirit to say no to sin and become perfect in love in this present life if they completely surrender to God.

Three major doctrinal statements define Methodist belief:

• The Apostles' Creed, which is often recited during church services.

- The 25 Articles of Religion, which is John Wesley's revision of the 39 Articles of the Church of England.

- The Doctrines and Discipline of the Methodist Church, which is reissued every four years.

AFRICAN METHODIST EPISCOPAL CHURCH

Founded: 1816
Members: 1,857,186
Congregations: 7741

Beginnings

In 1787, a group of African-American parishioners at Saint George's Church in Philadelphia left the congregation over the racial prejudice they encountered there. The church had predominantly white members, but African-Americans had also been welcome with the understanding that they would be segregated away from white worshippers (in the "gallery" of the church).

One day an African-American, Absalom Jones, was kneeling in prayer in the wrong section of the church when some white trustees forcefully pulled him up from his knees and removed him to the back of the church. When the congregational leadership went along with this open display of racial discrimination, former slave Richard Allen led the African-American membership away from the church in protest.

Allen promptly purchased a blacksmith shop with his own money, and this facility became the meeting place for a new church of African-Americans: the Bethel Church for Negro Methodists in Philadelphia. Allen became their preacher. For a time, the whites in the Methodist denomination tried to prevent

Allen and his congregation from controlling their own property. (To be fair, local Methodist churches do not normally control their own property, even among white churches.) In 1816, however, the Pennsylvania Supreme Court sided with Allen.

About this same time, Allen became aware that similar congregations of African-Americans had cropped up around the city. In 1816, he took the lead in organizing the groups into a new denomination: the African Methodist Episcopal Church. Allen was elected the denomination's first bishop, and he was personally ordained by the Anglo-American bishop Francis Asbury of the Methodist Episcopal Church.

Beliefs

Bible. The Bible contains all things necessary to salvation. The Holy Spirit guides people in understanding Scripture.

God. The one true and living God is everlasting, infinitely powerful, all-wise, and good. He is the Creator and Preserver of all things. The unity of the Godhead includes three persons who are of one divine substance: the Father, the Son, and the Holy Spirit.

Jesus Christ. Jesus, the Son of God, is eternal God, of one substance with the Father. He is Lord and Savior. In the Incarnation, He took on man's nature, having been born of the Virgin Mary, so that two natures—the human and the divine—were joined together in one person. He suffered on the cross for human sin, thereby reconciling human beings to God. He was dead and buried, rose from the dead, and ascended into heaven. Jesus is the only Mediator between God and man.

Holy Spirit. The Holy Spirit proceeds from the Father and the Son and is one in substance, glory, and majesty with the Father and the Son. He is eternal God.

Sin and Salvation. Because of Adam's sin, all human beings are born with such a corrupt nature that they are very far from original righteousness and continually inclined to evil. Human beings cannot turn in their own natural strength and works to faith, and therefore they are in need of the grace of God. Those who respond to God's grace by faith are justified—accounted righteous before God. After people have been justified, they can fall back into sin and depart from God's grace. However, if they repent and turn back to God again, restoration to God is possible.

Church. The visible church is a congregation of faith in which the pure Word of God is preached and the sacraments are properly administered. The mission of the African Methodist Episcopal Church is socially oriented. Members seek to preach the gospel, feed the hungry, clothe the naked, house the homeless, bring cheer to the fallen, provide jobs for the homeless, encourage thrift and economic advancement, and minister to those in prison, hospitals, nursing homes, senior citizen's homes, and other social facilities.

Government involves conferences with increasing levels of authority: the Local Church Conference, the District Conference, the Annual Conference, and the General Conference. Women are welcome to serve in any official capacity in the church.

Sacraments. Baptism is not only a sign of one's profession of faith in Christ but also a sign of regeneration and the new birth. Young children may participate in the sacrament. The mode can be pouring, sprinkling, or immersion. The Lord's Supper is not only a sign of the love Christians share among each other but also a sign of our redemption in Christ.

End Times. Christ will one day come again to judge the living and the dead. Heaven is the abode where believers will enjoy eternal fellowship with God. Hell is the abode where there will be a complete absence of God.

Website

www.amecnet.org

FAST FACTS ON
the Equality of the Races

- God loves *all* human beings (John 3:16).

- *All* human beings descended from Adam (Acts 17:26).

- God does not desire that *any* perish (2 Peter 3:9).

- God's redeemed will be from *every* tribe and tongue and people and nation (Revelation 5:9).

- Conclusion: *All* human beings are equal in God's sight.

CHRISTIAN METHODIST EPISCOPAL CHURCH

Founded: 1870
Members: 850,000
Congregations: 2980

Beginnings

Following the emancipation of slaves, African-American members of the Methodist Episcopal Church (South)—embracing some 80,000 African-Americans—amicably split off from white members and organized the Colored Methodist Episcopal Church in America in Jackson, Tennessee, in 1870. More than 80 years later, at its 1954 General Conference in Memphis, Tennessee, an overwhelming majority voted to change "Colored" to "Christian." The official name of the denomination became Christian Methodist Episcopal Church. The denomination presently reaches not only across the United States but also into Haiti, Jamaica, Nigeria, Ghana, and Liberia.

Beliefs

Bible. Scripture is the work of inspired human beings. Through the power of the Holy Spirit, the words of Scripture are "God-breathed."

God. There is one true and living eternal God. Within the unity of the Godhead are three persons of equal divine substance, power, and eternity: the Father, the Son, and the Holy Spirit.

Jesus Christ. Jesus is the Son of God. In the Incarnation, He was very God and very man, having been conceived by the Holy Spirit and born of a virgin. He died for the sins of all human beings upon the cross. He rose from the dead and ascended into heaven.

Holy Spirit. The Holy Spirit is the third person of the Trinity.

Sin and Salvation. Man is fallen in sin, but salvation is a gift of God through Jesus Christ. It is received through faith in Christ as made possible by the grace of God. Those who are truly Christians receive a witness from the Holy Spirit that gives them a sense of inner certainty that they indeed are children of God. Christians can live in such a way that they reject the grace of God and fall from salvation.

Church. The church is the people of God. Church government is episcopal, with bishops overseeing the denomination. The General Conference has highest legislative authority. Women can be ordained as pastors, elders, and deacons.

Sacraments. A sacrament is a visible sign of an inward and spiritual grace instituted by Christ. In baptism, the believer is cleansed and incorporated into Christ by death, burial, and resurrection. It is for children, youth, and adults, and the mode can be sprinkling, pouring, or immersion. In infant baptism, the parents must commit to raise the child in Christian nurture and support.

The Lord's Supper involves use of the bread and the cup as a memorial of Christ's sacrifice. The broken bread and shared cup are vessels that bear the presence of Christ.

End Times. Jesus will one day come again to judge the living and the dead. Heaven is the destiny of believers, who will there enjoy a perfect relationship with God. Hell is the destiny of unbelievers, where no such relationship with God will be possible.

Distinctives. This denomination espouses a form of Christian perfectionism. It is believed that even though a perfect, sinless life has never actually been attained, nevertheless such a life is possible through God's enabling grace. Every Christian must therefore strive toward perfection and should give some evidence in that direction.

Website

www.c-m-e.org

CONGREGATIONAL METHODIST CHURCH
Founded: 1852
Members: 14,738
Congregations: 187

Beginnings

The Congregational Methodist Church was founded in 1852 as a result of lay members who were dissatisfied with certain policies of the Methodist Episcopal Church (South). There were three primary objections:

1. Lay members had no voice in the government of the church.

2. They desired more church autonomy, including the freedom for the church to own its own building and call its own ministers.

3. Many of these individuals were already involved in ministry, winning souls to the Lord, but were not permitted to serve as pastors until they met their denomination's stringent educational qualifications for ordination. They wanted more reasonable requirements for ordination.

The dissatisfaction continued to escalate until a group of lay people and lay ministers in the north-central part of Georgia decided to sever their relationship with the Georgia Conference of the Methodist Episcopal Church (South). They organized a new church that gave a voice to lay people, allowed affiliate churches to call their own pastors and own their own land, and had reasonable requirements for the ordination of ministers. The church met in the home of Mickleberry Merrit on May 8, 1852, and elected William Farbough as its chairman.

Beliefs

Bible. The Bible is preached and taught in every church. All Scripture is divinely inspired.

God. The one true living God is infinite in power, wisdom, and goodness. He is the Creator and Sustainer of all things in the universe. Within the unity of the Godhead are three persons who are equal in substance, power, and eternity: the Father, the Son, and the Holy Spirit.

Jesus Christ. Jesus is full deity. He was born of a virgin, died on a cross for the redemption of humankind, physically rose from the dead, and ascended into heaven.

Holy Spirit. The Holy Spirit is the third person of the Trinity, equal in substance to the Father and the Son.

Sin and Salvation. Man is fallen in sin. The new birth (regeneration) is necessary for salvation. Redemption is based on the death of Christ at the cross and is received through faith. Christians can be assured of salvation because the Holy Spirit bears witness in their hearts that they are children of God. Entire sanctification is viewed as a second definite work of grace that is subsequent to regeneration.

Church. Unlike most other Methodist churches, in this denomination each local church calls its own pastor, owns its own property, and sets its own budget. There are no bishops. There are, however, local church conferences, an Annual Conference, and a General Conference. Women may participate in church ministries and government.

Sacraments. Baptism is a sign of regeneration or the new birth. It is administered in the name of the Father, the Son, and the Holy Spirit, and it is performed by a licensed minister. The mode may be sprinkling, pouring, or immersion. The Lord's Supper is open to all Christians.

End Times. The second coming of Christ will be premillennial. The final destiny of the righteous is heaven. The final destiny of the wicked is hell.

Website

www.congregationalmethodist.net

THE EVANGELICAL CHURCH OF NORTH AMERICA

Founded: 1968
Members: 12,475
Congregations: 164

Beginnings

The Evangelical Church of North America was established in 1968 by members of the Evangelical United Brethren who refused to participate in the planned merger of their denomination with the Methodist Church, a merger that would form the United Methodist Church. Their new denomination was organized at Portland, Oregon, and affiliate churches are scattered across the nation, with heaviest concentration in the Northwest.

Beliefs

Bible. The Bible is the written Word of God. Scripture is inspired and inerrant in its entirety.

God. The one true living God is eternal, infinitely powerful, all-wise, and all-good. He is the Creator and Preserver of the universe. Within the unity of the Godhead are three persons equal in substance, power, and eternity: the Father, the Son, and the Holy Spirit.

Jesus Christ. Jesus is the Son of God and is full deity. He is the eternal Savior and Mediator. In the Incarnation, He was truly God and truly man, the eternal Word made flesh. He was conceived by the Holy Spirit and born of a virgin. He suffered and died on the cross, was buried, rose from the dead, and ascended bodily into heaven.

Holy Spirit. The Holy Spirit proceeds from and is one being with the Father and the Son. He convicts the world of sin, righteousness, and judgment. He comforts, sustains, empowers, and sanctifies the faithful. He guides them into all truth.

Sin and Salvation. Because of Adam's transgression, humanity is fallen from original righteousness and is separated from the grace of our Lord Jesus Christ, entirely destitute of holiness. Human beings are inclined to evil, and that continually. A person in his or her own strength, without divine grace, cannot do good works pleasing and acceptable to God. However, people who are influenced and empowered by the Holy Spirit and the prevenient grace of God are enabled to exercise their will to turn to God, place their faith in Jesus Christ, and do good works. Those who repent of their sins and place faith in Jesus are regenerated (born again) and justified (accounted righteous before God).

The Holy Spirit bears witness to this work of God in people's hearts and assures regenerate believers that they have passed from death to life. However, after the experience of regeneration, believers may depart from grace, fall into sin, and, if remaining unrepentant, lose salvation. Through renewed repentance and faith, the person can be restored to righteousness and true holiness.

Church. The church is a community of born-again believers under the lordship of Christ. It is a fellowship of the redeemed who hear the preaching of the Word of God and receive the sacraments. The denomination is split into districts, with conference superintendents overseeing each district and Annual Conference. The highest authority is a General Conference that meets quadrennially.

Sacraments. Baptism signifies entrance into the household of faith and symbolizes repentance and inner cleansing from sin. It is administered only to those who receive Jesus as Lord and Savior. Since children are heirs to the kingdom, they too can be baptized. Believing parents must see to it that they are nurtured and led to a personal acceptance of Christ and by profession of faith confirm their baptism. The mode can be sprinkling, pouring, or immersion.

The Lord's Supper signifies our redemption and is a memorial of the suffering and death of Jesus Christ. It points to the love and union Christians have with Christ and with each other. It is to be celebrated until He comes again.

End Times. Christ will one day bodily return, thereby fulfilling many biblical prophecies. He will triumph over all evil. Both the righteous and the unrighteous will be resurrected. Heaven is the final destiny of the righteous; hell is the final destiny of the wicked.

Distinctives. Entire sanctification is viewed as a second, definite, instantaneous work of God that is wrought in the heart of the fully consecrated believer. It is subsequent to regeneration. In this act, God cleanses the heart from all inherited sin and fills the soul with the Holy Spirit, enabling people to love God with their entire heart. It involves total death to inherited sin. This work, however, does not deliver believers from the infirmities, ignorance, and mistakes common to humanity, nor from the possibility of further sin. The Christian must continue to guard against temptation and seek spiritual victory.

Website

www.theevangelicalchurch.com

EVANGELICAL CONGREGATIONAL CHURCH

Founded: 1928
Members: 21,463
Congregations: 168

Beginnings

In 1796, Methodist itinerant preacher Jacob Albright (1759–1808) founded a movement known as the Evangelical Association.

Long after his death, the organization suffered a division in 1891 due to differences of opinion and practice, especially relating to episcopal authority. This led to the formation of a split-off group in 1894 called the United Evangelical Church. These two groups reconciled and re-merged in 1922, but some of those affiliated with the United Evangelical Church did not approve of the merger. They remained separate and in 1928 took the name of Evangelical Congregational Church.

Beliefs

Bible. The Bible is inspired by God. It contains all one needs to know regarding salvation in Jesus Christ.

God. The one true God is eternally manifest in three persons who are equal in substance and power: the Father, the Son, and the Holy Spirit.

Jesus Christ. Jesus is the Son of God. In the Incarnation, two natures—the human and the divine—were perfectly united in the one person of Christ. He is the sole Mediator between God and man.

Holy Spirit. The Holy Spirit is the third person of the Trinity. He is equal in substance to the Father and the Son.

Sin and Salvation. Man is fallen and depraved. Salvation is only through repentance and personal faith in Jesus. Those who believe are justified (acquitted of guilt and declared righteous) and regenerated (born again). Members reject the Calvinist idea of limited atonement (salvation for the elect only), arguing instead for human free will and the belief that God's grace is available to all.

Church. The church is a fellowship of followers of Jesus Christ. Local churches are partially autonomous in the sense that they can own and manage their own property. They are governed by local conferences, Annual Conferences, and a General Conference (the highest authority).

Sacraments. Baptism is performed in the name of the Father, the Son, and the Holy Spirit. It is a visible sign and seal that the participant stands in a covenant relationship with God and His people. The Lord's Supper is a memorial of the sufferings of Christ in attaining our salvation. Participants who partake of the elements receive the body and blood of Christ in a spiritual manner.

End Times. Jesus will one day come again in great power and glory. All people will be resurrected, the righteous to eternal life and the unrighteous to punishment. All human beings will be judged. Heaven is the final destiny of believers. Hell is the final destiny of the wicked, where they will be tormented eternally.

Distinctives. Like many Methodist churches, the Evangelical Congregational Church espouses the doctrine of entire sanctification. This is a state of Christian perfection attainable by every Christian through the power of the Holy Spirit, and it should be earnestly sought by all. Such a state of perfection, however, does not prohibit one from making human mistakes.

Website

www.eccenter.com

THE EVANGELICAL METHODIST CHURCH

Founded: 1946
Members: 8615
Congregations: 105

Beginnings

The Evangelical Methodist Church was founded in 1946 in Memphis, Tennessee, in reaction to the modernism that had infiltrated their parent body, the Methodist Church. Those who participated in the founding meeting saw an ever-widening chasm developing between the conservative and liberal elements in the church, and they felt that this chasm could never be healed. Therefore the Evangelical Methodist Church was founded to preserve the distinctive biblical doctrines of the historic Wesleyan position. Dr. J.H. Hamblen was elected chairman of this meeting, as well as the first General Superintendent at the organizational conference in November of that year.

Beliefs

Bible. The Bible is the inspired Word of God and is to be received as the revealed will and way of God for daily life.

God. The one true and living God is the Creator, Sustainer, and Ruler of the universe. He is infinite, eternal, and unchangeable. Within the unity of the Godhead are three persons of one substance, power, and eternity: the Father, the Son, and the Holy Spirit.

Jesus Christ. Jesus Christ, born of the Virgin Mary, was both God and man. He lived a sinless life and died a substitutionary death on the cross, thereby attaining human redemption. He physically rose from the dead and ascended into heaven. He is now our High Priest and Advocate.

Holy Spirit. The Holy Spirit, the third person of the Trinity, reveals Jesus to Christians and empowers them to serve God.

Sin and Salvation. All people are fallen in sin. Salvation is a gift of God's grace. It cannot be gained or made more secure by good works but is freely bestowed on all who place faith in the finished work of Jesus at Calvary. All who believe in Jesus are redeemed by His shed blood. Each person must acknowledge the lordship of Jesus to be born again. Every Christian is expected to live a holy life, one that is truly Christian.

Church. The denomination affirms both the local and the universal church, which is the body of Christ on earth. Church government is congregational yet connectional. It is congregational in the sense that each congregation calls its own pastor and owns its own property. It is connectional in the sense that the denomination as a whole is governed by the conference system. The highest body is the General Conference, which meets every four years.

Sacraments. The two sacraments are baptism and Holy Communion. The mode of baptism is left to the conscience of the individual.

End Times. Jesus will one day literally return again. Church members are premillennialists. All human beings will be resurrected from the dead, believers to eternal life and unbelievers to everlasting punishment.

Distinctives. Entire sanctification follows regeneration, whereby believers are cleansed from the pollution of sin, saved from its power, and enabled through grace to love God with all their heart.

Website

www.emchurch.org

FREE METHODIST CHURCH OF NORTH AMERICA

Founded: 1860
Members: 61,202
Congregations: 971

Beginnings

The Free Methodist Church of North America was founded in western New York in 1860 by ministers and lay people who had been expelled from the Methodist Episcopal Church for insubordination. The reason for the expulsion is that these individuals, under the leadership of Reverend Benjamin Titus Roberts (1823–1893), voiced concern that the church had departed from the doctrines and lifestyle of early Methodism. The expelled individuals therefore called a meeting, and on August 23, 1860, the Free Methodist Church of North America came into being. The new denomination dealt with all the issues that caused them concern with the Methodist Episcopal Church:

- Whereas the Methodist Episcopal Church refused to take a stand on the issue of slavery, the Free Methodist Church of North America felt that all people—including African-Americans—should be *free*.

- Whereas the Methodist Episcopal Church rented and sold pews to wealthier members, thereby forcing the poor to sit in the back, the Free Methodist Church of North America believed that all seating should be *free*.

- Whereas dissenters felt that the Methodist Episcopal Church had dead formalism in its church services, the Free Methodist Church of North America felt that worship style should be *free*.

- Whereas the Methodist Episcopal Church was open to members participating in secret societies, the Free Methodist Church of North America felt there should be no participation in such societies so that truth might be shared openly and *freely*.

Beliefs

The denomination is among the most conservative of Methodist bodies.

Bible. The Bible is God's written Word and is uniquely inspired by the Holy Spirit. It bears unerring witness to Jesus Christ, the living Word. It is a trustworthy record of God's revelation and is completely true in all that it affirms.

God. The one true and living God is the Creator and Sustainer of all things. In the unity of the Godhead are three persons who are equal in eternity, purpose, power, wisdom, and goodness: the Father, the Son, and the Holy Spirit.

Jesus Christ. In the Incarnation, Jesus was conceived by the Holy Spirit and born of a virgin, thereby joining in one person perfect deity and perfect humanity. The Son of God suffered, was crucified, died, and was buried. He poured out His life as a blameless sacrifice for human sin and transgressions. He rose from the dead, ascended into heaven, and now sits at the right hand of the Father as exalted Lord.

Holy Spirit. The Holy Spirit proceeds from the Father and the Son. He is equal in deity, majesty, and power with the Father and the Son. He seeks to reveal, interpret, and glorify the Son. He is also the effective agent in conviction of sin, regeneration, sanctification, and glorification. He equips the church with witnessing power.

Sin and Salvation. Because of Adam's sin, Adam's offspring are corrupted in their nature from birth so that they are inclined to sin. They are unable in their own strength to restore themselves to God and merit eternal salvation. However, the Holy Spirit acts to impart new life and put people into a right relationship with God as they repent and their faith responds to His grace. Those who respond are justified, regenerated, and adopted into God's family.

Christians can willfully sin and sever their relationship with Christ. By repentance before God, however, forgiveness can be granted and the relationship with Christ restored.

Church. The church is the people of God, a fellowship of the redeemed *and* the redeeming—preaching the Word of God and properly administering the sacraments. Jesus is the head of the church. Local congregations exist in 32 districts across the United States. Church government involves Annual Conferences and a General Conference that meets every four years. Women are permitted to participate in all areas of church leadership and ministry.

Sacraments. The sacraments are means of grace through faith and tokens of our profession of faith. By them, God works within us to quicken, strengthen, and confirm our faith.

Baptism signifies acceptance of the benefits of the atonement of Jesus Christ to be administered to believers. It is a declaration of faith in Jesus as Savior. It is a symbol of the new covenant of grace, just as circumcision was a symbol of the old covenant. Baptism is for infants too because they are included in the atonement. Parents must give them Christian training so that in time they can express personal faith in Christ for themselves.

The Lord's Supper is a sacrament of our redemption by Christ's death. Those who partake of the elements spiritually partake of the body and blood of Christ. The sacrament is a sign of the love and unity Christians have among themselves. It is only for those who are repentant and trust in Christ alone for salvation.

End Times. Jesus will one day come again and triumph over evil. There will be a bodily resurrection from the dead. Those who have done good will be resurrected unto life, whereas those who have done evil will be resurrected unto damnation. God will judge the world in righteousness. Those who trust in Christ will live in eternal glory and blessedness in heaven. Those who do not believe in Christ will experience everlasting punishment in hell.

Distinctives. Entire sanctification is that work of the Holy Spirit, subsequent to regeneration, by which fully consecrated believers, upon exercise of faith in the atoning blood of Christ, are cleansed in that moment from all inward sin and empowered for service. The resulting relationship is attested by the witness of the Holy Spirit and is maintained by faith and obedience. Entire sanctification enables believers to love God with all their heart and love their neighbors as themselves.

Website

www.freemethodistchurch.org

SOUTHERN METHODIST CHURCH

Founded: 1939
Members: 7686
Congregations: 82

Beginnings

The Southern Methodist Church was founded in Columbia, South Carolina, in 1939. The founding congregations were a part of the Methodist Episcopal Church (South) who did not go along with the 1939 merger of this denomination with the Methodist Episcopal Church (North) because they believed this latter body was tainted with apostasy and heresy. They also felt that such a merger would overly centralize ecclesiastical control in one body. Rather than go along with the merger, they began a new denomination.

Beliefs

Bible. The Bible contains all things necessary to salvation. The Holy Spirit guides people in understanding Scripture.

God. The one true and living God is everlasting, infinitely powerful, all-wise, and good. He is the Creator and Preserver of all things. The unity of the Godhead includes three persons who are of one divine substance: the Father, the Son, and the Holy Spirit.

Jesus Christ. Jesus, the Son of God, is eternal God, of one substance with the Father. He is Lord and Savior. In the Incarnation, He took on man's nature, having been born of the Virgin Mary, so that two natures—the human and the divine—were joined together in one person. He died on the cross for human sin, thereby reconciling human beings to God. He was buried, rose from the dead, and ascended into heaven. Jesus is the only Mediator between God and man.

Holy Spirit. The Holy Spirit proceeds from the Father and the Son and is one in substance, glory, and majesty with the Father and the Son. He is eternal God.

Sin and Salvation. Because of Adam's sin, all human beings are born with such a corrupt nature that they are very far from original righteousness and continually inclined to evil. Human beings cannot turn in their own natural strength and works to faith, and therefore they are in need of the grace of God. Those who respond to God's grace by faith are justified—accounted righteous before God. People who have been justified may fall back into sin and depart from God's grace, thereby losing salvation. However, if they repent and turn back to God again, restoration to God is possible.

Church. The visible church is a congregation of faith in which the pure Word of God is preached and the sacraments are properly administered. Local churches can control their own property and call their own pastors, but the call must be approved by the Annual Conference. The highest legislative body is the General Conference. Women cannot be ordained into the ministry, though they can be involved in a variety of unordained ministry roles.

Sacraments. Baptism is not only a sign of one's profession of faith in Christ but also a sign of regeneration and the new birth. Young children may participate in the sacrament. The mode can be pouring, sprinkling, or immersion. The Lord's Supper is a sign of the love Christians share among each other and of our redemption in Christ.

End Times. Christ will premillennially come again to judge the living and the dead. In heaven, believers will enjoy eternal fellowship with God. In hell, God's presence will be completely absent.

Website

www.southernmethodistchurch.org

THE UNITED METHODIST CHURCH
Founded: 1968
Members: 8,298,145
Congregations: 24,162

Beginnings

The United Methodist Church emerged in Dallas, Texas, on April 23, 1968 as a result of a merger of two other Methodist bodies—The Methodist Church and The Evangelical United Brethren Church. The merger became a reality when Bishop Reuben H. Mueller, representing The Evangelical United Brethren Church, and Bishop Lloyd C. Wicke, of The Methodist Church, joined hands at the constituting General Conference in Dallas, Texas, and said, "Lord of the Church, we are united in Thee, in Thy Church and now in The United Methodist Church."

A merger seemed to make good sense in view of the fact that both shared similar doctrines, had similar books of discipline, and their preachers often spoke in each other's pulpits. These two denominations themselves had been the result of earlier mergers in Methodist history.

When founded, the denomination had some 11 million members. Today it has less than 8.3 million. Membership has declined significantly in the United States and Europe, though it has increased in Africa and Asia.

Beliefs

Bible. Scripture is the primary source and criterion for Christian doctrine. Scripture is an authority in matters of faith. It reveals all humans need to know about salvation. High value is given to human reason, for it is by reason that one reads and interprets the Bible.

God. The one true and living God is everlasting, infinitely powerful, all-wise, and all-good. He is the Creator and Sustainer of the universe. Within the unity of the one God are three persons of equal substance, power, and eternity: the Father, the Son, and the Holy Spirit.

Jesus Christ. Jesus is eternal deity and is of the same substance as the Father. In the Incarnation, Jesus took on a human nature so that in one person, there was a perfect unity of very God and very man. Jesus truly suffered, was crucified, died a sacrificial and atoning death on our behalf, and was buried. He rose from the dead, thereby triumphing over evil and death.

Holy Spirit. The Holy Spirit is the third person of the Trinity.

Sin and Salvation. Man is fallen in sin, having broken his covenant with God, and is therefore estranged from Him. God truly loves us despite our willful sin. Salvation is provided in and through Jesus Christ. God summons us to repentance, seeking to pardon us, desiring to receive into fellowship those who respond to the grace given to us in Jesus Christ.

Prevenient grace is available to all humanity, which makes acceptance of God possible. Through faith in Jesus Christ we are forgiven, reconciled to God, and transformed as people of the new covenant. One's justification and conversion may be sudden and dramatic, or it may be gradual and cumulative.

Christians can have an assurance of salvation when the Holy Spirit bears witness with our spirit that we are children of God. It is possible, however, for Christians to depart from grace and fall into sin. They can be restored only by repentance and turning back to God, as enabled by God's grace.

Church. United Methodists confess one holy, catholic, and apostolic church. They understand themselves to be a part of Christ's universal church. The local church is the community of believers, which the Spirit has brought into existence for the healing of nations. The church should be a community in which all persons, regardless of racial and ethnic background, can participate in every level of its connectional life and ministry. One is initiated and incorporated into this community of faith by baptism.

Church government involves a hierarchy of conferences: Annual Conferences (divided into districts), Jurisdictional Conferences (encompassing certain geographical areas), and the General Conference (the main legislative body).

Women are welcome to participate at all levels of church life, including pastoral positions. Presently, 17 percent of ordained clergy are women.

Sacraments. Baptism is a sacrament that initiates a covenant that connects God, the church (faith community), and the believer being baptized. The mode can be sprinkling, pouring, or immersion.

The Lord's Supper is a sacrament of redemption. People who partake of the elements spiritually receive the body and blood of

Christ. Communion may be celebrated as often as desired and is open to all Christians.

End Times. Jesus will one day return in glory to judge humankind. All humanity will be resurrected from the dead—the righteous to eternal life, and the unrighteous to endless condemnation.

Distinctives. Similar to other Methodist bodies, this denomination espouses a doctrine of sanctification whereby those who are born again can be cleansed from sin in their thoughts, words, and deeds. They are enabled to live in full accordance to God's will. All Christians should therefore strive for holiness, without which no one will see God.

Website

www.umc.org

14

ORTHODOX CHURCHES

THE ORTHODOX CHURCH, ONE OF the three major branches of Christianity, includes the national churches of Russia, the Ukraine, Bulgaria, Albania, Romania, Serbia, Greece, and Cyprus. These Orthodox churches agree on doctrinal essentials, but each has unique cultural and historical distinctives. Presently there are more than 200 million Orthodox believers around the world.

The word *orthodox* has two meanings among Orthodox believers. First, the word means "true glory." Church members believe the primary purpose in life is to give glory to God, which includes a worshipful attitude. The heart of such worship, for the Orthodox believer, is the Eucharist. The Lord Jesus is believed to be mystically present in the sanctified elements, and when participants receive them, their bond is deepened with each other and with Christ.

A second meaning of *orthodox* is "true doctrine" or "straight teaching." Orthodox believers claim to live in continuity with the first-century church and the teachings of the original apostles. They believe they have been uniquely guided by the Holy Spirit in preserving and teaching the authentic Christian faith, free from man-made additions, distortions, and innovations.

The Orthodox church has a rich history. Christianity, after its founding, soon spread far beyond the boundaries of Jerusalem, eventually moving into Hellenized (Greek) Gentile cultures, including Greece, Syria, Egypt, and Asia Minor. By the middle of the second century, Christianity spread into the Coptic and Syriac subcultures.

The Greek Fathers played a foundational role in the doctrine and practice of the Orthodox church. Included in this group are such notables as Athanasius (328–373), John Chrysostom (344–407), Cyril of Alexandria (412–444), Basil the Great (of Caesarea) (330–379), Gregory the Theologian (of Nazianzus) (330–390), and Gregory of Nyssa (d. 394). Among Orthodox believers, the writings of these Fathers are considered to be a part of tradition, just as the Bible is—and therefore both are authoritative.

History documents that the early Christian church was a martyr's church. Christians were persecuted and martyred by one Roman emperor after another. All this changed, however, with the reign of Constantine (280–337). As a Christian himself, Constantine gave legitimacy—and protection—to Christianity. He also called the first ecumenical council of the Christian church in A.D. 325.

Constantine had an agenda in calling this council. At the time, Christians were experiencing significant divisions regarding doctrine and practice. Because this was not good for the empire, Constantine desired to bring unity to the church. He attempted to settle Christian differences by calling a council, inviting church leaders to assemble in his presence to agree upon and clearly define correct doctrine and tradition. His reasoning was that if church leaders could be brought to unity, the people who followed them would soon imitate their example. He determined that whatever these church leaders decided by consensus, he would proclaim as law.

While Constantine's strategy seemed sound, the reality was that heresies continued to emerge in early church history, and more councils eventually became necessary following Constantine's time. The second ecumenical council—the First Council of Constantinople (381)—was convened by Theodosius I to confirm victory over Arianism, a heresy that denied the Trinity and the full deity of Jesus. The third ecumenical council—the Council of Ephesus (431)—was convened by Theodosius II to deal with the Nestorian heresy, which argued that the divine and human natures in Christ were not united.

The fourth ecumenical council—the Council of Chalcedon (451)—was held in response to the Monophysite faction (who believed the humanity of Jesus was absorbed into God's divinity, thereby making Jesus solely divine). The council affirmed the doctrinally orthodox position that Jesus in the Incarnation was wholly divine *and* wholly human in one person.

This council also affirmed five official centers of Christianity: Rome, Constantinople, Alexandria, Antioch, and Jerusalem, each headed by a bishop or "patriarch." The Patriarch of Rome (in the West) was considered the first among equals. Significantly for the Orthodox Church, the Patriarch of Constantinople (in the East) eventually attained the status of *second* among equals.

The fifth ecumenical council—the Second Council of Constantinople (553)—was convened by Justinian I to settle a dispute involving moderate Monophysites. The sixth ecumenical council—the Third Council of Constantinople (680)—was convened by Constantine IV to deal with Monotheletism (the view that Christ had only one will). The council affirmed that Christ had two wills, with the human will subject to the divine. The seventh ecumenical council—the Second Council of Nicaea (787)—was convened by Byzantine Empress Irene to refute iconoclasm, which prohibited the use of images in worship.

Meanwhile, out of the five centers of Christianity mentioned earlier, only Rome (the West) and Constantinople (the East) were destined to remain in power. By the early to mid seventh century, the other three centers diminished as a result of being overcome by Islamic armies.

The East-West Split. During these years the division between the Western and Eastern churches increased. Cultural differences were unavoidable because the East was Greek in speech and attitude, and the West was Latin and Roman in speech and attitude. Political differences and doctrinal disagreements also widened the divide for years. Western theology had been heavily influenced by Augustine of Hippo (354–430), while Eastern theology was influenced by the Greek Fathers.

Another bone of contention related to the so-called Filioque clause. Recall that in John 15:26, Jesus said, "When the Counselor comes, whom I will send to you *from the Father*, the Spirit of truth who goes out *from the Father*, he will testify about me" (italics added). Based on this verse, the original Nicene Creed noted that the Holy Spirit proceeds from the Father. However, the Western church added the Filioque clause to the original text. *Filioque* is a Latin term meaning "and the Son." Hence, the Western version of the Nicene Creed says the Holy Spirit proceeds from the Father *and the Son*. The Eastern church rejected this insertion because John 15:26 provides no warrant for it. This issue caused a rift between the Roman Pope Leo IX (1049–1054) and the Patriarch of Constantinople, Michael Caerularius (1043–1058).

Further friction emerged due to the consensus that soon developed in the Western church that the *entire* church should be ruled by a single ecclesiastical institution with a single head (the Roman pope). Understandably, Michael Caerularius, Constantinople's patriarch, would not go along with this consensus. In A.D. 1054 the estrangement between the two churches became permanent when the Roman Catholic pope and Constantinople's patriarch excommunicated each other and their followers. From this point forward, the Roman Catholic church of the West and the Orthodox church of the East have remained separate wings of Christianity. *Emergence in the United States.* Fast-forward to the eighteenth century. In 1741, the Russians discovered Alaska, and the Church of Russia (part of the Orthodox church) founded a Christian mission there in 1794. About a century later, in 1891, a single Orthodox congregation was founded in San Francisco. The Orthodox church had a humble beginning in the United States.

The late nineteenth century, however, brought a massive immigration of Orthodox believers from Greece, Russia, the Balkans, Asia Minor, and the Middle East. During this time, various national Orthodox churches exploded on American soil. These churches enabled the immigrants to keep connection with their homeland, language, and customs, even while adjusting to their new environment. Today there are some five million Orthodox believers in the United States.

Beliefs

Nicene Creed. The Nicene Creed is at the very heart of Orthodox theology. It is recited whenever the Orthodox liturgy is celebrated.

Rejection of Roman Catholic Doctrines. Orthodox believers reject distinctive Roman Catholic doctrines, including the pope as the sole vicar of Christ on earth, papal infallibility, the immaculate conception of Mary, the bodily assumption of Mary, the treasury of merits of the saints, indulgences, and purgatory.

The Bible and Tradition. For Orthodox believers, authority is rooted in tradition. *Tradition* refers to that which has been passed on and given over from the time of the apostles to the present. It is believed to include the Bible, the decisions of the seven ecumenical councils (especially the Nicene Creed), the writings of the Greek Fathers, the writings of the Latin Fathers prior to the eleventh century, and the testimony of the divine liturgies. The Bible is important, but it is viewed as a book *of* the church to be interpreted *by* the church. After all, both the Old and New Testaments emerged within the context of the believing community (the church) and thus can only be understood within the context of that believing community. The Orthodox church is viewed as the guardian, custodian, and interpreter of Holy Scripture.

God. God is almighty, faithful and true, and absolutely holy. He is characterized by goodness, truth, love, wisdom, knowledge, unity, purity, joy, and simplicity. An important emphasis in Orthodox theology is that God is a *mystery* who is utterly transcendent and wholly beyond the reach of finite human minds. He is "wholly other," and His true essence cannot even begin to be captured in finite human words. In view of this, the very contemplation of God involves wonder, marvel, and awe. Although God in His essence is beyond human comprehension, He can be known in the context of His activities in the midst of the faith community. He can be known *experientially* as He acts in concrete historical situations.

The Orthodox church affirms the doctrine of the Trinity—that is, there is one true God, and within the unity of the Godhead, the Father, Son, and Holy Spirit are distinct persons who share the same divine essence or substance. There is one "what" (divine essence) and three "whos" (persons). Each is related to the others in a bond of love. Each shares in the presence and activities of the others. No person of the Trinity acts independently of or in isolation from the others.

Jesus Christ. Jesus is Lord, Savior, and Messiah. He is the only-begotten Son of God, of one essence with the Father. The Incarnation of Jesus is the core event of divine revelation. He was born of the Virgin Mary by the power of the Holy Spirit. Absolute deity was united with full humanity (body, soul, mind, and will) so that both maintained their distinct characteristics, all the while being brought together in a single person: the God-man, Jesus Christ. Anyone who denies either the absolute deity or the full humanity of Jesus is outside the confines of Orthodoxy. After dying on the cross, Jesus rose from the dead on the third day and ascended into heaven, where He now sits at the right hand of the Father.

The Holy Spirit. The Holy Spirit, the third person of the Trinity, is the Lord and Giver of life. He proceeds from the Father and is of the same divine essence as the Father and the Son. He seeks to manifest Jesus to every person in every age. He also seeks to unite believers to Christ, enabling them to share in the divine nature and empowering them to love.

The Church. The Orthodox church considers itself the one true church on earth. Church members view their church as the only Christian church that has been kept pure and undefiled from heresy. It is viewed as the kingdom of God on earth, glorifying God with its correct doctrine and correct worship.

There is no single overarching governing body of the church, as is the case in Roman Catholicism. Each expression of the Orthodox tradition—whether the Greek Orthodox, the Russian Orthodox, the Ukrainian Orthodox, or some other jurisdiction—has its own bishop who is independent of all other orthodox bishops. Each national body is said to have its own "autocephalous hierarchy." (*Autocephalous* refers to being governed by one's own head bishops.) In each, there is a synod of bishops overseen by an elected archbishop.

There are three orders in ministry: deacons, priests, and bishops. Deacons assist priests in parish work and in administering the sacraments. Priests carry on the work of ministry in local parishes. They are allowed to get married before ordination, but marriage is forbidden following ordination. Bishops are chosen from among monastic communities and live under a life-long vow of poverty, chastity, and obedience.

Unique to Orthodox worship is its liturgy, which celebrates Christ's incarnation, crucifixion, and resurrection. Through participating in Orthodox liturgy, one communicates with God, learns about God and His ways, and even becomes more God-like. The liturgy makes use of many varied artistic expressions, including unique architecture, icons (of revered persons and events), music, incense (representing prayers), candles, sculptures, poetry, and the like. By making use of such artistic expressions, one *experiences* God in worship, *experiences* the kingdom of God on earth, and moves from the external realm of the material world to the inner world of spiritual mystery.

The Sacraments. The seven sacraments are also called mysteries: baptism, chrismation, holy communion, marriage, anointing the sick, confession, and holy orders. Baptism celebrates Christ's death and resurrection, and participants become regenerated (baptismal regeneration). Chrismation is the same as confirmation. During this ritual, the participant receives the seal of the gift of the Holy Spirit.

Holy communion, or the Eucharist, is the sacrament of sacraments and mystery of mysteries. It is believed that the Holy Spirit descends on the elements of the bread and wine by liturgical invocation. At consecration by the Holy Spirit through the priest, the elements are mystically changed into the body and blood of Jesus. Those who participate share a banquet of the kingdom of God. Only those committed to Christ in the Orthodox church through baptism and chrismation may participate.

In the sacrament of marriage, human love is transformed into divine love, and one's union is sanctified and made eternal. In the sacrament of anointing the sick, human suffering is consecrated with Christ's suffering. In the sacrament of confession, believers repent and receive forgiveness. In the sacrament of holy orders, continuity is maintained in the church from the first century to the present in terms of its bishops.

Sin and Salvation. The sin of humanity's first parents does not pass on a sinful, corrupt nature to human beings. There is no inherited guilt. Children remain innocent until they personally choose to sin. However, the very fact of becoming mortal invariably brings about sin. Sinfulness is a *consequence* of mortality. By becoming mortal, humans ultimately have a greater yearning for sin because they now have appetites and bodily needs that must be satisfied. As a result of the sin human beings individually commit, a barrier is erected between them and God that they cannot cross by their own efforts.

Since human beings cannot possibly do away with this barrier by their own self-efforts, God made a path to humanity via the Incarnation of Jesus. The Incarnation reopens the bridge to God for human beings.

A key aspect of salvation in Orthodox theology involves Christians sharing in the divine nature with God. In this view, God shared fully in human life through the Incarnation so that believers might be enabled to share fully in the divine life. This is called "deification" *(theosis).* The idea is that "God became man so that man might become God." This does not mean humans actually become God *ontologically* (so that the Trinity is no longer a Trinity but encompasses innumerable persons within the Godhead). Rather it has to do with the believer being transfigured into the image and likeness of God through a life of virtue that is rooted in one's personal relationship with Jesus Christ.

The backdrop to this idea is the teaching in Genesis that humans were created in the image and likeness of God. As a result of the fall, humans lost their likeness to God but still remain in possession of the image of God. This image includes humanity's rationality and freedom. The Orthodox church teaches that Christians are presently in the process of seeking a restoration of the lost likeness. This likeness involves assimilation to God through Christian virtue and hinges on our moral choices. By following the teachings of the Orthodox church, people can be restored in their God-likeness. This likeness is a goal toward which human beings must perpetually aim.

End Times. Christ will one day come again to judge the living and the dead. Those who reject God's gift of life in communion with God are allowed to experience the fruit of their choice—that is, living eternally with the devil and his angels. For those who love the Lord, His presence will be infinite joy, paradise, and eternal life.

ORTHODOX CHURCH IN AMERICA
Founded: 1970
Members: 1,000,000
Congregations: 725

Beginnings

Princess Olga, a Christian ruler over Kiev, was baptized in the Orthodox faith in A.D. 875. Her high-profile commitment to Orthodoxy caused the Orthodox church to become widely known throughout the Ukraine, the center of the original Russian state. Her grandson, Vladimir the Great, eventually accepted Orthodox Christianity in A.D. 988 and commanded that all in his kingdom do the same. His religious proclamation caused Orthodoxy to become the official religion throughout the Ukraine. It was only a matter of time before Orthodoxy spread throughout the rest of Russia.

As noted earlier, the Russian Orthodox church eventually penetrated American soil via Alaska. In 1794, eight Orthodox missionaries from Russia traveled to Alaska (then a part of Russia) and made a profound impact on the native Alaskan population, bringing many to the Orthodox Christian faith. In 1840, a Russian Orthodox bishop was assigned to the area.

The United States purchased Alaska from Russia in 1867. Within five years (1872), the seat of orthodoxy moved from Alaska to San Francisco. At that time, the church was known as the Russian Orthodox Greek Catholic Church of America. Parishes soon emerged throughout the United States. The denomination thrived as a result of immigrants pouring in from central, eastern, and southern Europe, as well as the Middle East, in the late nineteenth and early twentieth centuries. In 1905, the headquarters for the denomination relocated to New York City.

The denomination reached a milestone in 1970 when the patriarch of Moscow (His Holiness Alexis) granted the Russian Orthodox church in America the freedom to operate as an independent, indigenous body. At this time the name of the denomination changed to the Orthodox Church in America. The denomination then invited all the various national Orthodox church jurisdictions to join with it in unity. The denomination now embraces the Romanian Orthodox Episcopate, the Albanian Orthodox Archdiocese, and the Bulgarian Orthodox Diocese.

Beliefs

The beliefs and practices of the Orthodox Church in America are in keeping with those of other Orthodox Christians, holding firmly to the Nicene Creed. (See the earlier discussion of the beliefs of Orthodox churches.)

Website

www.oca.org

ANTIOCHIAN ORTHODOX CHRISTIAN ARCHDIOCESE OF NORTH AMERICA

Founded: 1895
Members: 70,000
Congregations: 230

Beginnings

Antioch has an interesting biblical history. It was a strategic city in the Roman province of Syria, and it was one of the first cities to be evangelized by the apostles. It was also the city in which believers in Jesus were first called "Christians" (Acts 11:26). This occurred around A.D. 42, about a decade after Christ died on the cross and was resurrected from the dead. The followers of Jesus had previously referred to themselves by such terms as "brothers" (Acts 15:1,23), "disciples" (Acts 9:26), "believers" (Acts 2:44), and "saints" (Romans 8:27). But now, in Antioch, they are called Christians. In view of the "ian" ending (meaning "belonging to the party of"), the Antiochians apparently viewed Christians as "those who belonged to the party of Christ."

We noted earlier that the fourth ecumenical council—the Council of Chalcedon (A.D. 451)—affirmed the five official centers of Christianity: Rome, Constantinople, Alexandria, Antioch, and Jerusalem, each headed by a bishop or "patriarch." Christianity obviously became a stronghold in Antioch, and the form of Christianity that took root there was of the Orthodox variety.

Fast-forward to the late nineteenth century. During this time, large numbers of Antiochian Christians immigrated to North America. They first affiliated with the Syro-Arabian Mission of the Russian Orthodox church (Arabic became the language of Antioch early in its history). Then, in 1895, a Syrian Orthodox Benevolent Society was established by Antiochian immigrants in New York City. Dr. Ibrahim Arbeely, a prominent Damascene physician, served as its first president. This marks the beginning of what would eventually evolve into the Antiochian Orthodox Christian Archdiocese of North America.

Arbeely used his skills of persuasion to convince Raphael Hawaweeny, both a clergyman and a professor of the Arabic language in Russia, to relocate to New York City to establish and pastor an Arabic-speaking Orthodox church. Hawaweeny met the challenge, came to New York City, and was promptly consecrated as an Orthodox bishop in 1904. He was a man with a mission and engaged in wide travels across the United States, gathering scattered immigrants into Orthodox parishes. He also published liturgical books in Arabic for use in these Antiochian Orthodox parishes.

For a time the denomination suffered a rupture as a result of various factors, including the emergence of World War I in 1914, the sudden, premature death of Hawaweeny in 1915, and the Russian revolution in 1917. These factors brought financial and administrative chaos to the Orthodox churches in the United States and caused the various ethnic Orthodox churches to divide into ecclesiastical factions. It would take some 60 years before the rupture was healed. In 1975, Metropolitan* Philip Saliba of the Antiochian Archdiocese of New York and Metropolitan Michael Shaheen of the Antiochian Archdiocese of Toledo (Ohio) signed Articles of Reunification. This brought restored unity to the Antiochian Orthodox Christians in the United States and Canada.

Today the mission of the Antiochian Orthodox Christian Archdiocese of North America is to bring America to the ancient Orthodox Christian faith. In so doing, they seek to join and cooperate with other Orthodox jurisdictions.

Beliefs

The beliefs and practices of the Antiochian Orthodox Christian Archdiocese of North America are in keeping with those of

---
* Presiding bishop

other Orthodox Christians, holding firmly to the Nicene Creed. (See the earlier discussion of the beliefs of Orthodox churches.)

Website

www.antiochian.org

SERBIAN ORTHODOX CHURCH IN THE USA AND CANADA

Founded: 1921
Members: More than 65,000
Congregations: 140

Beginnings

Cyril (d. 869) and Methodius (d. 884) were brothers and Greek missionaries who were sometimes referred to as "apostles to the Slavs." Christianity emerged in the ninth century among the Serbian people due to the efforts of these brothers.

As the Serbian Orthodox church grew, it was difficult for its members to maintain independence and autonomy. From the time of the Serbian church's founding until the early thirteenth century, the Patriarchate of Constantinople maintained control over it. In 1219, however, the church managed to attain independence and autonomy from Constantinople's control under the leadership of Archbishop St. Sava.

The freedom was short-lived. From the fourteenth through the early nineteenth centuries, the Serbian people found themselves under the control of Muslim Turks, and the church understandably suffered severe persecution during this time. In the nineteenth century, Muslim control weakened, and the Serbian church was revived.

A massive immigration of Serbians into the United States began in 1890, primarily motivated by a less-than-desirable political climate in their homeland. Finding no already existing Serbian churches, these immigrants initially worshipped in Russian Orthodox churches. In 1892, Archimandrite* Firmilian arrived in America and began to organize Serbian Orthodox churches, first in Jackson, California, and then in Chicago, in Douglas, Alaska, and in McKeesport, Steelton, and Pittsburgh, Pennsylvania. All these parishes remained under the jurisdiction of the Russian Orthodox church.

Almost three decades later, in 1921, the Serbians separated from the Russian Orthodox church and the Serbian Orthodox Diocese in the USA and Canada was formally organized, with the full approval of the Serbian Patriarchate of Yugoslavia. Five years later, in 1926, the Serbian church consecrated its first American bishop, Archimandrite Mardary Uskokovich.

In 1963, the Serbian Orthodox Diocese in the USA and Canada eventually reorganized into three separate dioceses: the Diocese of the Eastern United States and Canada, the Diocese of the Mid-West United States, and the Diocese of the Western United States. In 1983, a separate diocese was created for Canada alone.

Despite the autonomy of the Serbian church, it still maintains hierarchical and spiritual ties to the Serbian Orthodox Patriarchate in Belgrade.

Beliefs

The Serbian Orthodox Church in the USA and Canada agrees doctrinally with other Orthodox churches. (See the earlier discussion of the beliefs of Orthodox churches.)

Website

www.serbian-church.net

---

* Superintendent, or superior abbot.

GREEK ORTHODOX ARCHDIOCESE OF NORTH AMERICA

Founded: 1922
Members: More than 1,500,000
Congregations: 555

Beginnings

The Greek Orthodox Archdiocese of North America is one of the largest Orthodox religious bodies in America. The Christian church emerged in Greece in the earliest years of Christianity. Indeed, as noted earlier, Christianity quickly spread beyond the boundaries of Jerusalem, soon moving into various Hellenized (Greek) Gentile cultures, including Greece, which became a vital center of Christianity.

The Greek Orthodox church penetrated North America when a small Greek Orthodox colony was set up near St. Augustine, Florida, in 1768. About a century later, in 1864, some Greek merchants founded Holy Trinity Church (a Greek Orthodox church) in New Orleans.

After these humble beginnings, the Greek Orthodox church in America experienced an explosive influx of immigrants from Greece and Asia Minor from 1880 to about 1920. This caused a significant escalation in the number of Greek Orthodox parishes in the United States. The number of Greek Orthodox parishes grew from 35 in 1910 to 150 by 1920. Overseeing each of these parishes were priests who came to the United States with the approval of either the Patriarchate of Constantinople or the Church of Greece.

Why two different sources of authority? A confusing shift of authority occurred from 1908 to 1922. First, the Greek Orthodox churches in America were under the supervision of the Patriarchate of Constantinople. But this authority was transferred to the Church of Greece, perhaps due to the political instability among the Balkans. Meanwhile, by 1922, the Greek Orthodox Archdiocese had been formally incorporated in New York City during a visit of the Metropolitan Meletios from Athens. That same year, after Meletios was elected as the new Patriarchate of Constantinople, he reversed the 1908 decision and restored the jurisdiction of the Greek Orthodox Church in America back to the Patriarchate of Constantinople.

In any event, the new denomination experienced significant growth due to the efforts of Archbishop Spyrou of Corfu, who became the head of the Greek Orthodox church in America in 1931. Under his leadership, the denomination grew to include more than 280 parishes.

Since 1999, Archbishop Demetrios, the sixth archbishop of the denomination, has led the church in America. The denomination remains under the broad jurisdiction of the Ecumenical Patriarchate of Constantinople.

Beliefs

The beliefs and practices of the Greek Orthodox Archdiocese of North America are in keeping with those of other Orthodox Christians, holding firmly to the Nicene Creed. (See the earlier discussion of the beliefs of Orthodox churches.)

Website

www.goarch.org

UKRAINIAN ORTHODOX CHURCH OF THE USA

Founded: 1924
Members: 8000
Congregations: 115

Beginnings

Ancient tradition reveals that the apostle Andrew made his way to what is now Kiev, the capital of the Ukraine, and preached the gospel there. It would be many centuries later, however, before Christianity took a firm root in this part of the world. As noted earlier, in A.D. 875, Princess Olga, a Christian ruler over Kiev, was baptized in the Orthodox faith. Her high-profile commitment to orthodoxy caused the Orthodox Church to become widely known throughout the Ukraine. Her grandson, Vladimir the Great, also accepted Orthodox Christianity (in 988) and commanded that all in his kingdom do the same.

Almost a millennium later (the early 1920s), the Ukrainian church found its way to American soil through immigrants. Metropolitan John Teodorovych arrived in America in 1924 and became the first bishop of the Ukrainian Orthodox church in America. He had been consecrated in the episcopate a few years earlier in Kiev (1921) and shepherded the Ukrainian Orthodox Church of the USA until he died in 1971. Following his death, the Archbishop Mstyslav, who immigrated to the United States in 1950, shepherded the church until his death in 1993. Metropolitan Constantine then took over the reins.

Today the Ukrainian Church of the USA has churches in 25 states in the United States.

Beliefs

The beliefs and practices of the Ukrainian Orthodox Church of the USA are in keeping with those of other Orthodox Christians, holding firmly to the Nicene Creed. (See the earlier discussion of the beliefs of Orthodox churches.) One distinction is that this denomination stresses that music in the church should be strictly vocal and not instrumental.

Website

www.uocofusa.org.

15

PENTECOSTAL CHURCHES

PENTECOSTALISM IS A TWENTIETH-CENTURY movement that takes its name from the Holy Spirit's working on the day of Pentecost in Acts 2. Proponents of the movement believe the same phenomena depicted in Acts—that is, a baptism of the Holy Spirit accompanied by the gift of speaking in tongues—should be normative in the church today.

The Pentecostal movement has its roots in the holiness movement, which emphasized the "second blessing" or "second work of grace" called entire sanctification. In this theology, people first get saved—that is, they are justified and born again. Following this, they experience a period of growth in which they progressively become more holy in daily living. This ultimately culminates in a "second work of grace" whereby the Holy Spirit cleanses their heart of original sin, literally eradicating all inbred sin, and then imparts His indwelling presence to them, empowering them to live the Christian life in perfection. This is the baptism of the Holy Spirit. It happens instantaneously as believers present themselves as living sacrifices to God with an attitude of full consecration. Pentecostals took this doctrine of the "second blessing" or "second work of grace" and related it to empowerment by the Holy Spirit, evidenced by speaking in tongues.

Modern Pentecostalism began in Topeka, Kansas, in 1901. In January of that year, a young woman named Agnes Ozman—a student at Bethel Bible College—spoke in tongues while at the church of Holiness minister and evangelist Charles Fox Parham (1873–1929). Three days later, Parham himself spoke in tongues. The movement soon spread from Kansas to Houston, Texas, where Parham opened a Pentecostal school. An African-American holiness minister named William J. Seymour (1870–1922) attended the school and, after studying the apostle Paul's epistles, became convinced that Parham's views were correct. Parham and Seymour agreed on three basic works of grace in the life of the believer: (1) salvation, (2) sanctification, and (3) empowerment. This empowerment is from the Holy Spirit and is evidenced by supernatural manifestations such as speaking in tongues. Seymour insisted that the gift of tongues was the true test of being filled with the Spirit.

Seymour then went to California, where the famous Azusa Street revival broke out in Los Angeles from 1906 to 1909. This revival, led by Seymour, received some unexpected publicity. Seymour had warned the people that if they did not repent and turn to God, God would judge them. One week later, a powerful earthquake hit San Francisco, and suddenly Pentecostalism was bigtime news. Thousands of people from around the United States traveled to Azusa Street and then carried the Pentecostal message back to their communities.

Out of the Azusa Street revival emerged a number of different Pentecostal churches and groups, including the Pentecostal Holiness Church, the Church of God in Christ, the Church of God (Cleveland, Tennessee), the Apostolic Faith (Portland, Oregon), the Assemblies of God, the International Church of the Foursquare Gospel, and the Full Gospel Business Men's Fellowship. One of the reasons various new denominations emerged was that those who spoke in tongues were no longer welcome in many traditional (non-Pentecostal) churches.

In the 1960s and 1970s, however, the Pentecostal experience started to penetrate some mainline churches and crossed denominational lines. Such churches experienced what became known as the charismatic renewal movement. A case in point is the Pentecostal outbreak that took place at (Roman Catholic) Duquesne University. A course had been offered that focused on how to restore spirituality. Required textbooks included *The Cross and the Switchblade* by David Wilkerson and *They Speak with Other Tongues* by John L. Sherrill—both of which are Pentecostal in nature. Soon, people on campus were speaking in tongues. Since then, the movement has grown phenomenally in the Catholic Church. In 1973, some 30,000 Catholic Pentecostals had a conference at Notre Dame University (a Catholic university) entitled, "How to Speak in Tongues." By 1980, Pentecostalism had penetrated Catholic churches in over 100 countries around the world.

In what follows, I will narrow my attention to some of the more prominent Protestant Pentecostal denominations that have emerged on American soil.

ASSEMBLIES OF GOD, THE GENERAL COUNCIL OF

Founded: 1914
Members: More than 2,600,000
Congregations: 12,100

Beginnings

As noted above, a primary problem for many who experienced the Pentecostal phenomenon of speaking in tongues was that they were not welcomed into fellowship by many established churches. Soon, participants in the Pentecostal movement found themselves without an existing religious body with which to affiliate. This led to the emergence of hundreds of distinctly Pentecostal congregations around the country.

In time, the need developed for formal recognition of ministers, the approval and support of missionaries, the production of gospel literature in keeping with Pentecostal beliefs, proper Bible training, and the like. Concerned leaders in the Pentecostal movement decided that to protect and preserve the precious revival of the Spirit that so many had experienced, they should unite into a cooperative fellowship. In 1914, some 300 preachers and lay people from 20 states met in Hot Springs, Arkansas. A cooperative fellowship emerged out of that meeting and was incorporated under the name The General Council of the Assemblies of God. Most of the leaders at the meeting had no interest in forming a new denomination, so they purposefully structured the fellowship to provide unity but allow local churches to be self-governing and self-supporting. This small meeting of 300 people eventually mushroomed into more than 2.6 million people in the United States and more than 48 million people overseas.

Beliefs

Bible. The Bible is the verbally inspired Word of God. It is the infallible, authoritative rule of faith and conduct.

God. The one true God is the Creator and Redeemer of humankind. In the perfect unity of the one God are three persons: the Father, the Son, and the Holy Spirit. The Father is the Begetter, the Son is the Begotten, and the Holy Spirit is the one proceeding from the Father and the Son.

Jesus Christ. Jesus is fully divine. He is the eternal Son of God. In the Incarnation, He was fully God and fully man. He lived a sinless life and performed many miracles, thereby attesting to His identity. He died a substitutionary death on the cross, rose bodily from the dead, and ascended into heaven, where He is now exalted at the right hand of the Father.

Holy Spirit. All believers are entitled to and should seek the promise of the Father—the baptism of the Holy Spirit. With this baptism comes the endowment of power for life and service, an overflowing fullness of the Spirit, a deepened reverence for God, an intensified consecration to God, and a more active love for Christ. This baptism is witnessed by the initial sign of speaking with other tongues as the Spirit gives utterance.

Sin and Salvation. By voluntary transgression, man fell and thereby incurred both physical and spiritual death. Humanity's only hope of redemption is through the blood of Jesus, shed at the cross. Salvation is received through repentance toward God and faith in the Lord Jesus Christ. The two evidences of salvation are the inward direct witness of the Holy Spirit and the outward evidence of a life of righteousness.

Church. The church is the body of Christ and the habitation of God through the Spirit. Each believer, born of the Spirit, is an integral part of the church. The church is called to be an agency of God for evangelizing the world, a corporate body in which human beings may worship God, and a channel of God's purpose to build a body of saints being perfected in the image of His Son.

Church government is congregational at the local level and presbyterial at the national level. The General Council has centralized control over missionary, educational, and ministerial concerns. Women are welcome to participate in all levels of ministry, including ordination to ministry.

Sacraments. All who repent and trust in Christ as Savior and Lord are to be baptized. By this ordinance, believers declare to the world that they have died with Christ and have been raised to newness of life. The Lord's Supper is a symbol of the believer's sharing the divine nature of the Lord Jesus Christ, a memorial of His suffering and death on the cross, and a prophecy of His soon second coming.

End Times. Christ will come one day to rapture His saints. This will be followed by the visible return of Christ, at which time Christ will set up His millennial kingdom and rule for 1000 years. There will be a final judgment. The wicked will be consigned to everlasting punishment in the lake of fire, while believers look forward to a new heavens and a new earth.

Distinctives. Divine healing is an integral part of the gospel. Deliverance from sickness is provided in the atonement.

Website

www.ag.org

FAST FACTS ON
the Healing Debate

Healing *is* in the Atonement	Healing *is not* in the Atonement
Isaiah 53:5 says we are healed through Christ's wounds.	The healing in Isaiah 53:5 is spiritual healing (from sin), not physical healing.
Going to a doctor reveals a lack of faith.	Jesus Himself said, "It is not the healthy who need a doctor, but the sick" (Matthew 9:12).
God's will is that no one becomes sick.	Sometimes God has a purpose in allowing us to go through times of suffering (1 Peter 4:15-19).
God healed people in biblical times.	God allowed Epaphroditus (Philippians 2:25-27), Trophimus (2 Timothy 4:20), Timothy (1 Timothy 5:23), Job (Job 1–2), and Paul (2 Corinthians 12:9) to suffer periods of sickness.
Physical healing is guaranteed in the atonement.	Ultimate physical healing (in the resurrection body) is guaranteed in the atonement.

CHURCH OF GOD
(CLEVELAND, TENNESSEE)

Founded: 1886
Members: 932,024
Congregations: 4564

Beginnings

The Church of God (Cleveland, Tennessee) had a humble beginning in 1886 when eight Christians, under the leadership of Baptist minister R.G. Spurling (1810–1891), gathered at the Barney Creek Meeting House on the Tennessee–North Carolina border. They were not satisfied with formalism and spiritual indifference, and had a deep desire for a closer relationship with Christ. They were not convinced that the churches they attended could be reformed, so they established a new church with the objective of restoring sound scriptural doctrines, encouraging deeper consecration, and promoting evangelism and Christian service. Originally known as "Christian Union" (1886), then the "Holiness Church" (1902), the movement eventually took the name "Church of God" (1907). From the initial eight Christians that met in 1886 grew a movement that is today one of the largest Pentecostal denominations in the world.

Beliefs

Bible. The Bible is verbally inspired, inerrant, and infallible.

God. The one God eternally exists in three persons: the Father, the Son, and the Holy Spirit.

Jesus Christ. Jesus is absolute deity and is the Son of God. In the Incarnation, He was conceived by the Holy Spirit and born of a virgin. At the cross He gave His life as an atoning sacrifice for the sins of the world. He was buried, rose from the dead, and ascended to the right hand of the Father, where He now makes intercession for us.

Holy Spirit. The Holy Spirit ministers among the people of God. The baptism of the Holy Spirit is subsequent to regeneration and a clean heart, and its initial evidence is speaking in tongues.

Sin and Salvation. All have sinned and fall short of the glory of God. Repentance is commanded of God for all and is necessary for the forgiveness of sins. Justification, regeneration, and the new birth are wrought by faith in the blood of Jesus. Sanctification is subsequent to the new birth and takes place through faith in the blood of Jesus, through the Word of God, and by the Holy Spirit. Holiness is God's standard for all His people.

Church. The government of the church is centralized. Authority is vested in the General Assembly, which meets every two years and is made up jointly of ministers and laity. The benefits of centralized government include the uniformity of doctrine and practice, mutual accountability, cooperative decision making, and a united effort in world missions and evangelism. Women can be ordained in the ministry.

Sacraments. Water baptism must be by immersion. It is for all who repent and are committed to following Christ (no infants). It should be performed in the name of the Father, Son, and Holy Spirit. The Lord's Supper is open to all believers. Foot washing is also practiced.

End Times. Jesus will premillennially come again in bodily form. His followers will be caught up to meet Him in the air. Christ will set up His millennial kingdom and reign for 1000 years. All people will be resurrected from the dead—the righteous to eternal life and the wicked to everlasting punishment. Heaven is the final destiny of the righteous. Hell is the final destiny of the wicked.

Website

www.churchofgod.cc

CHURCH OF GOD IN CHRIST

Founded: 1907
Members: 5,499,875
Congregations: 28,988

Beginnings

Charles Harrison Mason was born September 8, 1866, on the Prior Farm near Memphis, Tennessee. His father and mother, Jerry and Eliza Mason, were converted during the days of American slavery and were members of a Missionary Baptist Church.

Charles converted in November of 1878, and in 1893 began work in Christian ministry in a Baptist church in Preston, Arkansas. As he and some of his associates conducted revivals, he found Baptist doors closing because some of the things happening at his revivals seemed extreme (including "theophanic manifestations").

In 1907 Mason decided to visit Azusa Street in Los Angeles, California, where a famous Pentecostal revival had broken out. While there, he had his first experience of speaking in tongues.

> There came a wave of Glory into me and all of my being was filled with the Glory of the Lord…. There came a light which enveloped my entire being above the brightness of the sun. When I opened my mouth to say Glory, a flame touched my tongue which ran down me. My language changed and no word could I speak in my own tongue. Oh! I was filled with the Glory of the Lord. My soul was then satisfied.[1]

That same year Mason called for a meeting in Memphis, Tennessee, of ministers who were enthusiastic about Pentecostal theology. At that meeting he organized a general assembly of the

Church of God in Christ. He was named the general overseer of the assembly and retained this position until his death in 1961. The denomination is the largest African-American Pentecostal organization in the United States.

Beliefs

Bible. The Bible is the Word of God. It is fully inspired and is infallible. It is the only authority in religious matters.

God. The one true God is the Creator of all things in the universe. Within the unity of the Godhead are three persons who are equal in eternity and power: the Father, the Son, and the Holy Spirit.

Jesus Christ. Jesus is the Son of God. He is of the same substance as the Father. In the Incarnation, He took on a human nature and was born of a virgin. He was a "suffering servant" who provided redemption and reconciliation to God by His death on the cross. He then rose from the dead and ascended into heaven.

Holy Spirit. The Holy Spirit proceeds from the Father and Son. He is of the same substance, equal in power and glory, as the Father and the Son. He equips and empowers believers for service. He teaches and guides believers into the truth.

The baptism of the Holy Spirit is an experience subsequent to conversion and sanctification. In the early church, tongue-speaking was the consequence of the baptism in the Holy Spirit. The same experience should be mandatory for all today.

Sin and Salvation. Adam's sin has brought a depraved human nature to all his descendants. Humans are sinful by nature. Being born in sin, humans now need to be born again, sanctified, and cleansed from all sins by the blood of Jesus Christ. Human beings become saved by confessing and forsaking sins and believing on the Lord Jesus Christ. Salvation requires repentance toward God and faith toward the Lord Jesus Christ. One is then born again and adopted into the family of God. The Christian should then go on to claim the inheritance of the sons of God, namely, the baptism of the Holy Spirit.

Church. The church forms a spiritual unity of which Christ is the divine head. The church is animated by the Spirit of Christ and is God's agency for communicating spiritual blessings to believers. This body of believers professes one faith, clings to one hope, and serves one King.

Church government is basically episcopal. An ascending hierarchy includes overseer (pastor), state overseer, and general overseer. The General Assembly is the highest legislative body.

Sacraments. There are three ordinances. Baptism is an outward demonstration that one has already had a conversion experience and has accepted Christ as Savior. Immersion is the preferred mode, for it corresponds to the death, burial, and resurrection of our Lord. It also symbolizes regeneration and purification more than any other mode.

The Lord's Supper symbolizes the Lord's death and suffering for the benefit and in the place of His people. It represents not just the death of Christ but also its effect—giving life, strength, and joy to the soul.

Foot washing is an ordinance that represents how humility characterizes greatness in the kingdom of God. The ceremony should be subsequent to the Lord's Supper.

End Times. Jesus will one day come again personally, visibly, and bodily. Church members hold to premillennial theology.

Distinctives. Divine healing is provided in the atonement.

Website

www.cogic.org

Congregational Holiness Church

Founded: 1921
Members: 9565
Congregations: 190

Beginnings

The Congregational Holiness Church was organized in 1921 as a result of a controversy in Georgia the previous year over the issue of healing in the Pentecostal Holiness Church. Some in the church who believed in divine healing felt that Christians should never need to go to a doctor. Another faction in the church believed in divine healing but felt that medicinal science may be a provision of God that can bring about healing. The controversy escalated, and the leaders of the pro-medicine faction—Watson Sorrow and Hugh Bowling—were removed from the ministerial roll. They promptly withdrew and on January 29, 1921, organized the Congregational Holiness Church. The founding meeting had just 12 churches represented. Today some 190 congregations are affiliated with the denomination.

Beliefs

Bible. The Bible is the inspired Word of God.

God. The one true and living God is the Creator of the universe. The one Godhead includes three persons: the Father, the Son, and the Holy Spirit.

Jesus Christ. Jesus is the Son of God. In the Incarnation, He was virgin born and lived a sinless life. He accomplished a substitutionary atonement at the cross, died, was buried, rose from the dead, and ascended into heaven. He is exalted at the Father's right hand.

Holy Spirit. The Holy Spirit is involved in various ministries among believers in the church. The baptism of the Holy Spirit is evidenced by speaking in tongues as the Spirit gives utterance. There are nine gifts of the Spirit that can be manifested in believers' lives.

Sin and Salvation. Human beings are fallen in sin. Those who repent of sins and believe in Jesus are justified. Those who are faithful to the end will receive eternal redemption. The denomination does not believe in "once in grace always in grace" regardless of conduct.

Church. The bride of Christ is composed of the entire spiritual church. Since this is true, local churches should cooperate—even when they are from different denominations. Women are permitted to be ordained in the ministry.

Church government is congregational. Local churches are grouped into geographical districts, each having a presbytery. The General Conference is the highest ruling body.

Sacraments. There are three sacraments—baptism, the Lord's Supper, and foot washing. Baptism should be performed by an ordained minister, using the mode of immersion, in the name of the Father, the Son, and the Holy Spirit. The Lord's Supper and foot washing should be celebrated by all Christians.

End Times. The rapture of the church is imminent. There will be a personal and premillennial second coming of Jesus. The saved will share Christ's glory forever in heaven. The unsaved will be punished eternally.

Distinctives. Sanctification is a definite work of grace that is subsequent to salvation.

Website

www.chchurch.com

FAST FACTS ON
the Speaking in Tongues Debate

The Case for Speaking in Tongues	The Case Against Speaking in Tongues
Speaking in tongues is an evidence of the baptism of the Holy Spirit (Acts 2:4).	Not all the Corinthians spoke in tongues (1 Corinthians 14:5), but all were baptized (12:13).
Speaking in tongues should be normative among Christians today.	The Holy Spirit bestows spiritual gifts (1 Corinthians 12:11). Not every Christian has every gift.
Speaking in tongues is the test of being filled with the Holy Spirit.	The fruit of the Holy Spirit (Galatians 5:22-23) does not include speaking in tongues. Therefore, Christlikeness does not require speaking in tongues.
Speaking in tongues is a biblical doctrine.	Most of the New Testament writers are silent on tongues. Only three books (Mark, Acts, and 1 Corinthians) mention it.
Speaking in tongues is an inheritance of the sons of God.	There are more important gifts than tongues, and these are to be sought (1 Corinthians 12:28,31).

ELIM FELLOWSHIP

Founded: 1933
Members: 21,000
Congregations: 190

Beginnings

The Elim Fellowship began in 1933 as an informal fellowship of churches, ministers, and missionaries. It developed from the efforts of individuals who had trained at Elim Bible Institute, a school founded by the Reverend and Mrs. Ivan Spencer in 1924 for the training of students for full-time revival ministry. From the beginning, the fellowship has been "Pentecostal in conviction and charismatic in orientation."

Today Elim Fellowship is a worldwide revival fellowship that serves pastors, churches, missionaries, and other Christian ministers. It seeks to provide various forms of assistance to those in ministry and missions, including counseling individuals in ministry, credentialing ministers, establishing new churches, providing mutual accountability, and providing ministry resources. The fellowship also sponsors leadership seminars in the United States and abroad.

Beliefs

Bible. The Bible is the inspired, infallible, and authoritative Word of God.

God. The one God eternally exists in three persons: the Father, the Son, and the Holy Spirit.

Jesus Christ. The fellowship affirms Jesus' full deity, virgin birth, sinless life, miracles, vicarious death and atonement at the cross, bodily resurrection, ascension into heaven, and present priestly ministry.

Holy Spirit. The baptism in the Holy Spirit is evidenced by charismatic gifts and ministries. (As it was on the day of Pentecost, so it should be today.) The Holy Spirit is involved in producing spiritual fruit in believers' lives.

Sin and Salvation. Humanity is sinful and lost. Salvation is provided in Jesus Christ, who atoned for sins at the cross. Regeneration by the Holy Spirit is absolutely essential. Security of salvation is rooted in the keeping power of God.

Church. The church is the bride of Christ. God's design for the church is sanctification, holiness, and the overcoming life. Each local church is autonomous in making decisions. An annual assembly meets in Lima, New York. Women can be credentialed in the Elim Fellowship, though there is diversity of opinion among affiliate churches on the role of women.

Sacraments. Baptism is for believers only and is to be done by immersion. It bears witness to the gospel of Christ's death, burial, and resurrection, and points to the new life we have in Him. The Lord's Supper, when shared by believers, witnesses to the saving power of the gospel and looks forward to Christ's victorious return.

End Times. The second coming of Christ is imminent. The saved will be resurrected to eternal life, and the lost will be resurrected to everlasting punishment. Christ will establish everlasting dominion.

Distinctives. (1) The Elim Fellowship statement of faith specifically stipulates the need for sexual purity among God's people. (2) Divine healing is obtained on the basis of the atonement of Jesus Christ.

Website

www.elimfellowship.org

FELLOWSHIP OF
CHRISTIAN ASSEMBLIES

Founded: 1922
Members: Unknown
Congregations: More than 125

Beginnings

The Fellowship of Christian Assemblies is a family of autonomous, evangelical churches with historical roots in the modern Pentecostal movement. In 1922, some 25 ministers who were affiliated with three Scandinavian-oriented Christian groups decided to come together under a common, informal banner, calling their new fellowship the Independent Assemblies of God. By 1935, 54 pastors and evangelists and 21 foreign missionaries affiliated with the fellowship. The group's first national convention was held in 1936 at Brooklyn, New York.

During the 1940s, turmoil erupted within the group's ranks due to the latter rain movement—a movement that advocated the restoration of the prime role of apostles and prophets today. Some of the churches affiliated with their new fellowship defected to this movement, and this motivated the remaining body of churches to more clearly define their identity and bring about a more cohesive practical cooperation. In 1973, the group adopted a new name—the Fellowship of Christian Assemblies.

Beliefs

Bible. The Bible is the inspired, infallible, and authoritative Word of God.

God. The one God eternally exists in three persons: the Father, the Son, and the Holy Spirit.

Jesus Christ. The fellowship affirms Jesus' full deity, virgin birth, sinless life, miracles, vicarious and atoning death on the cross, bodily resurrection, and ascension to the right hand of the Father.

Holy Spirit. The baptism of the Holy Spirit is an experience distinct from regeneration. The Holy Spirit indwells Christians, enabling them to live godly lives. He supernaturally gifts and empowers the church for its work, life, and worship.

Sin and Salvation. Human beings are sinful and lost. Justification by faith in the atonement of Jesus Christ and regeneration by the Holy Spirit are absolutely essential for salvation.

Church. The prime agency for the work of God's kingdom is the local church functioning under the sovereignty of the Lord Jesus. Local churches in the fellowship are autonomous.

Sacraments. The two ordinances are believer's baptism and the Lord's Supper.

End Times. Jesus will return in power and glory to consummate His kingdom. At the resurrection of all human beings, the saved will be raised to eternal life and the lost unto damnation.

Website

www.foca.org

INDEPENDENT ASSEMBLIES OF GOD INTERNATIONAL

Founded: 1914
Members: Unknown
Congregations: Unknown

Beginnings

The Assemblies of God denomination (see above) was organized in 1914. Among the congregations that did not merge into this Pentecostal body were those consisting of Scandinavian immigrants. A few years later, in 1918, a new organization was founded called the Scandinavian Assemblies of God in the United States of America, Canada and Foreign Lands, and the organization continued under this name from 1918 to 1935. At that time, the organization merged with the Independent Pentecostal Churches, and the new merger was called the Independent Assemblies of God International.

Beliefs

Bible. The Bible is the inspired and infallible Word of God.

God. The one true God is eternally existent in three persons: the Father, the Son, and the Holy Spirit.

Jesus Christ. Jesus was virgin-born. He suffered a vicarious and atoning death at the cross, was bodily resurrected, and ascended into heaven.

Holy Spirit. The baptism of the Holy Spirit is subsequent to regeneration and is evidenced by speaking in tongues. The Holy Spirit enables believers to live holy lives.

Sin and Salvation. Man is fallen in sin. Salvation is through the blood of Christ. People who fall into sin and turn away from God can lose salvation.

Church. Local churches are autonomous and sovereign over their own affairs, but they can voluntarily work together on common ministries. Women are permitted to be ordained in the ministry.

Sacraments. Baptism is by immersion and follows one's conversion to Christ. The Lord's Supper is a memorial of Christ's death on our behalf.

End Times. The second coming of Jesus is imminent. Believers who are alive at Christ's coming will be translated into their bodies of glory, and believers who have fallen asleep (died) will be resurrected. Those who have not accepted Jesus as Savior will experience final judgment. They will suffer for all eternity in the lake of fire.

Distinctives. Divine healing is available through the redemptive work of Christ on the cross.

Website

www.iaogi.org

INTERNATIONAL CHURCH OF THE FOURSQUARE GOSPEL

Founded: 1927
Members: 269,349
Congregations: 1834

Beginnings

The International Church of the Foursquare Gospel was founded by Aimee Semple McPherson (1890–1944). Her mother had been a member of the Salvation Army, and she dedicated Aimee to the ministry. When Aimee was 17, she heard the gospel, was converted, and was baptized in the Holy Spirit. She soon married evangelist Robert Semple, but he died of malaria soon after they went to China in 1910 as missionaries. Once back in the United States, she eventually married Harold McPherson, and they began holding Pentecostal evangelistic meetings. After her divorce from McPherson, she continued in the work of evangelism.

Aimee settled in Los Angeles, California, and in 1923, with help from her supporters and lots of fund-raising efforts, she built and dedicated Angelus Temple, which seats 5300 people. At this temple she used unconventional means to communicate the gospel, including dramas, oratorios, and illustrated messages. A woman of obvious oratory skill, Aimee was soon drawing huge crowds. She often preached the "Foursquare gospel" to the masses: Christ as Savior, Christ as Baptizer with the Holy Spirit, Christ as the Healer, and Christ as the soon-coming King.

Four years after the dedication ceremony of the temple, in 1927, the International Church of the Foursquare Gospel was incorporated in California. It has since grown to embrace nearly 2000 congregations in the United States.

The "Foursquare Gospel": Jesus Christ Is...	
Savior of the World	Isaiah 53:5
Baptizer with the Holy Spirit	Acts 1:5,8
Healer	Matthew 8:17
Soon-Coming King	1 Thessalonians 4:16-17

Beliefs

Bible. The Bible is God-inspired. It is true, immutable, steadfast, and as unchangeable as its author, the Lord Jehovah.

God. The one true God is eternally manifest in three persons: the Father, the Son, and the Holy Spirit.

Jesus Christ. Jesus is full deity. In the Incarnation, He was fully God and fully man, having been conceived by the Holy Spirit and born of a virgin. He bore our sins at the cross by shedding His blood and purchased redemption for all who would believe on Him. Jesus is the Savior, the Baptizer with the Holy Spirit, the Healer, and the soon-coming King.

Holy Spirit. God desires the Christian to walk in dependence on the Holy Spirit daily. Spiritual fruit is an evidence of a Spirit-filled life. The purpose of the baptism in the Holy Spirit is to endue the believer with power to be a witness to the uttermost parts of the earth. The evidence of the baptism in the Holy Spirit is speaking in tongues.

Sin and Salvation. Humanity is fallen in sin. While we were yet sinners, however, Christ died for us, and God pardons all who believe on Him. Upon sincere repentance and a whole-hearted acceptance of Jesus Christ, we are justified before God. God's will is that Christians be sanctified daily and grow in the faith from the moment of conversion. Believers are secure in their salvation so long as they maintain their trust in the Savior. If they apostatize and do not repent, they can fall away from salvation. Yet God's mercy is always available to any who repent and return to God.

Church. Each local church is a subordinate unit of the International Church of the Foursquare Gospel. The pastor is appointed by a Board of Directors and is responsible for the spiritual welfare of the church. Soul-winning is the most important responsibility of the church. Women are (obviously) welcomed to be licensed and ordained in ministry. Presently 30 percent of ordained clergy are women.

The church is governed by a Board of Directors, a Foursquare Cabinet, and an Executive Council. The highest authority is the Annual Foursquare Convention.

Sacraments. Baptism is by immersion, for believers only, and is an outward sign of an inward work. It points to the Lord's death on the cross and our own death to sin. The Lord's Supper is to be celebrated as a commemoration using bread and juice. It serves to remind the participant of the broken body and blood of Christ, shed upon the cross. It should be preceded by a time of self-examination.

End Times. The second coming of Christ will be personal and is imminent. All will stand before God's judgment and receive either eternal life or death. Heaven is the indescribably glorious and joyful eternal home of born-again believers. Hell is the place of eternal torment and deep sorrow for all who reject Jesus as the Savior.

Distinctives. The International Church of the Foursquare Gospel emphasizes that the experience and daily walk of the believer should never lead him into extremes of fanaticism.

Website

www.foursquare.org

INTERNATIONAL PENTECOSTAL HOLINESS CHURCH

Founded: 1911
Members: 209,922
Congregations: 1886

Beginnings

The International Pentecostal Holiness Church emerged from a series of mergers of religious bodies that had been influenced by the Azusa Street revival in Los Angeles, California, in 1906–1907. More specifically, the Fire-Baptized Holiness Church (Iowa) merged with the Pentecostal Holiness Church (Goldsboro, North Carolina) to form the Pentecostal Holiness Church in 1911. Then, in 1915, the Tabernacle Pentecostal Church was added in Canon, Georgia. The church adopted its present name in 1975.

Beliefs

Bible. The Bible is the Word of God and is a full and complete revelation of the plan and history of redemption. It is verbally and entirely inspired.

God. The one true and living God is of infinite power, wisdom, and goodness. He is the Creator and Sustainer of all things. Within the unity of the Godhead are three persons of one substance and eternal being: the Father, the Son, and the Holy Spirit.

Jesus Christ. Jesus is the Son of God. He is of one substance with the Father. He took man's nature in the womb of the Virgin Mary, and so two whole and perfect natures—perfect deity and perfect humanity—were joined together in one person, never to be divided. He was crucified for human sin, rose from the dead, and ascended into heaven.

Holy Spirit. The Holy Spirit proceeds from the Father and the Son. He is of one substance, majesty, and glory with the Father and Son, and is very and eternal God. The Pentecostal baptism of the Holy Spirit is obtainable by a definite act of faith on the part of the fully cleansed believer. The initial evidence of this experience is speaking in tongues as the Spirit gives utterance.

Sin and Salvation. Man is fallen in sin. Jesus shed His blood for the complete cleansing of the justified believer from all indwelling sin and from its pollution. Justification is by faith alone. Salvation is secure unless one willfully rejects the grace of God.

Church. The church is the body of Christ. A primary goal of the church is to carry out the Great Commission. Church government is episcopal. A general board of administration, which includes a bishop and other officers, oversees the affairs of the denomination. Women can be licensed and ordained in the ministry.

Sacraments. Those who repent and unite with a local church on profession of faith shall further confess Christ by receiving water baptism. It is to be administered in the name of the Father, the Son, and the Holy Spirit, preferably by immersion. The Lord's Supper commemorates our redemption by Christ's blood. It is to be administered to all Christians at least once a year. While foot washing is not viewed as an ordinance, church members are free to follow their own conscience regarding whether they wish to observe the practice.

End Times. Believers await an imminent, personal, and premillennial second coming of the Lord Jesus Christ. Eternal life with God in heaven is the destiny of all the finally righteous. Everlasting banishment from God and unending torture in hell comprise the destiny of the persistently wicked.

Distinctives. Sanctification is initiated in regeneration (when one is born again) and is consummated in glorification (when one goes to heaven). However, a definite and instantaneous work of grace in sanctification is achieved by faith and occurs subsequent to regeneration. It delivers the believer from the power and dominion of sin. It is then followed by a lifelong growth in grace and knowledge of Jesus Christ.

Website

www.iphc.org

OPEN BIBLE STANDARD CHURCHES
Founded: 1935
Members: 37,000
Congregations: 482

Beginnings

The Open Bible Standard Churches originated from two revival movements: the Bible Standard Conference, founded in 1919 in Eugene, Oregon, and the Open Bible Evangelistic Association, founded in 1932 in Des Moines, Iowa. These two groups were similar in doctrine and structure, and they amalgamated in

1935 as the Open Bible Standard Churches. Roots of both parent groups go back to the Azusa Street revival that broke out in Los Angeles, California, in 1906.

Beliefs

Bible. The Bible is the inspired Word of God. It is the only infallible guide and rule of faith and practice.

God. The one true God is eternal, all-powerful, all-knowing, everywhere-present, and unchangeable. He is the Creator of all things. In the unity of the Godhead are three persons who are equal in every divine perfection and attribute: the Father, the Son, and the Holy Spirit. They fulfill distinct but complementary roles in the great work of redemption.

Jesus Christ. Jesus is the Son of God. In the Incarnation, He took upon Himself human form, being conceived by the Holy Spirit and born of a virgin. He died on the cross for human sin, reconciling the human race to God. He rose bodily from the dead, ascended into heaven, and is seated at the right hand of the Father, where He makes intercession for us.

Holy Spirit. The Holy Spirit convicts the world of sin, leads believers into all truth, and empowers and equips the church to carry out Christ's work on earth. He indwells every believer at the moment of salvation. The baptism in the Holy Spirit is distinct from salvation and releases the power of the Holy Spirit through faith. Believers should anticipate that the Spirit baptism will be accompanied by speaking in tongues.

Sin and Salvation. Humankind is fallen from its original, created goodness because of the sin of Adam and Eve. However, Jesus shed His blood on the cross to make provision for human salvation. Because humans are not able to save themselves, salvation is by God's grace alone. It is received by faith with repentance and acceptance of Jesus Christ as personal Savior.

Church. Christians should assemble regularly for edification, worship, fellowship, and the proclamation of the gospel. All believers should be involved in the work of ministry in the local church according to their spiritual gifts and should seek the fulfillment of the Great Commission.

Churches are congregationally governed. They are grouped into districts, governed by district superintendents. These districts are grouped into regions, governed by regional superintendents. The highest governing body is the General Convention, which meets biennially.

Sacraments. Baptism should be by immersion in the name of the Father, the Son, and the Holy Spirit. It is an outward sign of an inward work. The Lord's Supper involves partaking of bread and the cup in remembrance of the Lord's death, burial, and resurrection. Open communion is celebrated—meaning it is for all believers, regardless of church affiliation.

End Times. The second coming of Christ will be personal, visible, and triumphant. There will be a final judgment for all unbelievers. Hell is the final destiny of unbelievers and will entail suffering, bitter sorrow, and remorse. Heaven is the final destiny of the saved and is a place of happiness and security.

Distinctives. Healing is provided for in Christ's atonement.

Website

www.openbible.org

VINEYARD CHURCHES INTERNATIONAL

Founded: 1983
Members: Unknown
Congregations: More than 850

Beginnings

The Vineyard Churches International is a group of churches that have collaborated together to advance God's kingdom by communicating the gospel of Jesus Christ. Founded in 1983, the movement's most influential leader in theology and practice has been John Wimber. Wimber had earlier been influenced by theologian George Eldon Ladd, especially in regard to his writings on the kingdom of God. The concept of God's kingdom is at the very heart of Vineyard theology.

Beliefs

Bible. The Bible is inspired and is without error in the original manuscripts. It is our final, absolute authority. It is our only infallible rule of faith and practice.

God. The one true God is our eternal King. He is infinite, unchangeable, Spirit, perfect in holiness, wise, good, just, powerful, and loving. From all eternity He exists as the one living God in three persons of equal substance: the Father, the Son, and the Holy Spirit. God's kingdom is everlasting. Contrary to God's kingdom is Satan, who has sought to usurp God's rule and establish a counter-kingdom of darkness and evil on the earth.

Jesus Christ. God honored His covenants with Israel by sending His Son Jesus into the world. In the Incarnation, He was conceived by the Holy Spirit and born of the Virgin Mary. He inaugurated God's kingdom reign on earth. He overpowered Satan's counter-reign by resisting temptation, healing the sick, casting out demons, raising the dead, and preaching the good news of God's kingdom. His sinless life met the demands of God's law. His atoning death took God's judgment for sin. He rose from the dead, ascended into heaven, and now rules at the right hand of the Father.

Holy Spirit. The Holy Spirit is equal in substance to the Father and the Son. He convicts the world of sin. He was poured out on believers on the day of Pentecost, releasing spiritual gifts to them. All the gifts of the Spirit should be active in the church today, useful for ministry and driving back the kingdom of Satan. The Holy Spirit brings the permanent indwelling presence of God to us. He builds up the church. He is our Helper, Teacher, and Guide.

Sin and Salvation. God created human beings in His image, not only to engage in a relationship with Him but also to govern on earth. Under Satan's temptation, Adam and Eve fell from grace, thereby bringing sin, death, and judgment to the earth. Humans are now born in sin and are captive to Satan's kingdom of darkness. They are under just condemnation from God.

God, however, did not abandon His rule over the earth. He maintained His rule through various covenants made with people throughout biblical history, including Abraham and David. The Davidic covenant, in particular, promised that one of David's heirs would restore God's kingdom reign over His people as Messiah forever. This was fulfilled by Jesus of Nazareth.

Through the preaching of the good news of Jesus and the ministry of the Holy Spirit, those who repent and trust in Jesus as Lord and Savior are regenerated, justified, adopted into God's family, and sanctified. They are thus released from Satan's domain and brought into God's kingdom reign.

Church. There is one, holy, universal church. All who repent of their sins and trust in Jesus as Lord and Savior are regenerated by the Holy Spirit and form the living body of Christ, of which He is the head. The church is an instrument of God's kingdom on earth.

Sacraments. The two ordinances are water baptism and the Lord's Supper.

End Times. One day God's kingdom will be consummated in the glorious, visible, and triumphant second coming of Christ. At His return, He will definitively defeat Satan and his minions. At the resurrection from the dead, the wicked will experience eternal conscious torment, and the righteous will experience eternal blessing. God's rule and reign—His kingdom—will be fulfilled in the new heavens and the new earth.

Website

www.vineyardusa.org

16

PRESBYTERIAN CHURCHES

PRESBYTERIANS DERIVE THEIR NAME from the Greek word *presbuteros,* which means "elder." Presbyterian churches are so-named because they are governed by elders or presbyters.

Presbyterian churches are ultimately rooted in the work of two men—John Calvin and John Knox. In the next chapter, which deals with Reformed churches, I will focus attention on John Calvin (1509–1564), who was truly the driving force behind the emergence of Reformed churches. In the present chapter, it is enough to acknowledge that Calvin was also instrumental in the rise of Presbyterian churches. While Calvin did not *found* the Presbyterian Church, he certainly laid the *foundation* on which Presbyterianism emerged in Switzerland, Holland, France, England, Scotland, and Ireland. He sought to establish a church government based on the New Testament concept of the office of elder.*

Though Calvin laid the groundwork, the real founder of Presbyterianism is John Knox (1513–1572). Knox was born in Scotland, educated at the University of Glasgow, and ordained to the Roman Catholic priesthood in 1530. He became a convert to Protestantism around 1545 as a result of studying the Bible and the works of Augustine and Jerome. This was a huge turning point in his life.

---

* Calvin noted, though, that elder rule is not the only legitimate form of church goverment.

Knox became a thunderous preacher, willing to confront anyone—whether religious leaders or political leaders. He was a strong and vitriolic opponent of Roman Catholicism and often used scathing language to describe this church. He earned the reputation of being the "ruffian of the Reformation." He even carried a sword with him wherever he went.

Knox exerted an extraordinary influence on the religious landscape of his day. He preached in England for a number of years and even participated in the formation of the 39 Articles of the Church of England. He exited England, however, when Mary Tudor rose to power. Tudor, a staunch Catholic, stood against the emerging Protestantism with everything that was in her, burning some 300 people at the stake. No wonder she became known as Bloody Mary. Understandably, Tudor's ascension to the throne motivated Knox to leave, and at that time he decided to study under his friend John Calvin in Geneva.

Knox also preached a great deal in Scotland, and in 1560 he helped write the Scottish Confession of Faith adopted by the Parliament. History shows that Knox was the prime driving force behind the Scottish Reformation. By 1567 the Reformed Church of Scotland—with a presbyterial style of church government—was legally recognized by the Parliament. It was only a matter of time before churches with presbyterial governments started cropping up all over Ireland, Holland, Switzerland, and other countries.

Some time later, an important creed was written that would become the primary confession of faith for Presbyterian churches—the Westminster Confession of Faith. This confession arose out of the stormy political scene in England during the reign of Charles I. In 1643 the English parliament commissioned the Westminster Assembly to develop the creed of the Church of England. The confession was written by 121 English Puritan ministers and was completed in 1646 after more than 1000 sessions. It strongly stresses the sovereignty of God as well as the five points of Calvinism, often represented by the acronym TULIP: total depravity, unconditional election, limited atonement, irresistible grace, and perseverance of the saints. The influence of this creed has been immeasurable.

It was inevitable that Presbyterian churches would eventually find their way to America. Indeed, the steady stream of immigrants into colonial America from countries like Scotland, Ireland, and England included many Presbyterians.

The first American presbytery or association of local Presbyterian churches was founded in Philadelphia in 1706. The First General Assembly of the Presbyterian Church was held in the same city in 1789. It was convened by the Reverend John Witherspoon, the only minister to sign the Declaration of Independence.

During the interim, in the 1720s, William Tennent Sr. (1673–1746) founded a small "Log College" in Neshaminy, Pennsylvania. It was a Presbyterian institution of higher learning that later became the College of New Jersey and then became Princeton University. This school produced many powerful Presbyterian preachers who played a major role in the Great Awakening in the early eighteenth century. They also played a role in the expansion of Presbyterianism in the United States. In what follows, I will summarize some of the more important denominations in the Presbyterian camp.

ASSOCIATE REFORMED PRESBYTERIAN CHURCH
Founded: 1782
Members: 35,181
Congregations: 209

Beginnings

As noted above, by 1567 the Reformed Church of Scotland, with a presbyterial style of church government, was legally recognized by the Scottish Parliament. Under the leadership of King William II, the Reformed Church of Scotland was reorganized in 1688 into the Established Presbyterian Church of Scotland.

Unfortunately, divisions in the church emerged in the early eighteenth century. Some believers saw the close alliance between the church and state as problematic and formed a separate Associate Presbytery. A decade later, other believers had a conflict with the national church over polity and worship and organized themselves into the Reformed Presbytery. Eventually, both of these bodies immigrated to Pennsylvania. Soon enough, the Associate and Reformed groups merged in 1782 to become the Associate Reformed Synod in Philadelphia. It embraced churches in Pennsylvania, New York, Ohio, North and South Carolina, and Georgia.

A complicated set of splits and mergers followed. By 1803 the church grew to establish four synods (overseeing the Carolinas, Pennsylvania, New York, and Ohio regions), and in 1804 the first General Synod was established. However, controversy soon swelled in the ranks of some of these synods over the issues of church government, closed communion (communion only for members of the church), and whether or not only psalms should be sung in church services. The controversy became heated and led to synodical defections. The defecting synods eventually merged to become the United Presbyterian Church in 1858. The one synod that remained outside of that union—the Synod of the Carolinas—continued on as the Associate Reformed Presbyterian Church.

Beliefs

Bible. The entire Bible is inspired by God. By God's care and providence, the biblical manuscripts were kept pure in all ages. The Bible is without error in all it teaches and has full authority as the rule of faith and life. It provides the whole counsel of God.

God. The only one true God is infinite in being and perfection. He is invisible, immutable, immense, eternal, incomprehensible, almighty, most wise, most free, most absolute, all-sufficient, abundant in goodness and truth, working all things according to the counsel of His own immutable will, and doing all for His own glory. In the unity of the one God are three persons equal in substance, power, and eternity: the Father, the Son, and the Holy Spirit. The Father is of none, neither begotten nor proceeding; the Son is eternally begotten of the Father; the Holy Spirit eternally proceeds from the Father and the Son.

Jesus Christ. Jesus is the Son of God. He is eternal God and is of the same divine substance as the Father. In the fullness of time, He took upon Himself a human nature, conceived by the Holy Spirit, born of a virgin. He was very God and very man in one person. He was crucified for the sins of the elect, died, was buried, rose from the dead, ascended into heaven to the right hand of the Father, and now lives to make intercession for us. By His perfect obedience in life and His perfect sacrifice ending in death, He fully satisfied the justice of the Father and purchased our reconciliation.

Holy Spirit. The Holy Spirit proceeds from the Father and the Son. He is of the same divine substance as the Father and the Son. He is present everywhere and is the Lord and Giver of life. He is the only efficient agent in the application of redemption: He convicts humans of their sin, moves them to repentance, persuades and enables them to place faith in Jesus, and regenerates them by His grace. He indwells believers as their Comforter and Sanctifier, and He seals them unto the day of redemption.

Sin and Salvation. Adam and Eve fell from their original righteousness and lost communion with God. They became dead in sin, and every aspect of their being became defiled. All humans since that time have been born with a corrupted nature.

Humanity's fall was so devastating that humans became unable to convert themselves by their own strength. They lost all ability of will to do spiritual good. For this reason, God Himself enables those who are elected to salvation to believe to the saving of their souls. The Holy Spirit convicts the elect of their sin, moves them to repentance, persuades and enables them to place faith in Jesus, and regenerates them by His grace.

Elect believers cannot totally or finally fall away from a state of grace but will persevere to the end and be eternally saved. The security of salvation among the elect is rooted in the immutability of God's decree of election, the abiding ministry of the Holy Spirit, and the continued intercessory ministry of Jesus Christ.

Elect infants who die are regenerated by Jesus Christ through the Holy Spirit.

Church. The universal church, which is invisible, is made up of all the elect who have been, presently are, or will be gathered into one body, with Christ as the head. The visible church consists of those throughout the world who profess faith in Jesus Christ. God's goal for the church is that it engage in ministry, faithfully administer the sacraments, and facilitate the gathering and perfection of the saints.

The church is governed by synods and councils. These institutions determine the order of public worship, settle controversies over doctrine, and deal with any complaints that may emerge. Women are permitted to be deacons but not elders.

Sacraments. Baptism is a sign and a seal of believers' engrafting into Christ, their regeneration, their remission of sins, and their walking in newness of life. It is to be performed in the name of the Father, the Son, and the Holy Spirit, utilizing the modes of sprinkling or pouring. Infants, as members of the covenant community, are baptized too.

The Lord's Supper is a sign and seal of believers' communion with Christ and with each other as members of His body. It seals the benefits of Christ's death to the believer. It is also a perpetual remembrance of the sacrifice of Jesus in His death. Christ is spiritually present in the elements. Members of all evangelical denominations are welcome to partake.

End Times. At death, the souls of believers go to heaven and await the resurrection of the body. The souls of the wicked are cast into hell and are preserved for a future day of judgment. On the last day, all will be raised. Believers will be raised to honor and will be made conformable to Christ's glorious resurrection body. Unbelievers will be raised to dishonor.

All humans will be judged and give an account for their thoughts, words, and deeds committed during mortal life. The righteous will go into everlasting life and receive the fullness of joy and the refreshing that comes from being in the presence of the Lord. The wicked will be cast into everlasting punishment, forever quarantined away from the presence of the Lord. The denomination takes no stance on millennial views.

Website

www.arpsynod.org

FAST FACTS ON
Infant Salvation

- Jesus loves the little children (Matthew 18:1-6).

- David knew he would see his dead infant again in heaven (2 Samuel 12:22-23).

- No infant is ever mentioned at the final judgment of the wicked (Revelation 20:11-13).

- Infants are not old enough to understand moral "oughts" and "shoulds" (James 4:17).

- God, in His justice, would not demand of an infant something he could not do (like exercise saving faith) (Zephaniah 3:5).

- Conclusion: God applies the benefits of Christ's death to infants who die, and brings them straight to heaven.

CUMBERLAND PRESBYTERIAN CHURCH

Founded: 1810
Members: 85,427
Congregations: 544

Beginnings

Two primary issues led to the founding of the Cumberland Presbyterian Church: a controversy over the ordination of ministers, and a disagreement regarding the Westminster Confession of Faith. More specifically, a particular Presbyterian synod—the Kentucky Synod—stood against some of the ordinations in connection with the Cumberland Presbytery because the ministers were uneducated. Further, those affiliated with the Cumberland Presbytery (including the newly ordained ministers) did not believe in the doctrine of election and reprobation as taught in the Westminster Confession of Faith. Hence, the Kentucky Synod ruled that these ordinations were invalid. The Cumberland Presbytery refused to submit to the ruling of the Kentucky Synod.

Meanwhile, three Presbyterian ministers in Dickson County, Tennessee—Finis Ewing (1773–1841), Samuel King (1775–1842), and Samuel McAdow (1760–1844), each of whom rejected the doctrines of election and reprobation—constituted a *new* presbytery in 1810, *again* calling themselves the Cumberland Presbytery. The new presbytery wanted more flexibility in ordaining ministers in the midst of unique circumstances intrinsic to the American frontier. However, the Kentucky Synod still would not budge. Hence, the Cumberland crowd decided to create several more presbyteries, after which they formed the Cumberland Synod in 1813 (three presbyteries are required to make a synod).

The new synod met in 1814 at the Beech Church in Sumner County, Tennessee. Attenders formulated a brief doctrinal statement that clearly distinguished their beliefs from those espoused in the Westminster Confession. They stipulated that (1) there are no eternal reprobates, (2) Christ died for all people, not just the elect (unlimited atonement), and (3) the Holy Spirit operates on the whole world (not just the elect), just as Christ died for the sins of the whole world (universal grace).

Beliefs

Bible. The Bible is the Word of God, fully inspired by the Holy Spirit. It is the infallible rule of faith and practice and is an authoritative guide for Christian living.

God. The one true God is eternal, immutable, wise, all-powerful, holy, just, good, and full of truth. He is the Creator of the universe and exercises providential control over all things. Within the unity of the one God are three eternal persons: the Father, the Son, and the Holy Spirit.

Jesus Christ. Jesus is God's Son and is the supreme revelation of God. When Jesus took on human flesh, He was truly divine and truly human but was without sin. He willingly suffered on the cross for sin, was buried, rose from the dead, appeared to the disciples, ascended into heaven, and now makes intercession for us at the right hand of the Father.

Holy Spirit. The Holy Spirit works in many ways, including through the Scriptures, the sacraments, the corporate worship of the church, the witness of believers in word and deed, and in many ways finite humans cannot understand. He convinces sinners of their sins and their need for salvation and seeks to incline them to repentance and faith toward God.

Sin and Salvation. Adam and Eve fell into sin and became inclined toward sin in all aspects of their being. Now all human beings are enslaved to sin and death. All people are guilty and are under divine wrath and judgment unless they respond to God's grace through Jesus Christ.

God has given all human beings the capacity and freedom to respond—or *not* respond—to divine grace. They are thus responsible for their choices and actions before God. Those who, in dependence on the Spirit, respond to God's grace in repentance and faith receive salvation (justification and regeneration). This call, however, can be resisted, and those who resist go into eternity lost. Those who *do* believe unto salvation are preserved in their salvation such that they will never fall away from it. God will bring believers into eternal life.

Church. The one, holy, universal, apostolic church is the body of Christ, Christ Himself being the head. The church is called "universal" because God's act of salvation in Jesus Christ cannot be limited to any place or time. It is called "apostolic" because it was proclaimed by the apostles.

The church includes all people of all ages—past, present, and future—who respond in faith to God's invitation to join His covenant community. It consists of all who respond in faith to God's saving grace and who enter into formal covenant with God and with each other. The church is called by God to engage in worship, to witness to all persons, and to reach out to all who have not experienced God's grace in Christ.

The church is governed by officers who make decisions that guide the life and ministry of the covenant community. This government involves sessions, presbyteries, synods, and the General Assembly, with progressively increasing levels of authority. These bodies determine matters of faith and practice, consider different forms of worship and witness, exercise discipline when needed, and resolve disputes.

Sacraments. All believers should seek baptism for themselves and their children, for it is an external sign of the covenant that marks membership in the community of faith. Pouring or sprinkling is believed to best represent baptism in the Holy Spirit, and the ceremony is performed in the name of the Father, the Son, and the Holy Spirit. It is administered to infants, with one or both parents present who affirm faith in Christ and who accept the responsibilities of the covenant.

The Lord's Supper is a means by which Christians remember Christ's passion and death on the cross. It is a means of celebrating the perpetual presence of the risen Lord until He returns again. The celebration should be preceded by solemn self-examination, reverence, humility, and a grateful awareness of Christ's spiritual presence.

End Times. When Jesus returns, the kingdoms of this world will become the kingdom of the Lord, and He shall reign forever. The redemption of the saved will be complete in the resurrection of the body. The unsaved will forever remain alienated from God.

Website

www.cumberland.org

EVANGELICAL PRESBYTERIAN CHURCH

Founded: 1981
Members: 70,000
Congregations: 190

Beginnings

The Evangelical Presbyterian Church began in late 1980 and early 1981 when a group of conservative pastors and elders held a series of meetings in St. Louis, Missouri, for the purpose of planning and prayer. These conservative pastors and elders were from mainline Presbyterian denominations like the United Presbyterian Church (northern churches) and the Presbyterian Church in the United States (southern churches). Their concern was the theological liberalism growing in their denominations. They sought to establish a new church and denomination free of theological liberalism, completely committed to the Word of God, and faithful to the theology of the historic confessions of faith.

The meetings culminated in a General Assembly that was convened in 1981 in Detroit, Michigan, at which time the Evangelical Presbyterian Church formally began.

Beliefs

This denomination takes a unified stand on the essential doctrines of Christianity but allows liberty of conscience on peripheral issues over which Christians are free to hold their own opinions.

Bible. The Bible is fully inspired by the Holy Spirit. It alone is our infallible authority for faith and practice. It is the supreme and final authority in all matters on which it speaks.

God. The one true God is the sovereign Creator and Sustainer of the universe. He is infinitely perfect and eternally exists in three persons: the Father, the Son, and the Holy Spirit.

Jesus Christ. Jesus is the Living Word and is one in substance with the Father and equal in deity. He became flesh by His miraculous conception by the Holy Spirit and His virgin birth. In the Incarnation, He was true God and true man in one person. He died as a sacrifice for sins on the cross, rose from the dead, and ascended into heaven to the right hand of Majesty, where He now intercedes for us as our High Priest.

Holy Spirit. A primary ministry of the Holy Spirit is to glorify Christ. He convicts humans of sin, draws them to the Savior, and applies the saving work of Christ to their hearts. He indwells believers, gives them new life, empowers them for ministry, and gives them spiritual gifts for service. He instructs and guides believers into all truth. He also seals believers for the day of redemption.

The denomination allows flexibility on the issue of charismatic gifts. Some churches in the denomination believe tongues and other such gifts are still for today; others do not. This illustrates the policy of the denomination: In essentials, unity; in nonessentials, liberty; in all things, charity.

Sin and Salvation. Sin is a harsh reality. However, people can be freed from guilt and the power of sin through repentance and personal faith in Christ. Christ alone is the ground of God's saving grace. God's grace alone is the only way to be reconciled to God. Faith alone is the only means of receiving God's grace. Those who put faith in Jesus are justified—declared righteous—and become heirs of eternal life. Such believers cannot completely or finally fall from a state of grace and lose their salvation.

Church. The church is composed of all who have placed faith in Jesus Christ and, through the work of the Holy Spirit, are united together in the body of Christ. Local churches are a visible though imperfect expression of this body of believers. These local churches preach the Word of God, properly administer the sacraments, maintain loving fellowship, and provide scriptural discipline when necessary.

Local churches control their own property, elect their own officers, and make decisions regarding worship style. Governance is according to the scriptural pattern of elders. Each congregation is also represented at presbytery and General Assembly meetings.

Individual congregations have the freedom to decide their own policies regarding women officers. Local churches can elect to have a woman pastor, though the decision is subject to presbytery approval.

Sacraments. Baptism is a sign and seal of membership in the covenant community of God. It points to the believer's union with Jesus in His death, burial, and resurrection. It is administered to believers and their children. The Lord's Supper constitutes a perpetual remembrance of Christ's sacrificial death on our behalf and provides spiritual nourishment for believers.

End Times. Jesus will one day come again personally, visibly, and bodily. He will then judge the living and the dead and consummate the eternal plan of God. Heaven is the destiny of believers. There they will live in God's presence and experience the full redemption of their bodies. Hell is the destiny of the wicked, where they remain in torment and complete darkness.

Website

www.epc.org

THE ORTHODOX PRESBYTERIAN CHURCH

Founded: 1936
Members: 18,414
Congregations: 204

Beginnings

The Orthodox Presbyterian Church is not affiliated with Eastern Orthodoxy but is "orthodox" in the sense of subscribing to historic, biblical Christianity. It embraces the Apostles' Creed and the Nicene Creed. It began in reaction to the rise of theological liberalism that swept across the United States in the early twentieth century.

More specifically, in 1924 a significant minority of Presbyterian ministers—1300 out of 10,000—signed the liberal Auburn Affirmation. This document denied the inerrancy of the Bible and declared that pivotal beliefs such as the substitutionary atonement of Christ and His bodily resurrection from the dead should not be made tests for ordination or for good standing in the church. In 1929, Princeton Theological Seminary in Princeton, New Jersey, hired some liberal professors for the faculty. In protest, four conservative professors at Princeton resigned and founded Westminster Theological Seminary in Philadelphia to continue teaching biblical Christianity. They were not about to remain at a seminary where some of its professors denied the full authority of the Bible and rejected the virgin birth of Jesus Christ.

Following this, Presbyterian missionaries began teaching liberal theology, and J. Gresham Machen (1881–1937), one of Christian history's greatest opponents of liberalism, campaigned against the liberal camp. Machen—a Presbyterian minister and professor at Princeton, and later Westminster—challenged the liberal tendencies in the foreign missions of the Presbyterian Church in the USA, but the General Assembly in 1933 decided not to take action.

Machen and his followers left and founded a new independent Board for Presbyterian Foreign Missions. The following year, the General Assembly of the Presbyterian Church in the USA condemned their action and deposed them from office. Machen, along with 34 ministers, 17 ruling elders, and 79 laymen met in Philadelphia in 1936 to found the Presbyterian Church of America. However, the Presbyterian Church in the USA filed suit over the name, so in 1939 Machen and his associates changed the name of their church and denomination to The Orthodox Presbyterian Church. The denomination has continued to oppose theological liberalism and emphasize the authority of Scripture.

Beliefs

Bible. The Bible is the inspired, infallible, inerrant Word of God. It is entirely trustworthy and without error. It is the only rule of faith and life and is the only source of special revelation for the church today.

God. The one true God is the Creator and Sustainer of the universe. He is an invisible Spirit, is completely self-sufficient, and is unbounded by space or time. He is personal, holy, just, loving, merciful, and in complete sovereign control of all things. Within the unity of the Godhead are three persons: the Father, the Son, and the Holy Spirit.

Jesus Christ. Jesus is the Son of God and is eternal deity. At the appointed time, He took upon Himself a human nature, being born of the Virgin Mary. In the Incarnation, He was fully God and yet fully man in one person. He lived a perfect sinless life and rendered a perfect sacrifice on the cross for sins, thereby securing salvation for His chosen ones. He rose from the dead, ascended into heaven, and now sits as Lord and rules over His kingdom.

Holy Spirit. The Holy Spirit convicts the elect of sin, draws them to Christ, and enables them to believe. He indwells them, sanctifies them, and enables them to increasingly stop sinning and to live in righteousness. Charismatic phenomena such as speaking in tongues, prophesying, and miraculous healings are explicitly rejected.

Sin and Salvation. Because of Adam's sin, all humans are now corrupt by nature, dead in sin, and subject to the wrath of God. However, God determined, by a covenant of grace, that sinners may receive forgiveness and eternal life through faith in Jesus Christ. Those whom God has predestined to salvation are effectually drawn to Christ by the inner working of the Holy Spirit as they hear the gospel. They are enabled by the Holy Spirit to repent and believe. Once they believe in Jesus, God justifies them, pardons their sins, accepts them as righteous, and imputes Christ's merits to them. They are adopted as children of God and indwelt by the Holy Spirit. The Holy Spirit continues His work in their lives, enabling them to increasingly cease sinning and act righteously. Such believers persevere to the end and thus have an assurance of salvation.

Church. The church is the body of Christ, of which He is the head. Christ established the church for the purpose of gathering and perfecting His people through the ministry of the Word of God, the sacraments, and discipline when necessary. Local churches are called to engage in worship, education, evangelism, ministries of mercy, and godly discipline.

Believers who have professed faith in Jesus Christ and have been baptized are called "communicant members." They are permitted to partake of the Lord's Supper and have voting rights. Baptized children are viewed as noncommunicant members and do not partake of the Lord's Supper or have voting rights.

Church government involves sessions, presbyteries, and a General Assembly. Sessions govern individual congregations. Presbyteries meet twice per year, oversee the well-being of congregations, and supervise ministers in their geographical area. The General Assembly meets once a year and oversees the entire denomination.

Sacraments. Baptism is administered to both believers and their children. In the Lord's Supper, the body and blood of Jesus are spiritually present to the faith of believers.

End Times. Jesus will one day come again to judge the living and the dead. The saved will enter into eternal life. The unsaved will be consigned to everlasting punishment. Many in the denomination are amillennialists, but some are postmillennialists, and a few are historic premillennialists. There is liberty in eschatology, except concerning dispensationalism, which is firmly rejected.

Website

www.opc.org

FAST FACTS ON
Election

Election is that sovereign act of God whereby He chooses certain individuals to salvation before the foundation of the world.

Foreknowledge View	Sovereignty View
God's election is based on His foreknowledge of who would respond favorably to the gospel.	God's election is based on His sovereign choice alone.
God's salvation has appeared to all human beings, not merely the elect (Titus 2:11).	Certain human beings have been given to Christ (John 6:37; 17:2), and the Father draws them to Christ (John 6:44).
Christ died for all (1 Timothy 2:6; 4:10; Hebrews 2:9; 2 Peter 2:1; 1 John 2:2).	Christ died for the church (Acts 20:28) and for His sheep (John 10:11).
People in general are called to turn to God (Isaiah 31:6), repent (Matthew 3:2), and believe (John 6:29).	All who are appointed to eternal life believe (Acts 13:48).

PRESBYTERIAN CHURCH IN AMERICA
Founded: 1973
Members: 306,000
Congregations: 1206

Beginnings

The National Presbyterian Church was founded in December of 1973 but was rechristened in 1974 as the Presbyterian Church in America. This is another denomination that emerged in reaction to the theological liberalism of American churches in the nineteenth and early twentieth centuries. A group of conservative believers split off from the Presbyterian Church in the United States (the southern churches) because of its escalating liberalism (which the conservatives saw as a gospel that tended toward humanism), an unbiblical view of marriage and divorce, the financing of abortion, a diluted theology, and an affiliation with the (liberal) National Council of Churches and World Council of Churches.

In view of such liberalism, the conservatives in the denomination met at Briarwood Presbyterian Church in Birmingham, Alabama, in December of 1973. They represented some 260 congregations with a total communicant membership of over 41,000 people. The denomination that emerged from this meeting was firmly committed to the Westminster Confession of Faith.

Beliefs

Bible. The entire Bible is inspired in the original manuscripts and is therefore free from error of fact, doctrine, and judgment. It is our only infallible rule of faith and life.

God. The one true God eternally self-exists in three persons: the Father, the Son, and the Holy Spirit. The Father is of none, neither begotten nor proceeding, the Son is eternally begotten of the Father, and the Holy Spirit eternally proceeds from the Father and the Son.

Jesus Christ. Jesus is the Son of God. He is eternal God, of one substance with the Father. In the fullness of time, He became a human being, conceived by the Holy Spirit and born of the Virgin Mary. In the Incarnation, He joined full Godhood and full manhood in one person. He died for the sins of the elect on the cross, rose from the dead, ascended into heaven, and makes intercession at the right hand of the Father.

Holy Spirit. The Holy Spirit guided the writers of Scripture so that they were kept free of error of fact, doctrine, and judgment. He quickens sinners (among the elect) so that they are enabled to believe in Christ as Savior and become born again.

Sin and Salvation. All humanity participated in Adam's fall from his original sinless state to a state of sin. Human beings are unable in themselves to reach out toward God.

In His grace, God has unconditionally elected some human beings to salvation. Nothing in any of these humans rendered them personally worthy of saving, but God sovereignly predestined some to everlasting life for no other reason than His own unfathomable love and mercy. Jesus died on the cross only for the sins of the elect, accomplishing a "particular atonement." The Holy Spirit effectually moves upon the hearts of the elect to apply the work of redemption. Through His irresistible grace, the Holy Spirit quickens the hearts of the elect, enabling them to believe in Jesus as Savior by the Word of God so that they become born again and justified (being clothed with the very righteousness of Christ). The elect are secure in their salvation. They will all persevere to the end.

Church. The church is God's covenant community on earth. One becomes a member of this elect community through personal faith in Jesus Christ through the enabling ministry of the Holy Spirit. Sessions govern the local church, regional presbyteries govern the sessions, and the General Assembly governs the presbyteries and all churches at the national level.

The offices of teaching and ruling elders can only be held by men. Sessions determine how women may exercise their gifts in other functions.

Sacraments. Baptism is a sign and seal of God's covenant and of the believer's engrafting into Christ, his regeneration, his remission of sins, and his walking in newness of life. It is properly administered to believers and their children in the name of the Father, the Son, and the Holy Spirit. The proper mode is pouring or sprinkling.

The Lord's Supper is a perpetual remembrance of Jesus' sacrifice and serves to seal all the benefits of His death to true believers. It is a bond and a pledge of believers' communion with Jesus and with other believers as members of the body of Christ. It provides spiritual nourishment to the believer.

End Times. At death, the bodies of all people return to dust. The soul of the Christian passes directly into the presence of God in heaven. The soul of the unbeliever is eternally separated from God and remains condemned until the future judgment day. Jesus will one day come again visibly and bodily. He will then consummate history and the eternal plan of God.

Website

www.pcanet.org

PRESBYTERIAN CHURCH (USA)

Founded: 1983
Members: 2,493,781
Congregations: 11,200

Beginnings

Presbyterianism suffered a major division in 1861 during the Civil War years. The two Presbyterian branches created by that division—the United Presbyterian Church in the United States of America (national) and the Presbyterian Church in the United States (southern)—were finally reunited in Atlanta, Georgia, in 1983 to form the Presbyterian Church (USA), now the largest Presbyterian group in the country. The reunion took place at a historic communion service celebrated by 15,000 persons in the Georgia World Congress Center in Atlanta. The event was televised.

Beliefs

Bible. The Bible is sacred Scripture and is inspired by the Holy Spirit. The Bible contains all we need to understand regarding how God has been present with humanity since the beginning of time and continues to be present today.

God. The one true God is the Creator of the world. In the unity of the one God are three persons who are equal in substance: the Father, the Son, and the Holy Spirit.

Jesus Christ. Jesus is the Son of God, the Lord of the universe, and is full deity. In the Incarnation, He was fully God and fully man in one person, having been born of a virgin. He was crucified for human sin, was raised from the dead, and ascended into heaven.

Holy Spirit. The Holy Spirit is everywhere the Giver and Renewer of life. He binds believers together in the one body of Christ, the church. The Holy Spirit convinces people of their sin, effectually moves them to repentance, and persuades and enables them to embrace Jesus by faith. Believers are accordingly justified—declared righteous before God.

Ministries of the Holy Spirit among believers include empowerment for service, enablement to live holy lives, and the production of spiritual fruit. God sent the Holy Spirit to be a companion, counselor, and guide for the believer.

Sin and Salvation. Because of Adam's sin, all human beings have violated the image of God in themselves and others, falling short of God's glory. They are now estranged from God and deserve God's condemnation.

Through the death of Jesus at the cross, God triumphed over sin and death. Those who repent and believe in Jesus Christ are saved and are made heirs with Christ. This salvation is based entirely on the grace of God. Believers become sealed by the Holy Spirit unto the day of redemption and are thus secure in their salvation.

Church. The church is God's covenant community on earth. Congregations are ruled by sessions, presbyteries, synods, and a General Assembly, with escalating levels of authority. Women can be ordained as elders and ministers.

Sacraments. Baptism is a one-time sacrament for believers and their children. The proper mode is sprinkling. The Lord's Supper is only for believers. Each believer should examine his or her life before partaking.

End Times. Jesus will one day return in great glory and will judge the earth in righteousness. The righteous will go into eternal life and receive the fullness of joy and refreshing in God's presence.

The wicked will be cast into eternal torment and everlasting punishment.

Website

www.pcusa.org.

17

REFORMED CHURCHES

REFORMED CHURCHES ARE ROOTED in the Swiss Reformation, whose greatest theologian and writer was John Calvin (1509–1564). Born in Noyon, France, in an influential family, Calvin's mental acumen was obvious to his parents, and they provided him with the very best education. At his father's urging, Calvin studied law, fully intending to enter this profession, when he experienced a sudden and dramatic conversion to Protestantism in 1533.

The year of his conversion, Calvin—not shy about sharing his views—was arrested for his activities as a reformer. He managed to escape to Geneva, where he continued his efforts at reformation. Calvin's stature in Geneva was larger than life, and under his forceful influence the city became somewhat of a theocracy, leading some to call Geneva "a Protestant Rome." His principles for civic activity extended to every area of life. In this God-ruled city, heretics were persecuted, and one well-known one—Michael Servetus, who denied the doctrine of the Trinity—was burned at the stake in 1553. By 1559, Calvin had established the University of Geneva, whose Reformed graduates spread Reformed theology far and wide throughout Germany, Italy, and Scotland.

Among his greatest accomplishments is his *Institutes of the Christian Religion*, which started out as an essay but was continually revised and expanded until it eventually became a substantial book in 1559. Among other things, the book sets forth Calvin's (now) well-known views on the sovereignty of God in creation and human salvation. The wonder of the printing press served to spread Calvin's Reformed ideas around the world.

Reformed churches eventually found their way to American soil, largely as a result of the heavy immigration of Dutch people (members of the Dutch Reformed Church) into the colonies. As well, many German Reformed Christians immigrated into Pennsylvania in the eighteenth century. (More than half the Germans in Pennsylvania at this time were proponents of Reformed theology.) Influential leaders in the Reformed tradition in America at that time include Johann Philip Boehm (1683–1749) and Michael Schlatter (1718–1790). Since colonial days, Reformed churches have permeated the United States.

Reformed churches generally subscribe to three key confessions of faith:

- *The Belgic Confession* was written by Dutch Reformed pastor Guido de Bres in 1561 to demonstrate to King Philip II of Spain that Reformed theology was not heretical. De Bres was martyred for his beliefs in 1567.

- *The Heidelberg Catechism*, written by Zacharias Ursinus and Caspar Olevianus in 1563 (during Reformation times), sought to mediate between Lutheran and Reformed theology.

- *The Canons of Dort* were written in 1618 to address the theological controversy over predestination and how God's sovereignty related to God's work of salvation. It outlined the five well-known points of Calvinism. As noted in an earlier chapter, these five points are often represented by the acronym TULIP: total depravity, unconditional election, limited atonement, irresistible grace, and perseverance of the saints.

CHRISTIAN REFORMED
CHURCH IN NORTH AMERICA

Founded: 1857
Members: 198,400
Congregations: 732

Beginnings

In the 1830s, the Dutch monarchy wanted to control the church in the Netherlands. Members of the Reformed Church wanted independence.

The Reformed Church, under the leadership of Hendrik DeCock, Henrik Scholte, and Albertus van Raalte, decided to split off from the government-controlled state church and form an independent body. This did not sit well with the government, however, and they were persecuted for their action. In 1847, these Dutch believers made the decision to immigrate to America.

From 1850 to 1857, these Dutch immigrants affiliated with the Reformed Church in America because this body initially rendered aid to them and seemed to share their same basic faith. It proved not to be a happy marriage, however. The Dutch believers became disenchanted with the Reformed Church in America, which (1) practiced open communion (serving all believers instead of just Reformed believers), (2) neglected catechism preaching, (3) lacked the piety the Dutch were used to, and (4) utilized inappropriate hymns in church services. The Dutch believers called a conference in Holland, Michigan, and founded a separate church in 1857. After going through a few name changes over the next two years, the group settled on the name Christian Reformed Church in 1859.

The emblem of the denomination is a cross inside a triangle. The cross represents belief in Jesus Christ. The triangle represents the Trinity (one God who is eternally manifest in three persons: the Father, the Son, and the Holy Spirit).

The denomination holds to the Belgic Confession, the Heidelberg Catechism, and the Canons of Dort. As well, the denomination subscribes to the Apostles' Creed, the Athanasian Creed, and the Nicene Creed.

Beliefs

Bible. The Bible in its entirety is God's Word. It is verbally and entirely inspired by the Holy Spirit and is therefore infallible and inerrant in all its parts. Scripture is the supreme and final authority in all matters on which it speaks. It is the final rule of faith and practice.

God. God is absolutely sovereign, and nothing is outside His control. No force in heaven or on earth can frustrate His sovereign plans. This one God is eternally manifest in three persons: the Father, the Son, and the Holy Spirit.

Jesus Christ. Jesus is the Son of God and is of the same divine essence as the Father. He is Savior and Lord. He died on the cross for human salvation, rose from the dead, ascended into heaven, and now rules over the world from heaven.

Holy Spirit. The Holy Spirit is of the same divine essence as the Father and the Son. He is involved in various ministries in the church and among Christians. Any teaching regarding a separate baptism of the Holy Spirit, or a "second blessing," is rejected.

Sin and Salvation. Due to the sin of Adam, humanity is now fallen in sin. Jesus was crucified on the cross to atone for human sin. Only faith in Christ the Savior brings salvation. Christians can have an assurance of salvation because of God's faithfulness. Nothing can take the Christian out of God's hand—not even the weaknesses and failings of Christians.

Church. The church is made up of Christians. In church worship services, congregants confess sin, ask for forgiveness, listen to a Scripture reading, hear a sermon, partake of the Lord's Supper, and participate in prayers of intercession.

Church polity is presbyterial: Councils oversee local churches, classes oversee the councils and the churches affiliated with them, and the General Synod oversees the entire denomination.

Women can be ordained to the offices of deacon, elder, minister, and evangelist.

Sacraments. The relationship Christians enjoy with God involves a covenant that stipulates that God fulfills His promises so long as Christians accept them with a repentant and believing heart. This covenant is celebrated through the sacraments of baptism and the Lord's Supper. Baptism is not just for adults but for infants too because they are part of the covenant community. The Lord's Supper—only for those who have professed faith in Jesus as Savior (of any denomination)—is celebrated at least four times a year (frequency is set by each individual church). This sacrament is a reminder to every Christian of the sacrifice Jesus made to make our salvation possible.

End Times. Jesus will one day come again and establish His perfect, eternal kingdom. The spoiled creation will finally be restored. The saved—those who have trusted in Christ the Savior—will live with Him for all eternity in heaven. Those who reject Jesus will suffer everlasting punishment.

Website

www.crcna.org

FAST FACTS ON
Descriptions of Heaven

- It is a heavenly country, filled with light, glory, and love (Hebrews 11:13-16).

- It is a holy city, full of purity and without sin (Revelation 21:1-2).

- It is the home of righteousness (2 Peter 3:13).

- It is a kingdom of light, where Christ, the light of the world (John 8:12) dwells (Colossians 1:12).

- It is the paradise of God, full of pleasure and delight (Revelation 2:7).

- It is the new Jerusalem, a massive city of the saints of all ages (Revelation 21:1-2,16).

REFORMED CHURCH IN AMERICA
Founded: 1628
Members: 173,463
Congregations: 735

Beginnings

The Reformed Church in America had a humble beginning. In the year 1628, a mere 50 Dutch Reformed immigrants met around a crude table in a mill loft in New Amsterdam—what is now Manhattan Island in New York. At this table they celebrated the Lord's Supper together, and at this moment their denomination was born. The first minister of the church was Domine Jonas Michaelius, from the Netherlands.

This initial church of the denomination exists even to the present day. It is the Collegiate Reformed Church in New York City and is widely known as the oldest evangelical church in North America with a continuous ministry.

During the early colonial days, the church was under the authority of the Classis of Amsterdam. This eventually became a problem for church members. Once these Dutch immigrants became Americanized, they sought independence from the church authorities in Holland. Under the able leadership of Reverend John Livingston, the group attained independence from the Classis of Amsterdam in 1776. The new denomination adopted its constitution in 1792, formally incorporated in the United States in 1819 as the Reformed Protestant Dutch Church, and then changed its name in 1867 to the Reformed Church of America. The denomination experienced consistent growth, primarily due to the steady wave of Dutch immigrants that poured into the United States in the late 1840s.

The denomination accepts the Heidelberg Catechism, the Belgic Confession, and the Canons of Dort, as well as the Apostles' Creed, the Athanasian Creed, and the Nicene Creed. All such creeds, however, are subject to evaluation in the light of Scripture.

Beliefs

Bible. The Bible constitutes God's Word for every person. It is a source of revelation for finding God's will and is the final authority in matters of faith and practice. It is the standard against which all teachers and teachings should be measured.

God. The one God is eternally manifest in three persons: the Father, the Son, and the Holy Spirit.

Jesus Christ. Jesus is the Son of God. He became a human, born of the Virgin Mary, for the purpose of rendering a perfect sacrifice for the sins of humankind. He then rose from the dead and ascended into heaven.

Holy Spirit. The Holy Spirit proceeds from the Father and the Son. All Christians receive the gift of the Holy Spirit. He enables Christians to live the Christian life and illumines the Word of God so they can understand it. There is no "second blessing" from the Holy Spirit.

Sin and Salvation. Adam and Eve disobeyed God, and this resulted in all humanity falling into a state of sin. Because of God's love for humanity, He has a plan to restore humans to a state of joy and peace. This plan involved sending Jesus, who lived a life of perfect obedience to the Father and then rendered a perfect sacrifice for human sin at the cross. Those who call on the name of Jesus are saved.

Church. The church is made up of those who have accepted Jesus as God's Son. The church is Christ's body on earth and has the responsibility of continuing Christ's work.

Each congregation is governed by a consistory. A group of congregations in a geographical area forms a classis, which supervises churches in that area. Regional synods are comprised of churches and classes within a broader geographical boundary. The General Synod is the highest ecclesiastical authority.

Women can become missionaries, teachers, study leaders, elders, deacons, and even ministers.

Sacraments. Baptism is a sign and seal of God's covenant of grace and demonstrates God's promise that we are cleansed in Christ's blood, buried with Him in death, and risen with Him in newness of life. In baptism God promises by His grace to forgive our sins, adopt us into His body (the church), send the Holy Spirit daily to renew and cleanse us, and resurrect us to eternal life. Infants are permitted to be baptized because they are a part of the covenant community of God. The mode may be sprinkling, immersion, or pouring.

The Lord's Supper is a sacrament in which Christ Himself is present (through the power of the Holy Spirit) and His life passes into us and is made ours. It is a means by which Christ continually strengthens, comforts, and nourishes believers. The sacrament is only for those who have been baptized into Christ.

End Times. Jesus will one day come again. He will judge the living and the dead. All believers will be resurrected and live with Him forever in heaven. Unbelievers are excluded from God's presence for all eternity.

Website

www.rca.org

FAST FACTS ON
Descriptions of Hell

- destruction (Matthew 7:13)
- a fiery furnace (Matthew 13:42)
- an eternal fire (Matthew 18:8)
- a lake of burning sulfur (Revelation 19:20)
- eternal punishment (Matthew 25:46)
- exclusion from God's presence (Luke 13:27)

UNITED REFORMED CHURCHES IN NORTH AMERICA

Founded: 1996
Members: Unknown
Congregations: 81

Beginnings

The United Reformed Churches in North America began on October 1, 1996, at a synod in Lynwood, Illinois. Most of the congregations that joined had a previous background in the Christian Reformed Church but wanted to return fully to the orthodoxy that is reflected in the Heidelberg Catechism, Belgic Confession, and Canons of Dort. They felt the Christian Reformed Church had drifted from the orthodoxy reflected in these creeds.

Beliefs

Bible. The Bible is inspired by the Holy Spirit and is fully authoritative in all matters of faith and practice.

God. The one true God is eternally manifest in three persons: the Father, the Son, and the Holy Spirit.

Jesus Christ. Jesus is full deity. In the Incarnation, He was fully God and fully man. He was a sinless person. He died for human sin, rose from the dead, and ascended into heaven.

Holy Spirit. The Holy Spirit, the third person of the Trinity, is engaged in a variety of ministries in the church and among individual believers.

Sin and Salvation. Man is fallen in sin. Salvation is found only in Jesus Christ. Nothing can separate the true believer from God.

Church. The church is the people of God on earth. Congregations exhibit a variety of worship styles. Government is by elder rule. Women are not allowed in the ministry. The General Synod meets at least once every three years, though it can meet every year if church officials deem it necessary.

Sacraments. The two sacraments are baptism and the Lord's Supper. Baptism is for both adults and infants. The Lord's Supper is only for professing Christians. It is a supervised sacrament. Non-members must obtain permission from an elder before participating.

End Times. The church has no official position on the end times. Many church members are amillennial in their eschatology; others are postmillennial. Heaven and hell are viewed as eternal destinies for the saved and unsaved.

Website

www.covenant-urc.org/urchrchs.html

NOTES

Beginnings

1. *Dictionary of Christianity in America*, ed. Daniel G. Reid, Robert Linder, Bruce Shelley, and Harry Stout (Downers Grove, IL: InterVarsity Press, 1990), p. 350.
2. Ibid.
3. Frank S. Mead and Samuel S. Hill, *Handbook of Denominations in the United States* (Nashville, TN: Abingdon Press, 2001), p. 19.
4. J.E. Wood, "Separation of Church and State," in *Dictionary of Christianity in America*, p. 268.
5. Quoted in Wood, p. 267.
6. Mead and Hill, p. 22.
7. Carmen Renee Berry, *The Unauthorized Guide to Choosing a Church* (Grand Rapids, MI: Brazos Press, 2003), p. 46.
8. Robert McAfee, *The Spirit of Protestantism* (Oxford, England: Oxford Press, 1961), p. 4.
9. See my book *The Challenge of the Cults and New Religions* (Grand Rapids, MI: Zondervan, 2001), pp. 19-35.
10. See *Dictionary of Christianity in America*, p. 351; Mead and Hill, p. 16.

Chapter 1—Adventist Churches

1. William Miller, cited in John Gerstner, *The Theology of the Major Sects* (Grand Rapids, MI: Baker Book House, 1960), p. 21.
2. Hank Hanegraaff explains: "Evangelicals have often been divided as to how Adventism should be classified. Adventism has long borne the stigma of being called a cult. Since Seventh-day Adventism does officially accept the foundational doctrines of historic Christianity (the inspiration and authority of the Bible, the Trinity, Christ's true deity, His bodily resurrection,

and salvation by grace through faith), we do not believe that it should be classified as a cult." See Hank Hanegraaff, "Seventh-day Adventism: Christian or Cultic?" Perspective CP0602, Christian Research Institute website: www.equip.org/free/CP0602.htm.

Chapter 2—Baptist Churches

1. Robert G. Torbet, *A History of Baptists* (Chicago, IL: The Judson Press, 1950), p. 59.
2. Ibid., p. 60.
3. Ibid., p. 62.
4. Ibid., pp. 60ff.

Chapter 4—Catholic Churches

1. Austin Flannery, "The People of God," in *Documents of Vatican II* vol. 1 (Grand Rapids, MI: Eerdmans Publishing Company, 1992), pp. 267-68.
2. Cited in Karl Rahner, ed., *Teaching of the Catholic Church* (Staten Island, NY: Albar, 1967), p. 203.
3. Rahner, p. 207.
4. *Catechism of the Catholic Church* (New York: Doubleday, 1994), p. 249.
5. Ibid., p. 292.
6. Council of Trent, session 22, "Teachings and Canons of the Most Holy Sacrifice of the Mass," canon 1.

Chapter 8—Friends (Quaker) Churches

1. Quoted in J. Gordon Melton, *Encyclopedia of American Religions* (Detroit, MI: Gale Research, 1999), p. 91.

Chapter 12—Mennonite Churches

1. The Dordrecht Confession of Faith, translated by J.C. Wenger, available online at www.bibleviews.com/Dordrecht.html.

Chapter 13—Methodist Churches

1. J. Gordon Melton, *Encyclopedia of American Religions*, sixth edition (Detroit, MI: Gale Research, 1999), p. 71.

Chapter 15—Pentecostal Churches

1. "The Story of Our Church," available online at www.cogic.org.

BIBLIOGRAPHY

The website addresses in this bibliography are accurate as of this book's publication. A regularly updated list of these websites may be found at www.ronrhodes.org.

General Resources

Ahlstrom, Sydney. *A Religious History of the American People.* 2 vols. New Haven: Yale University Press, 1972.

Berkhof, Louis. *The History of Christian Doctrines.* Grand Rapids: Baker Book House, 1981.

Berry, Carmen Renee. *The Unauthorized Guide to Choosing a Church.* Grand Rapids: Brazos Press, 2003.

Bromiley, Geoffrey W. *Historical Theology: An Introduction.* Grand Rapids: Eerdmans, 1978.

Gaustad, Edwin, and Philip Barlow. *New Historical Atlas of Religion in America.* New York: Oxford University Press, 2000.

Gerstner, John H. *The Theology of the Major Sects.* Grand Rapids: Baker Book House, 1960.

Lincoln, Eric, and Lawrence Mamiya. *The Black Church in the African-American Experience.* Durham: Duke University Press, 1990.

Linder, Robert D., Daniel G. Reid, Bruce L. Shelley, and Harry S. Stout, eds. *Dictionary of Christianity in America.* Downers Grove, IL: InterVarsity Press, 1990.

Marty, Martin. *Modern American Religion.* 2 vols. Chicago: University of Chicago Press, 1986.

Mead, Frank S., and Samuel S. Hill. *Handbook of Denominations in the United States.* Nashville: Abingdon Press, 2001.

Melton, J. Gordon. *Encyclopedia of American Religions.* Sixth edition. Detroit: Gale Research, 1999.

Steig, Shelly. *The 60-Second Guide to Denominations: Understanding Protestant Churches of North America*. Iowa Falls: World Bible Publishers, 2003.

Sweet, William W. *The Story of Religion in America*. Grand Rapids: Baker Book House, 1979.

Walker, Williston. *A History of the Christian Church*. New York: Scribner, 1985.

Adventist Churches

Kearney, Clarence J. "A Man Named Miller: The Advent Christian Story." Advent Christian Church website: www.adventchristian.org.

"Origin of the Seventh-day Adventist Reform Movement." Seventh-day Adventist Reform Movement website: www.sdarm.org.

"Seventh-day Adventist Reform Movement: This We Believe." Seventh-day Adventist Reform Movement website: www.sdarm.org.

"The Declaration of Principles." Advent Christian Church website: www.adventchristian.org.

"What We Believe: Fundamental Beliefs of Seventh-day Adventists." Seventh-day Adventist website: northamerica.adventist.org.

Baptist Churches

"10 Facts You Should Know About the American Baptists." American Baptist Churches website: www.abc-usa.org.

"About Us—Meet Southern Baptists." Southern Baptist Convention website: www.sbc.net.

"Abstract to the Doctrine of Salvation as Advocated by the Primitive Baptists." Primitive Baptists website: www.pb.org.

"American Baptists: A Brief History." American Baptist Churches website: www.abc-usa.org.

"An Affirmation of Our Faith." Baptist General Conference website: www.bgc world.org.

"Articles of Faith." General Association of Regular Baptist Churches website: www.garbc.org.

"Articles of Faith." National Association of Free Will Baptists website: www.nafwb.org.

Brackney, William. *The Baptists*. New York: Greenwood Press, 1988.

"Doctrinal Statement of the American Baptist Association." American Baptist Association website: www.abaptist.org.

"FAQ." Primitive Baptists website: www.pb.org.

"General Baptist Statement of Faith." General Association of General Baptist Churches website: www.generalbaptist.com.

"General Information." National Association of Free Will Baptists website: www.nafwb.org.

Grenz, Stanley J. *The Baptist Congregation: A Guide to Baptist Belief and Practice.* Valley Forge, PA: Judson Press, 1985.

Hastey, Stan. "Alliance Governance." Alliance of Baptist Churches website: www.allianceofbaptists.org.

————. "History Time Line." Alliance of Baptist Churches website: www.alliance ofbaptists.org.

Leonard, Bill, ed. *Dictionary of Baptists in America.* Downers Grove, IL: Inter-Varsity Press, 1994.

Nettles, Tom J., and Russell Moore, eds. *Why I Am a Baptist.* Nashville: Broadman and Holman, 2001.

"North American Baptist Conference Statement of Beliefs." North American Baptist Conference website: www.nabconference.org.

"Our Mission Statement." Alliance of Baptist Churches website: www.alliance ofbaptists.org.

"The Origin of the Progressive National Baptist Convention." Progressive National Baptist Convention website: www.pnbc.org.

"The Primitive Baptist Church of Christ Believes…" National Primitive Baptist Convention website: www.natlprimbaptconv.org.

Torbet, Robert G. *A History of Baptists.* Chicago: The Judson Press, 1950.

"What is GARBC?" General Association of Regular Baptist Churches website: www.garbc.org.

"Who We Are." Cooperative Baptist Fellowship website: www.cbfonline.org.

Brethren Churches

"A Quick Run Through of Our History." Church of the United Brethren website: www.ub.org.

"A Real Quick Overview." Church of the United Brethren website: www.ub.org.

"Articles of Faith and Doctrine of the Brethren in Christ Church." Brethren in Christ Church website: www.bic-church.org/index.htm.

"Brethren Belief and Practice." Church of the Brethren website: www.bre thren.org.

"Brethren History." Church of the Brethren website: www.brethren.org.

"Common Beliefs/Core Beliefs." Church of God (Anderson, Indiana) website: www.chog.org.

"Confession of Faith." Church of the United Brethren website: www.ub.org.

"Covenant Affirmations." Evangelical Covenant Church website: www.cov church.org.

"The Decision to Believe and Begin." Church of God (Anderson, Indiana) website: www.chog.org.

"Distinctives of the Evangelical Free Church of America." Evangelical Free Church of America website: www.efca.org.

Durnbaugh, Donald, ed. *The Brethren Encyclopedia.* 3 vols. Philadelphia: Brethren Press, 1983.

"Fact Sheet." Church of the United Brethren website: www.ub.org.

"The FGBC Story." Fellowship of Grace Brethren Churches website: www.fgbc.org.

"History." Brethren Church (Ashland, Ohio) website: www.brethrenchurch.org.

"History." Church of God (Anderson, Indiana) website: www.chog.org.

"History." Evangelical Covenant Church website: www.covchurch.org.

"History." Evangelical Free Church of America website: www.efca.org.

"The Message of the Faith." Brethren Church (Ashland, Ohio) website: www.brethrenchurch.org.

"Ministries." Moravian Church website: www.moravian.org.

"Moravian Church." Moravian Church website: www.moravian.org.

"The Moravian Church's History." Moravian Church website: www.moravian.org.

"Our History." Brethren in Christ Church website: www.bic-church.org/index.htm.

"Policy on Baptism." Evangelical Covenant Church website: www.covchurch.org.

"Statement of Faith of the Evangelical Free Church of America." Evangelical Free Church of America website: www.efca.org.

"The Statement of Faith of the Fellowship of Grace Brethren Churches." Fellowship of Grace Brethren Churches website: www.fgbc.org.

"Who We Are." Evangelical Covenant Church website: www.covchurch.org.

Christian Churches

"Discover the Disciples." Christian Church (Disciples of Christ) website: www.disciples.org.

Garrison, W.E., and A.T. DeGroot, *The Disciples of Christ: A History.* St. Louis: Bethany Press, 1958.

"Governmental Polity." Christian Congregation website: www.netministries.org /see/churches/exe/ch10619.

McAllister, Lester, and William Tucker. *Journey in Faith: A History of the Christian Church* (Disciples of Christ). St. Louis: Bethany Press, 1975.

"Our History." Christian Congregation website: www.netministries.org/ see/churches/exe/ch10619.

Congregational Churches

"About Us." Congregational Christian Churches (National Association) website: www.naccc.org.

"About Us." United Church of Christ website: www.ucc.org.

"Constitution." Conservative Congregational Christian Conference website: www.ccccusa.org.

"The Nature of Our Fellowship." Conservative Congregational Christian Conference website: www.ccccusa.org.

Rohr, John V. *The Shaping of American Congregationalism: 1620–1957*. Cleveland: Pilgrim Press, 1992.

"Statement of Mission." United Church of Christ website: www.ucc.org.

"UCC Statement of Faith." United Church of Christ website: www.ucc.org.

"What Is the Congregational Way?" Congregational Christian Churches (National Association) website: www.naccc.org.

Friends (Quaker) Churches

"An Affirmation of Faith." Evangelical Friends International website: www.evangelical-friends.org.

Blackmar, Mary K. "Friends and God." Friends General Conference website: www.fgcquaker.org.

Cadbury, Henry J. "Friends and the Bible." Friends General Conference website: www.fgcquaker.org.

"Declaration of Faith." Friends United Meeting website: www.fum.org.

"Friends History." Evangelical Friends International website: www.evangelicalfriends.org.

Hall, Francis. *Friends in the Americas*. Philadelphia: Friends World Committee, 1976.

Hoare, Ted. "Facts About Friends." Religious Society of Friends website: www.quaker.org/friends.

"The Quakers: Children of Light." Friends United Meeting website: www.fum.org.

Fundamentalist and Bible Churches

"A Brief History of the BBFI." Baptist Bible Fellowship International website: www.bbfi.org.

"The Christian and Missionary Alliance Doctrinal Statement." Christian Missionary and Alliance website: www.cmalliance.org.

"The Christian and Missionary Alliance Mission Statement." Christian Missionary and Alliance website: www.cmalliance.org.

"Declaration of Faith." Conservative Baptist Association of America website: www.cbamerica.org.

"Introduction to the AECC." American Evangelical Christian Churches website: www.aeccministries.com.

"Let Us Introduce Ourselves." IFCA website: www.ifca.org.

"Plymouth Brethren FAQ." Plymouth Brethren website: www.brethren online.org.

"Plymouth Brethren History FAQ." Plymouth Brethren website: www.brethren online.org.

"What Is an Independent Fundamental Church." IFCA website: www.ifca.org.

"What is IFCA International?" IFCA website: www.ifca.org.

"What We Believe." IFCA website: www.ifca.org.

"What We Believe: Articles of Faith." Baptist Bible Fellowship International website: www.bbfi.org.

"Where We Came From: A Brief History of the CBA." Conservative Baptist Association of America website: www.cbamerica.org.

Holiness Churches

"A History of the Wesleyan Church." Indianapolis: Wesleyan Publishing House, 2000.

"Answers to Your Questions." Church of the Nazarene website: www.nazarene.org.

"The Articles of Religion." Wesleyan Church website: www.wesleyan.org.

"COCHUSA Church History In Brief." Church of Christ (Holiness) website: www.cochusa.com.

"Core Values." Wesleyan Church website: www.wesleyan.org.

"Eight Agreed Statements." Church of the Nazarene website: www.nazarene.org.

"General Information." Church of God (Holiness) website: www.cogh.net.

"Our Values." Church of the Nazarene website: www.nazarene.org.

"Preamble and Articles of Faith." Church of the Nazarene website: www.nazarene.org.

"Standing Firm: The Wesleyan Church Speaks on Contemporary Issues." Indianapolis: Wesleyan Publishing House, 2000.

"Statement of Faith." Church of God (Holiness) website: www.cogh.net.

Synan, Vinson. *The Holiness-Pentecostal Movement in the United States.* Grand Rapids: Eerdmans, 1971.

"This We Believe." Indianapolis: Wesleyan Publishing House, 1996.

"The Way to Eternal Life." Churches of Christ in Christian Union website: www.cccuhq.org.

"What We Believe." Church of Christ (Holiness) website: www.cochusa.com.

"What We Teach." Churches of Christ in Christian Union website: www.cccuhq.org.

Lutheran Churches

"A Biblical View of the Sacraments: Church of the Lutheran Brethren." Fergus Falls, MN: Faith & Fellowship Press, 2004.

"A Brief History of the Evangelical Lutheran Synod." Evangelical Lutheran Synod website: www.EvLuthSyn.org.

"A Brief History: Church of the Lutheran Brethren." Fergus Falls: Faith & Fellowship Press, 2004.

"A Concise Doctrinal Statement of the Evangelical Lutheran Synod." Evangelical Lutheran Synod website: www.EvLuthSyn.org.

"AFLC History." Association of Free Lutheran Congregations website: www.aflc.org.

"AFLC Introduction." Association of Free Lutheran Congregations website: www.aflc.org.

"Basic Principles." American Association of Lutheran Churches website: www.taalc.com.

"Belief and Practice." Lutheran Church—Missouri Synod website: www.lcms.org.

"Confession of Faith." American Association of Lutheran Churches website: www.taalc.com.

"Constitution and Bylaws of the Church of the Lutheran Brethren of America." Fergus Falls, MN: Faith & Fellowship Press, 2001.

"Declaration of Faith." Association of Free Lutheran Congregations website: www.aflc.org.

"How We Came to Be: Church of the Lutheran Brethren." Fergus Falls, MN: Faith & Fellowship Press, 2004.

Kolb, Robert, and Timothy Wengert, eds. *The Book of Concord: The Confessions of the Evangelical Lutheran Church.* Philadelphia: Fortress, 2000.

Nafzger, Samuel H. *An Introduction to the Lutheran Church—Missouri Synod.* St. Louis: Concordia Publishing House, 1994.

Nelson, Clifford, ed. *Lutherans in North America.* Philadelphia: Fortress Press, 1975.

"Roots of the Evangelical Lutheran Church in America." Evangelical Lutheran Church in America website: www.elca.org.

Schlink, Edmund. *Theology of the Lutheran Confessions.* Trans. Paul Keohneke and Herbert Bouman. Philadelphia: Muhlenberg Press, 1961.

"This We Believe: A Statement of Belief of the Wisconsin Evangelical Lutheran Synod." Wisconsin Evangelical Lutheran Synod website: www.wels.net.

"What Do ELCA Lutherans Believe?" Evangelical Lutheran Church in America website: www.elca.org.

"What We Believe." Church of the Lutheran Brethren of America website: www.clba.org.

"Who We Are." Church of the Lutheran Brethren of America website: www.cl ba.org.

Mennonite Churches

"Articles of Faith and Practice." Missionary Church website: www.mcusa.org.

"Confession of Faith in a Mennonite Perspective, 1995." Mennonite Church website: www.MennoniteChurchUSA.org.

"Conservative Mennonite Statement of Theology." Conservative Mennonite Conference website: www.cmscrosedale.org.

Dordrecht Confession of Faith, translated by J.C. Wenger, Internet version: www.bibleviews.com/Dordrecht.html.

Loewen, Harry, and Steven Nolt, Carol Duerkson, and Elwood Yoder. *Through Fire and Water: An Overview of Mennonite History.* Scottdale, PA: Herald Press, 1996.

"What Do We Believe?" Conservative Mennonite Conference website: www.cmscrosedale.org.

"Who Are the Mennonites?" Mennonite Church website: www.Mennonite ChurchUSA.org.

Methodist Churches

"Articles of Faith of the Evangelical Church." Evangelical Church of North America website: www.theevangelicalchurch.com.

"Basic Christian Affirmations." United Methodist Church website: www.umc.org.

The Book of Discipline of the United Methodist Church. Nashville: The United Methodist Publishing House, 1992.

Bucke, Emory, ed. *History of American Methodism.* Nashville: Abingdon Press, 1964.

Collins, Kenneth J. *A Real Christian: The Life of John Wesley.* Nashville: Abingdon Press, 1999.

"The Congregational Methodist Church in a Few Words." Congregational Methodist Church website: www.congregationalmethodist.net.

Langford, Thomas. *Doctrine and Theology in the United Methodist Church.* Nashville: Kingswood Books, 1991.

"Methodist Beliefs." Christian Methodist Episcopal Church website: www.c-m-e.org.

"Our CME Heritage." Christian Methodist Episcopal Church website: www.c-m-e.org.

"Our History." Southern Methodist Church website: www.southernmethodist church.org.

"Sacraments." Christian Methodist Episcopal Church website: www.c-m-e.org.

"What We Believe—What Is the Evangelical Methodist Church?" Evangelical Methodist Church website: www.emchurch.org.

"Who Are Free Methodists?" Free Methodist Church in North America website: www.freemethodistchurch.org.

Pentecostal Churches

"A Brief History." International Pentecostal Holiness Church website: www.iphc.org.

"About Elim." Elim Fellowship website: www.elimfellowship.org.

"About the COG." Church of God (Cleveland, Tennessee) website: www.church ofgod.cc.

"Articles of Faith." International Pentecostal Holiness Church website: www.iphc.org.

"Articles of Faith." Open Bible Standard Churches website: www.openbible.org.

Burgess, Stanley, and Gary McGee, eds. *Dictionary of Pentecostal and Charismatic Movements.* Grand Rapids: Regency Reference Library, 1988.

"Congregational Holiness Church." Congregational Holiness Church website: www.chchurch.com.

"Declaration of Faith." International Church of the Foursquare Gospel website: www.foursquare.org.

"General Information." International Church of the Foursquare Gospel website: www.foursquare.org.

"History." Fellowship of Christian Assemblies website: www.foca.org.

"Identity and Vision." Independent Assemblies of God, International website: www.iaogi.org.

"Mission Statement." Fellowship of Christian Assemblies website: www.foca.org.

"Our History." General Council of Assemblies of God website: www.ag.org.

Pentecostal Church of God General Bylaws 2004. Joplin, MO: Pentecostal Church of God International Headquarters, 2004.

"Statement of Faith." Independent Assemblies of God, International website: www.iaogi.org.

"The Story of Our Church." Church of God in Christ website: www.cogic.org.

Synan, Vinson. *The Holiness-Pentecostal Movement in the United States.* Grand Rapids: Eerdmans, 1971.

"Welcome to Elim." Lima, NY: Elim Fellowship, 2004.

"What We Believe." Fellowship of Christian Assemblies website: www.foca.org.

Presbyterian Churches

"A Synopsis of the Beliefs of the Presbyterian Church in America." Presbyterian Church in America website: www.pcanet.org.

"About the Presbyterian Church in America." Presbyterian Church in America website: www.pcanet.org.

The Book of Confessions: Presbyterian Church (USA). Louisville: Office of the General Assembly, 1996.

"The Brief Statement of Faith." Presbyterian Church USA website: www.pcusa.org.

"Confession of Faith." Cumberland Presbyterian Church website: www.cumberland.org.

"Essentials of Our Faith." Evangelical Presbyterian Church website: www.epc.org.

Hart, D.G., and Mark Noll, eds. *Dictionary of the Presbyterian and Reformed Tradition in America.* Downers Grove, IL: InterVarsity Press, 1999.

Smylie, James H. *A Brief History of the Presbyterians.* Louisville: Westminster John Knox Press, 1996.

"Statement of Faith." Associate Reformed Presbyterian Church website: www.arpsynod.org.

"Where We Are Today." Orthodox Presbyterian Church website: www.opc.org.

"Where We Came From." Orthodox Presbyterian Church website: www.opc.org.

"Who We Are." Presbyterian Church USA website: www.pcusa.org.

Reformed Churches

"About the CRC." Christian Reformed Church in North America website: www.crcna.org.

Calvin, John. *Institutes of the Christian Religion,* ed. John T. McNeill, trans. Ford Lewis Battles. Philadelphia: The Westminster Press, 1960.

"Frequently Asked Questions." United Reformed Churches in North America website: www.covenant-urc.org/urchrchs.html.

Hart, D.G., and Mark Noll, eds. *Dictionary of the Presbyterian and Reformed Tradition in America.* Downers Grove, IL: InterVarsity Press, 1999.

"Our Beliefs." Reformed Church in America website: www.rca.org.

"RCA Historical Highlights." Reformed Church in America website: www.rca.org.

Smith, Paul. *The Westminster Confession: Enjoying God Forever.* Chicago: Moody Press, 1998.

INDEX OF DENOMINATIONS

INDEX OF PERSONS

CHART INDEX:
FAST FACTS ON...

About the Author

Dr. Ron Rhodes
Reasoning from the Scripture Ministries
P.O. Box 2526
Frisco, TX 75034

Web site: www.ronrhodes.org

E-mail: reasoning@aol.com

Free newsletter available upon request.

HARVEST HOUSE
PUBLISHERS

Other Harvest House Books
You Can Believe In by Ron Rhodes

THE COMPLETE BOOK OF BIBLE PROMISES

Bible promise books abound—but not like this one! Two hundred alphabetized categories of verses include explanatory headings, insights from the original languages, and deeply moving quotes from famous Christian authors and hymns.

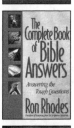

THE COMPLETE BOOK OF BIBLE ANSWERS

This great resource addresses the difficult Bible questions that arise during Bible sudies and witnessing—covering topics that range fom the conflicts between science and the Bible to reconciling God's sovereignty with man's free will.

FIND IT FAST IN THE BIBLE

A quick reference that lives up to its name! With more than 400 topics and 800-plus references, this comprehensive, topical guide provides one-line summaries of each verse. Perfect for research, discussions, and Bible studies.

FIND IT QUICK HANDY BIBLE ENCYCLOPEDIA

Complete enough to be called an encyclopedia but compact enough to be quick and easy to use, this reference book includes approximately 1500 entries, each containing pronunciations, concise definitions, interesting information, and Scripture references.

WHY DO BAD THINGS HAPPEN IF GOD IS GOOD?

Bible scholar, speaker, and author Ron Rhodes addresses this issue with the heart of a pastor and the mind of an apologist. Debunking non-Christian responses to the problem of pain, Ron explores the unshakable biblical truths that provide a strong foundation in stormy times.

HARVEST HOUSE
PUBLISHERS

More Harvest House Books
by Ron Rhodes

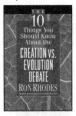

THE 10 THINGS YOU SHOULD KNOW ABOUT THE CREATION VS. EVOLUTION DEBATE

This helpful guide demonstrates why the two sides of the debate are mutually exclusive. You will deepen your appreciation for the wonder of creation and see how it points to the reality of the Creator.

ANGELS AMONG US

What are angels like? What do they do? Are they active today? Taking readers on a fascinating and highly inspirational tour of God's Word, Ron provides solid, biblically based answers to these questions and more.

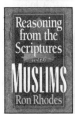

REASONING FROM THE SCRIPTURES WITH MUSLIMS

Who was Muhammad? What kind of inspiration and authority does the Quran have? How can Muslims be reached with the good news? Each chapter examines a Muslim belief and compares it with biblical Christianity.

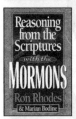

REASONING FROM THE SCRIPTURES WITH THE MORMONS

Powerful tools for sharing the truth of God's Word in a loving and gracious way are presented in a simple, step-by-step format.

REASONING FROM THE SCRIPTURES WITH THE JEHOVAH'S WITNESSES

Many outstanding features make this the *complete* hands-on guide to sharing the truth of God's Word in a loving, gracious way. Includes favorite tactics used by the Witnesses and effective biblical responses.

HARVEST HOUSE
PUBLISHERS